Thinking Kids®
Carson-Dellosa Publishing LLC
Greensboro, North Carolina

Thinking Kids®
Carson-Dellosa Publishing LLC
P.O. Box 35665
Greensboro, NC 27425 USA

ISBN 978-1-4838-3492-4
01-335157784

Contents

Awesome Activities for Practicing Math Skills

Guess Again: Addition, Place Value 8
Equation Sensation: Subtraction 9
Pattern Power: Counting 10
Quick Draw: Addition 11
Math Path: Subtraction, Counting by Twos 12
Shape Master: Understanding Shapes 13
Dare to Decode: Addition, Subtraction 14
On the Dot: Counting by Tens 15
Magic Square: Addition 16
Picture Perfect!: Telling Time 18
On the Lookout!: Addition 19
Number Cross: Counting, Addition 20
It Fits!: Counting by Tens, Place Value 21
Story Stumpers: Word Problems 23
Pattern Power: Counting by Tens 24
Math Path: Subtraction, Counting by Threes 25
Guess Again: Addition, Subtraction 26
A Show of Hands: Working with Data 27
Quick Draw: Drawing Shapes 29
Magic Square: Addition 30
Picture Perfect!: Telling Time 32
Equation Sensation: Subtraction, Counting 33
Dare to Decode: Comparing Numbers 34
Shape Master: Dividing Shapes 35
On the Dot: Addition, Subtraction, Understanding Shapes 36
On the Lookout!: Addition 37
Number Cross: Addition 38
It Fits!: Subtraction, Counting by Tens 39
Story Stumpers: Word Problems 41
Pattern Power: Counting 42
Picture Perfect!: Measuring Length 43
Magic Square: Comparing Numbers, Place Value 44
Guess Again: Addition, Subtraction 46
Quick Draw: Drawing Shapes 47
Math Path: Subtraction 48
A Show of Hands: Working with Data 49
Equation Sensation: Addition, Subtraction 51
Dare to Decode: Telling Time 52
Shape Master: Dividing Shapes 53
On the Dot: Subtraction, Counting by Tens, Understanding Shapes 55
Number Cross: Addition 56
On the Lookout!: Addition, Subtraction, Counting by Tens 57
Story Stumpers: Word Problems 58

It Fits!: Addition, Subtraction 59
A Show of Hands: Measuring Length, Comparing Length 61
Guess Again: Comparing Numbers, Addition, Place Value 63
Pattern Power: Addition, Subtraction, Counting by Tens 64
Picture Perfect!: Working with Data 65
Quick Draw: Drawing Shapes 66
Math Path: Addition, Subtraction 67
Magic Square: Addition, Counting by Tens 68
Equation Sensation: Counting by Tens, Place Value 70
Pattern Power: Telling Time 71
Story Stumpers: Word Problems 72
Shape Master: Measuring Length, Understanding Shapes 73
Dare to Decode: Addition 75
Number Cross: Subtraction 76
On the Dot: Addition, Subtraction 77
Guess Again: Comparing Numbers, Place Value 78
It Fits!: Measuring Length, Understanding Shapes 79
On the Lookout!: Addition, Subtraction 81
Picture Perfect!: Working with Data 82
Quick Draw: Dividing Shapes 83
Magic Square: Addition 84
Math Path: Telling Time 86
A Show of Hands: Comparing Numbers, Place Value 87
Pattern Power: Addition 89
Equation Sensation: Addition, Subtraction 90
Story Stumpers: Comparing Length, Word Problems 91
Number Cross: Addition, Subtraction, Counting by Tens 92
Shape Master: Understanding Shapes 93
Dare to Decode: Addition 94
It Fits!: Addition, Subtraction 95
Guess Again: Comparing Numbers, Place Value 97
On the Dot: Addition, Counting by Tens 98
Quick Draw: Drawing Shapes, Measuring Length 99
Magic Square: Addition, Place Value 100
Picture Perfect!: Dividing Shapes 102
A Show of Hands: Telling Time 103
Math Path: Addition, Subtraction 105
Pattern Power: Addition, Subtraction 106

Awesome Activities for Practicing Language Arts Skills

In Search Of: Adjectives 108
Picture This!: Categories 109
Jumbled Up: Nouns 111
Sudoku for You: Handwriting, Spelling 112
Sentence Scramble: Writing Sentences 113
Code Breaker: Vowel Sounds 114
Mirror, Mirror: Verbs, Spelling 115
Quiz Whiz: Conjunctions, Writing Sentences 116
Go on Across: Vowel Sounds 117
Word Math: Spelling, Handwriting 118
Picture This!: Consonant Blends, Handwriting 120
Jumbled Up: Spelling, Handwriting 121
Riddle Me: Prefixes, Base Words 122
Alpha-Challenge: Syllables, Vowel Sounds 123
Maze Craze: Prepositions, Writing Sentences 124
Mirror, Mirror: Nouns and Verbs 125
Prest-O Change-O!: Verbs, Handwriting 126
In Pieces: Categories 127
Riddle Me: Spelling, Context Clues 129
Sudoku for You: Pronouns, Handwriting 130
In Search Of: Writing Sentences 131
Jumbled Up: Suffixes, Base Words 132
Code Breaker: Using Capital Letters 133
Picture This!: Writing Sentences 134
Go on Across: Vowel Sounds, Spelling 135
Riddle Me: Context Clues, Spelling 136
Quiz Whiz: Writing Sentences, Vowel Sounds 137
Maze Craze: Articles, Writing Sentences 138
Code Breaker: Handwriting 139
In Search Of: Verbs 140
Prest-O Change-O!: Vowel Sounds, Handwriting, Spelling 141
Sentence Scramble: Writing Sentences 142
Jumbled Up: Writing Sentences 143
Sudoku for You: Verbs, Handwriting 145
Word Math: Consonant Blends 146
Mirror, Mirror: Using Commas 148
Alpha-Challenge: Nouns 149
Quiz Whiz: Prefixes, Suffixes 150
In Pieces: Vowel Sounds 151
Picture This!: Handwriting 153
Jumbled Up: Nouns 154
In Search Of: Prepositions 155
Maze Craze: Conjunctions 156

Go on Across: Verbs 157
Word Math: Syllables, Vowel Sounds, Handwriting 158
Quiz Whiz: Vowel Sounds, Spelling 160
Sentence Scramble: Writing Sentences 161
Sudoku for You: Pronouns, Handwriting 162
Prest-O Change-O!: Spelling, Handwriting 163
Picture This!: Consonant Blends 164
In Pieces: Prefixes, Base Words 165
Alpha-Challenge: Using Capital Letters 167
Code Breaker: Nouns and Verbs 168
Mirror, Mirror: Fiction vs. Nonfiction 169
Quiz Whiz: Writing Sentences 170
Go on Across: Vocabulary, Spelling 171
In Search Of: Categories 172
Jumbled Up: Syllables 173
Riddle Me: Prefixes, Base Words, Spelling 174
Picture This!: Vocabulary 175
Sudoku for You: Verbs, Handwriting 177
Sentence Scramble: Writing Sentences 178
Riddle Me: Consonant Blends, Context Clues 179
Quiz Whiz: Text Features 180
Jumbled Up: Using Commas 181
Picture This!: Adjectives, Nouns 182
Maze Craze: Prepositions 183
Word Math: Writing Sentences 184
Code Breaker: Handwriting 186
Riddle Me: Point of View 187
Code Breaker: Nouns and Verbs 188
Sudoku for You: Verbs, Handwriting 189
Jumbled Up: Vowel Sounds 190
Sentence Scramble: Writing Sentences 191
Alpha-Challenge: Sensory Words, Adjectives 192
In Pieces: Suffixes, Base Words 193
Maze Craze: Consonant Blends, Spelling 195
Quiz Whiz: Using Commas 196
Go on Across: Vocabulary 197
In Search Of: Spelling 198
In Pieces: Vowel Sounds 199
Sentence Scramble: Writing Sentences, Conjunctions 201
Word Math: Using Capital Letters 202
Riddle Me: Vowel Sounds, Using Capital Letters 204
Prest-O Change-O!: Spelling, Handwriting 205
Picture This!: Adjectives, Vocabulary 206

Answer Key 207

MATH

GUESS AGAIN

Use the clues to find each secret number.

It is more than 10.

It is less than 15.

Add the two digits and you get 4.

Secret Number:

Tens Ones

It is less than 18.

It is more than 14.

Add the two digits and you get 7.

Secret Number:

Tens Ones

Skills: Addition, Place Value

It is less than 20.

It is more than 16.

Add the two digits and you get 9.

Secret Number:

Tens Ones

It is more than 10.

It is less than 14.

Add the two digits and you get 2.

Secret Number:

Tens Ones

e(quation) / sen+sation

Skill: Subtraction

Fill in the missing numbers to complete the number sentences. Cross out gumballs in each machine to help you.

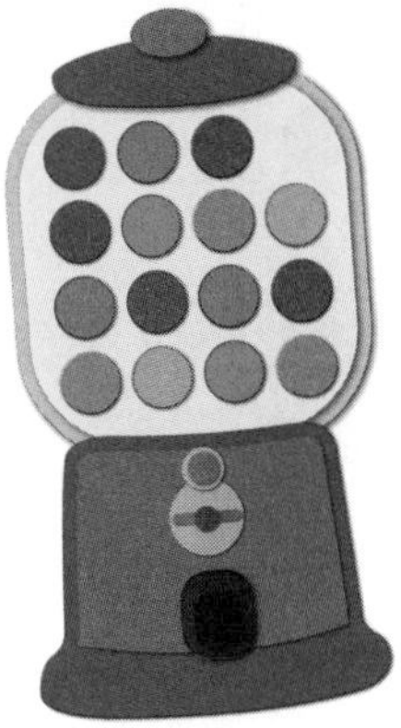

$15 - \square = 8$

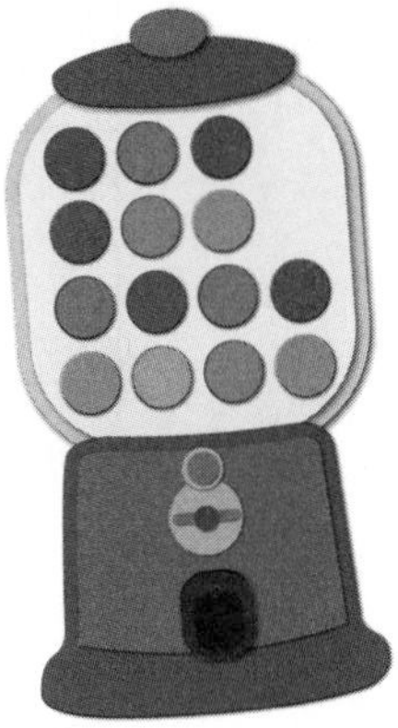

$14 - \square = 6$

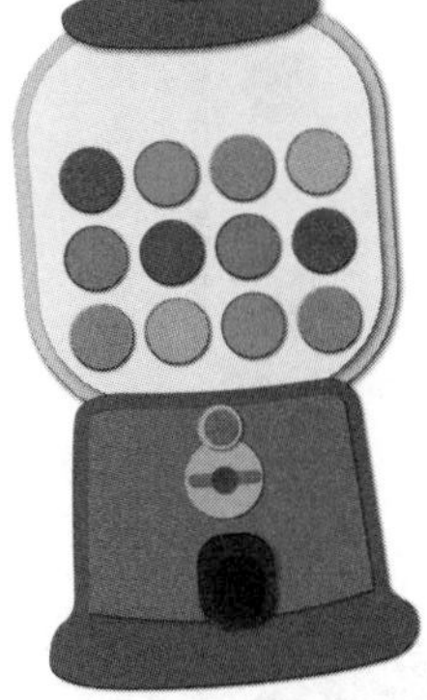

$12 - \square = 3$

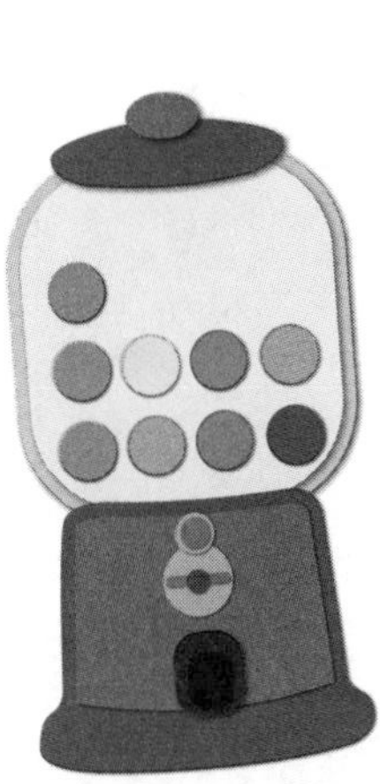

$9 - \square = 3$

PATTERN POWER

Skill: Counting

Find the pattern of dots in each row. Draw dots on the blank domino sides to complete the pattern.

QUICK DRAW

Write a number in each blank to make the number sentence true. Then, draw the missing apples.

Skill: Addition

7 + ☐ = 12

+ ☐ = 12

☐ + 10 = 14

☐ +

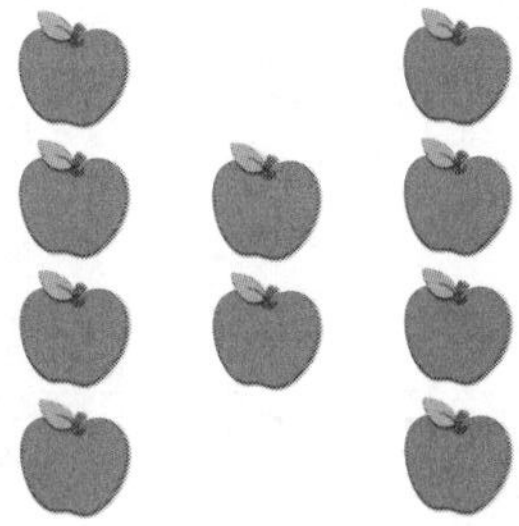

= 14

9 + ☐ = 15

+ ☐ = 15

9	8	6	4	2
11	7	10	9	5
13	9	15	12	6
17	19	16	14	4
20	18	17	15	8

Start at 20. Count backward by twos to find the path to the dog's bone.

Math path

	+		=	
=		=		=
3	+	1	=	
+		+		+
2	+	2	=	
+		+		+
1	+	4	=	

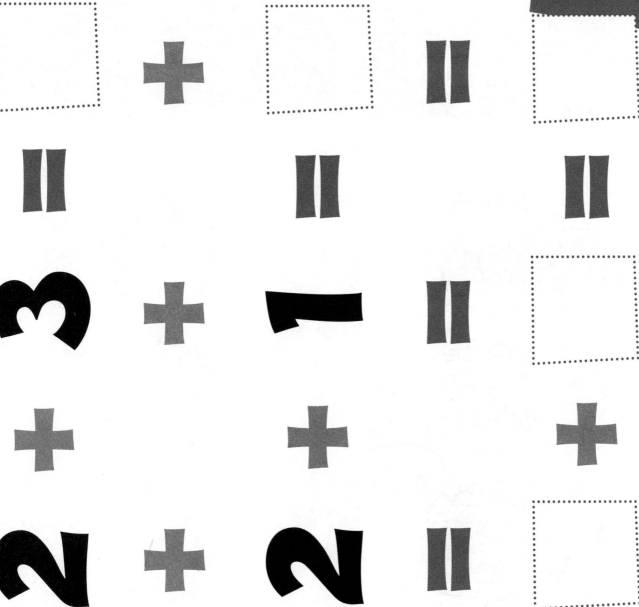

Read the time on the digital clock. Draw hands on the clock face to show the same time.

Picture Perfect!

On the Lookout!

Skill: Addition

Circle four addition problems in the puzzle. Write + and = signs to complete the number sentences. Then, write each numbe sentence yo found.

5	5	2	1
4	2	6	3
9	4	8	2
7	3	6	9

___ + ___ = ___

___ + ___ = ___

___ + ___ = ___

___ + ___ = ___

NUMBER CROSS

Skills: Counting, Addition

Read each clue. Write the numbers to fill the spaces in the puzzle.

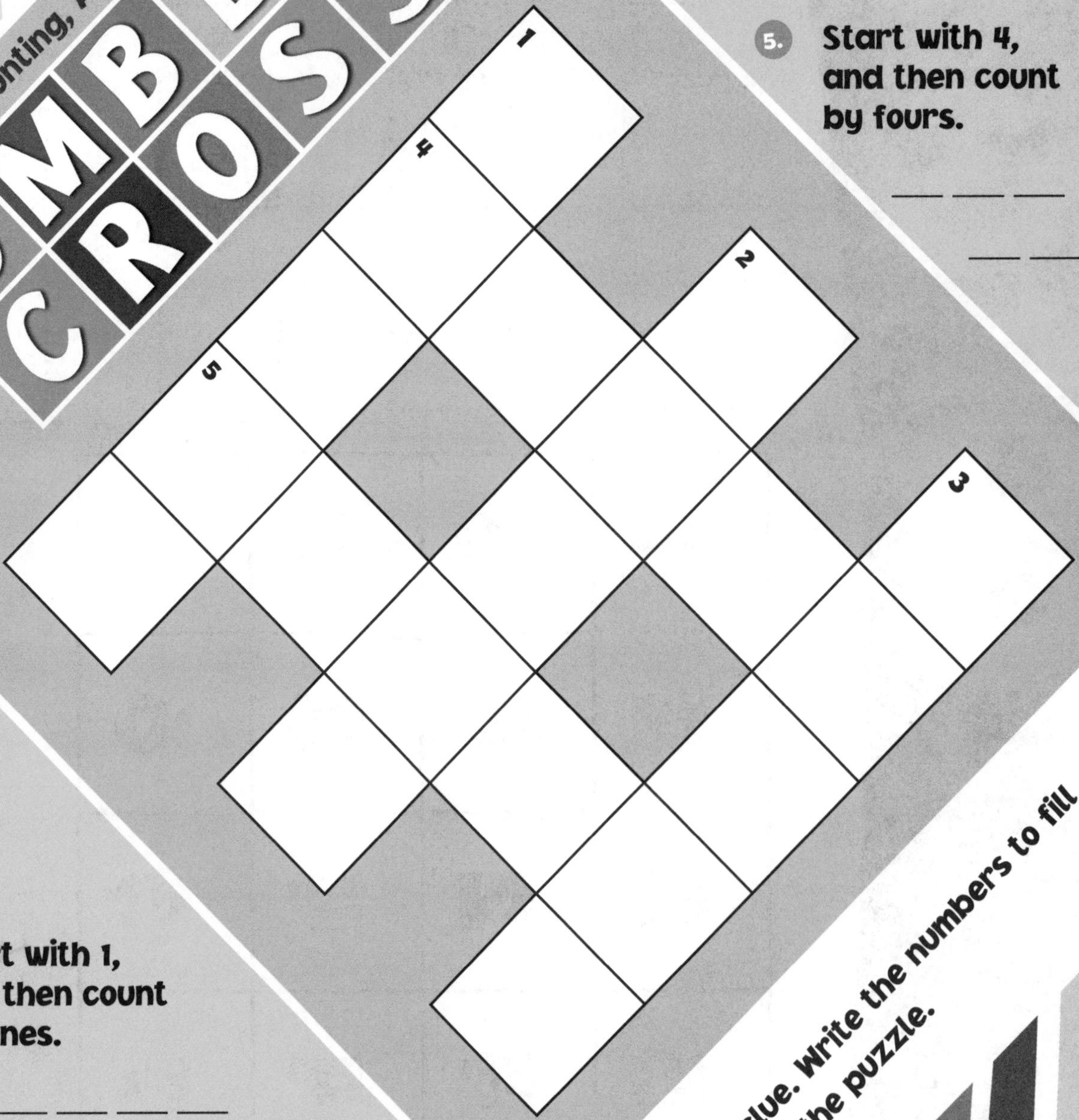

Across

4. Start with 2, and then count by twos.

___ ___ ___ ___ ___

5. Start with 4, and then count by fours.

___ ___ ___

___ ___

Down

1. Start with 1, and then count by ones.

___ ___ ___ ___ ___

2. Start with 3, and then count by threes.

___ ___ ___ ___ ___

3. Start with 5, and then count by fives.

___ ___ ___ ___ ___

IT FITS!

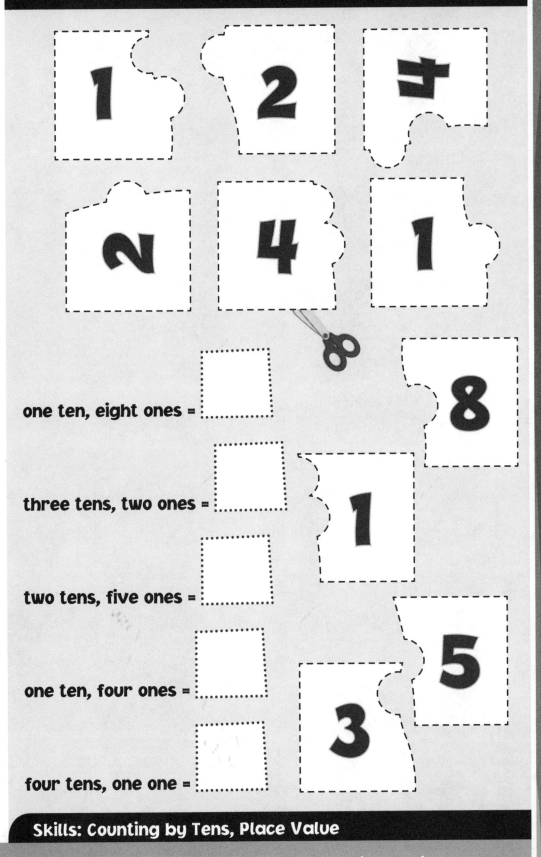

one ten, eight ones = ☐

three tens, two ones = ☐

two tens, five ones = ☐

one ten, four ones = ☐

four tens, one one = ☐

Skills: Counting by Tens, Place Value

Cut out the numbers. Use the clues to fit the pieces together to form two-digit numbers. Then, write the numbers you made.

13	10	7	6	3
16	18	14	9	7
19	20	16	19	12
22	21	18	15	11
24	19	16	13	10

Get a hit! Start at 24. Subtract 3 each time to find the path to the ball.

Math path

GUESS AGAIN

Use the clues to find each secret number.

Start [illegible]th 2.

Ad[illegible].

[illegible]ract 5, and you will [illegible] it.

[illegible]ecret Number:

Start with 17.

Subtract 4.

Add 10, and you will find it.

Secret Number:

Skills: Addition, Subtraction

Start with 3 more than 5.

Add 5 more.

Subtract 9, and you will find it.

Secret Number:

Start with 8 less than 20.

Add 3.

Add 2 more, and you will find it.

Secret Number:

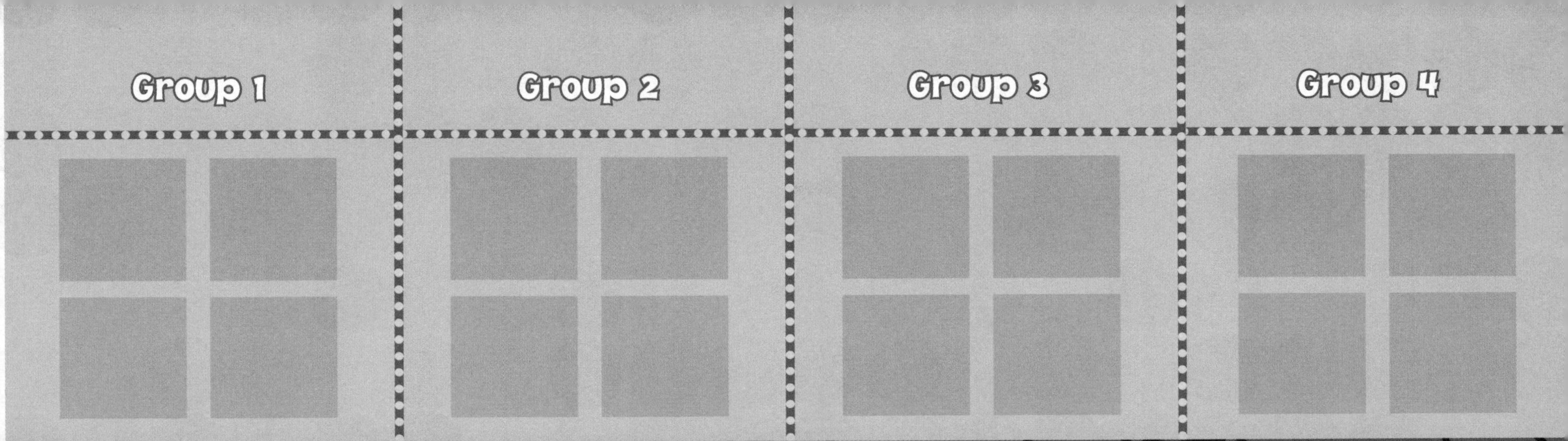

A Show of Hands

Skill: Working with Data

Cut out the pieces. Glue or tape them in the spaces to make four groups of fruits that are alike.

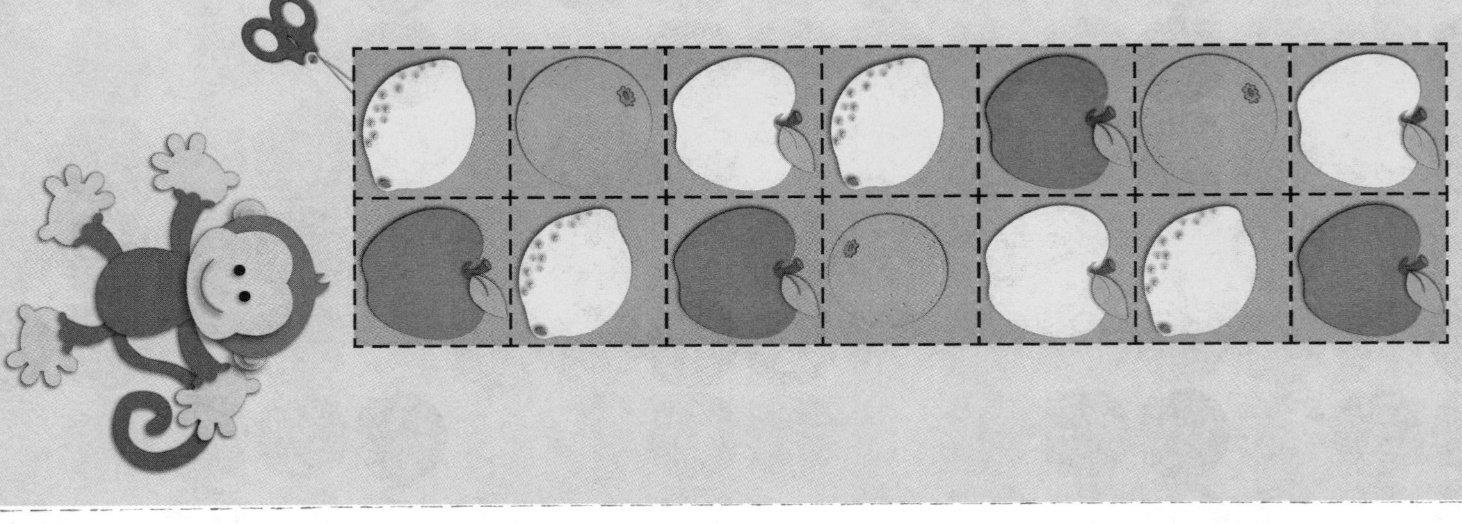

QUICK DRAW

Finish drawing each shape. Then, decorate the shapes with color.

Skill: Drawing Shapes

Magic Square

Place pennies in the empty spaces, or draw pennies. When you are done, each row and column should have the same number of pennies.

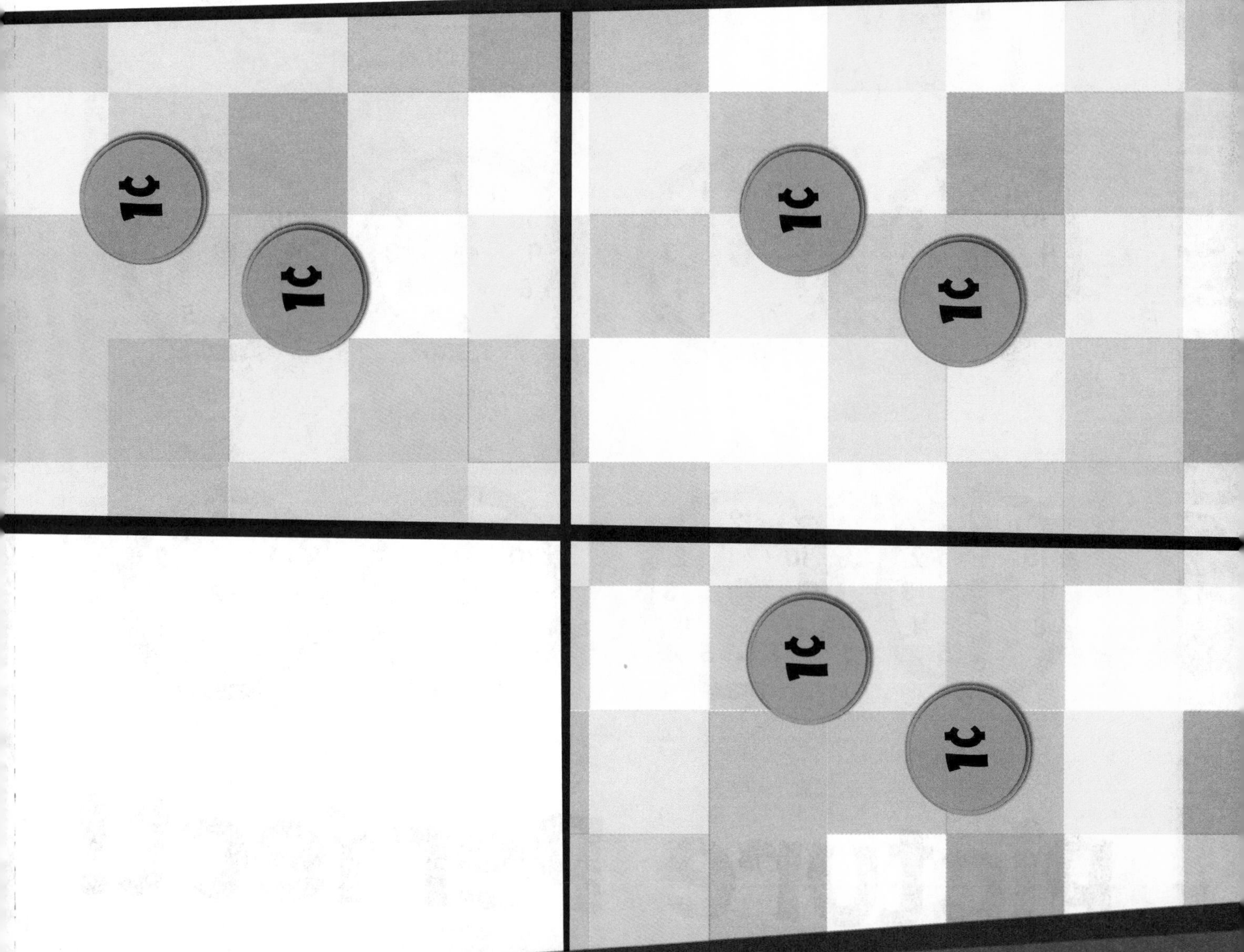
1¢
1¢
1¢
1¢
1¢
1¢

All of the clocks are a half-hour too fast! Draw the correct time on the blank clocks.

Picture Perfect!

e(quation) sen+sation

Skills: Subtraction, Counting

Write the missing numbers to complete the number sentences.

$$\square - 5 = \square$$

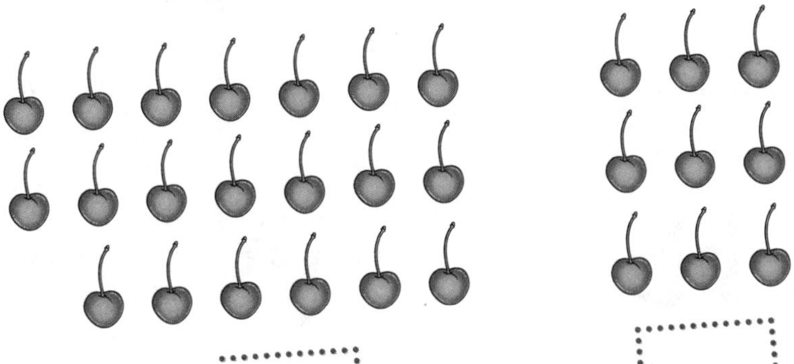

$$\square - 11 = \square$$

DARE TO DECODE

Skill: Comparing Numbers

Each comparison is written in code. Use the key to write the numbers. One comparison is wrong. Circle it.

Code Key

0	1	2	3	4	5	6	7	8	9
H	E	Y	M	P	W	B	C	A	L

YP > EA

☐ > ☐

MY < YL

☐ < ☐

MW < PC

☐ < ☐

YB > EC

☐ > ☐

SHAPE MASTER

Skill: Dividing Shapes

Which shapes can be divided into four equal parts (fourths)? Which shapes can be divided into only two equal parts (halves)? Draw lines to show your answers.

1. 5 + 7 = ____
2. 19 − 5 = ____
3. 4 + 13 = ____
4. 12 − 9 = ____
5. 7 + 8 = ____
6. 20 − 12 = ____
7. 2 + 9 = ____
8. 5 + 14 = ____
9. 15 − 3 = ____

ON THE DOT

Skills: Addition, Subtraction, Understanding Shapes

Solve each problem. Then, connect the dots in the order of your answers. Write the name of the shape you made.

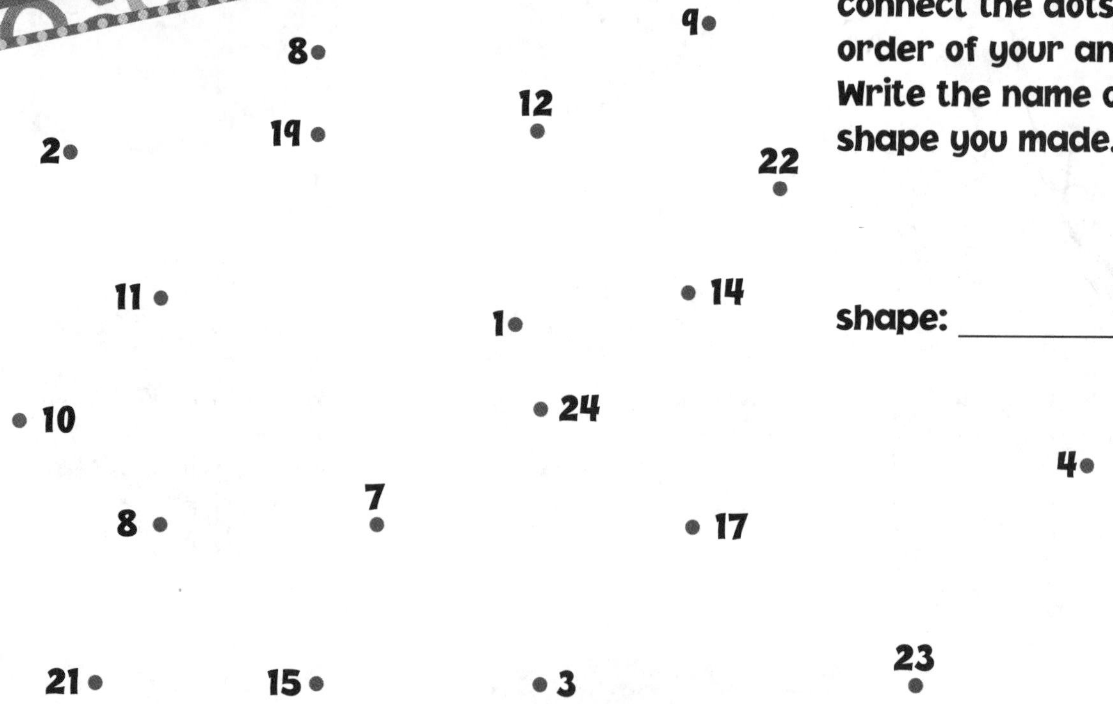

shape: ____________________

IT FITS!

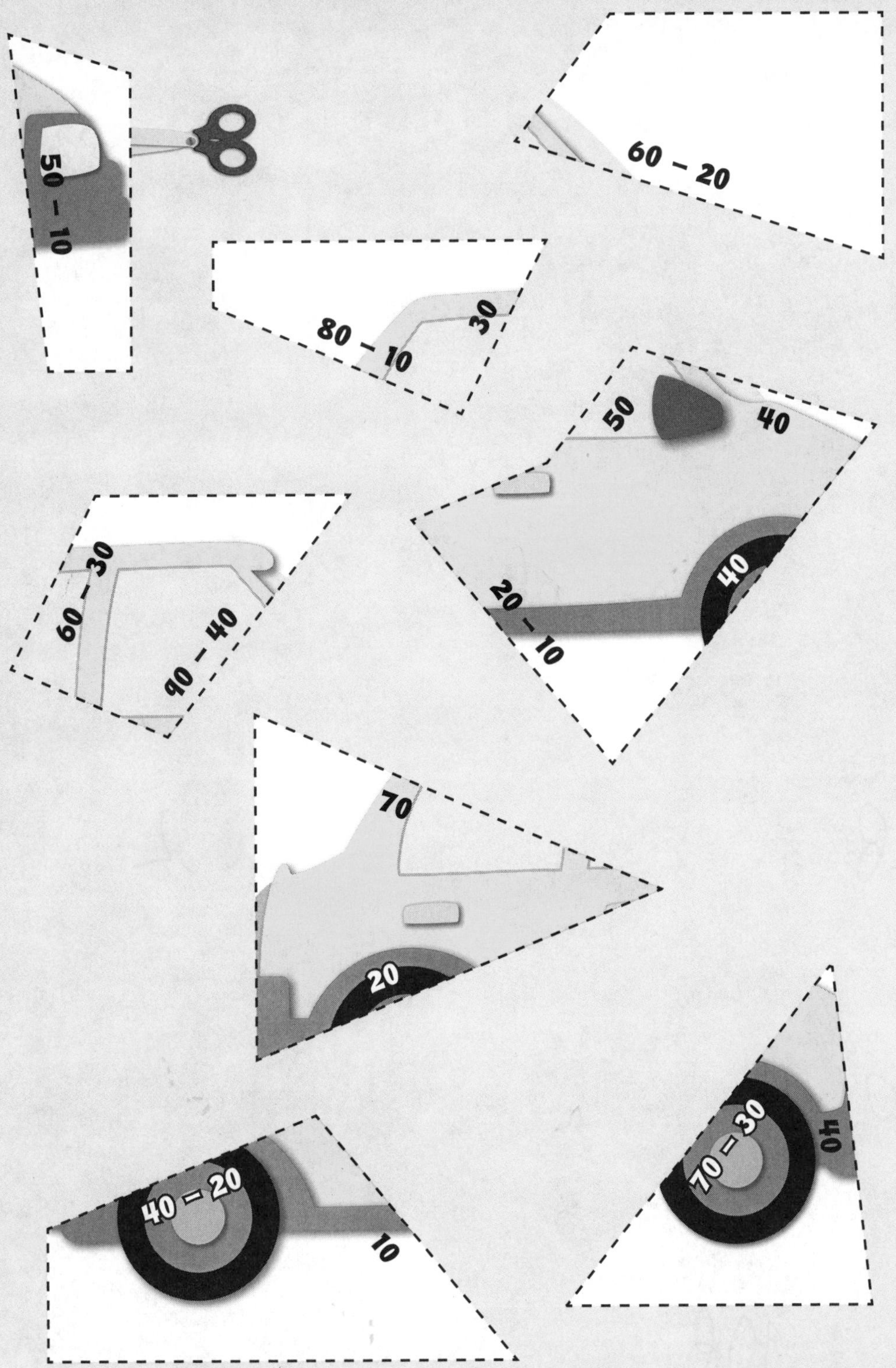

Skills: Subtraction, Counting by Tens

Cut out the puzzle pieces. Fit them together to make a picture. When you are done, each problem will be next to its answer.

Gather 20 pennies. Put rows of pennies below the pencils. Write how many pennies it took to measure the length of each pencil.

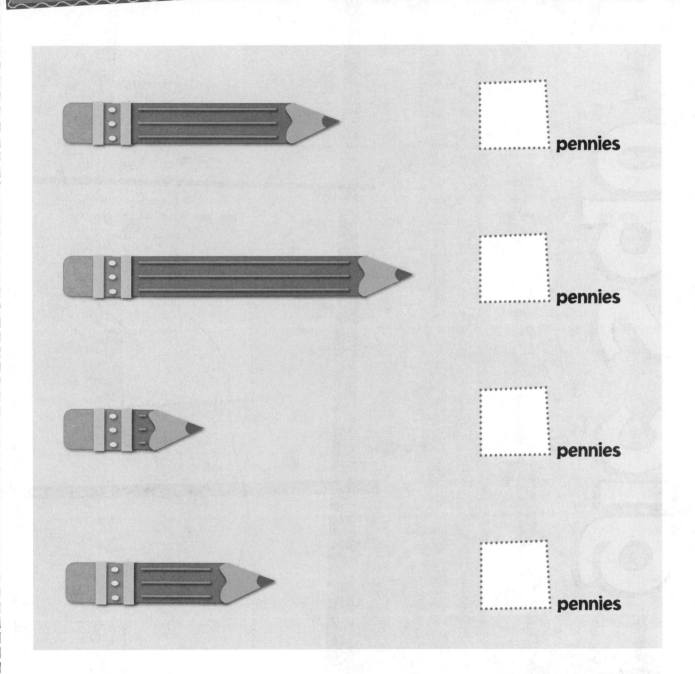

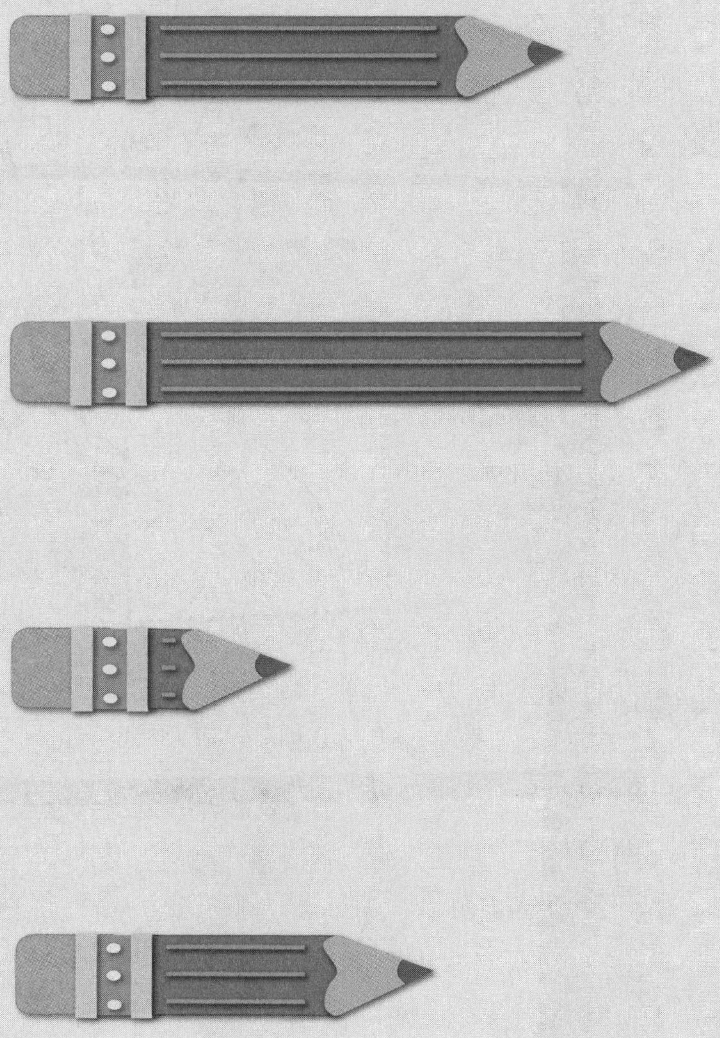

☐ pennies

☐ pennies

☐ pennies

☐ pennies

Picture Perfect!

Magic Square

Write the nine numbers in the magic square. One two-digit number goes in each square. Follow this rule: From top to bottom, and from left to right, the numbers must go from greatest to least.

77 24 34 84 28 16 95 65 51

Guess Again

Use the clues to guess each secret number.

Start with 22.
Subtract 9.
Subtract 5 more.
Secret Number:

Start with 31.
Add 4.
Add 10 more.
Secret Number:

Skills: Addition, Subtraction

Add 6 and 9.
Switch the two digits of your answer.
Add 4 to the new number.
Secret Number:

Start with 3 less than 40.
Add 10.
Switch the two digits of your answer.
Secret Number:

QUICK DRAW

Use only the shapes shown in the box to make a drawing. Here are some ideas for your drawing: a house, a face, a pattern, a spaceship, a map.

Skill: Drawing Shapes

9	8	20
4	10	6
5	3	0

2	10	5
20	3	4
12	0	4

5	20	1
3	7	0
6	1	3

2	2	0
5	8	9
7	4	20

For each puzzle, start at 20. Find a path that reaches 0 by subtracting each number you pass.

Math path

A Show of Hands

Skill: Working with Data

Eli saw animals at a farm. Cut out the pieces. Glue or tape them in the spaces to make three groups of animals that are alike. Circle the animal that Eli saw most.

Group 1

Group 2

Group 3

e(quation) sen+sation

Skills: Addition, Subtraction

Complete each number sentence. Fill in the missing numbers. Circle the correct math sign.

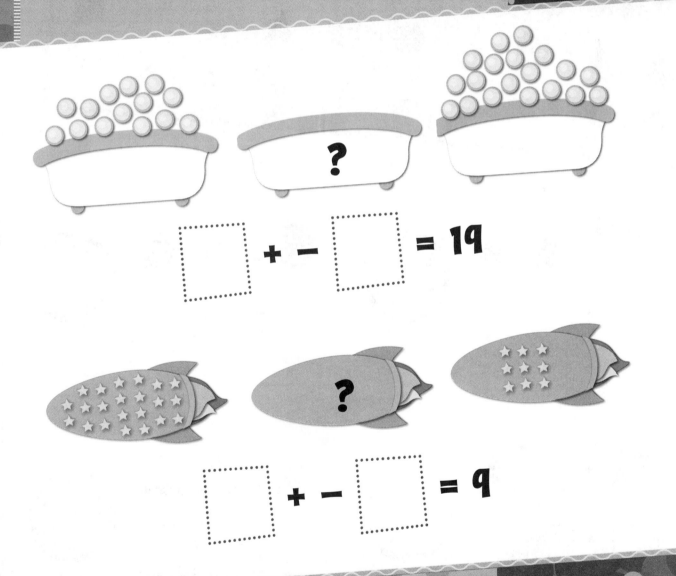

☐ + – ☐ = 19

☐ + – ☐ = 9

Dare to Decode

Skill: Telling Time

The times are written in code. Use the key to write the time in numbers. Then, draw hands on each clock to show the time.

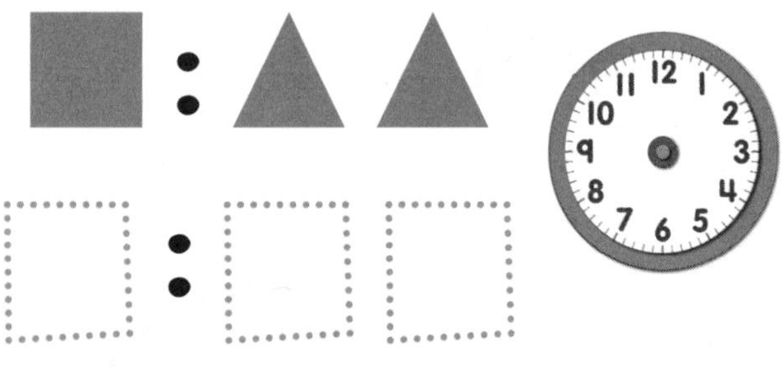

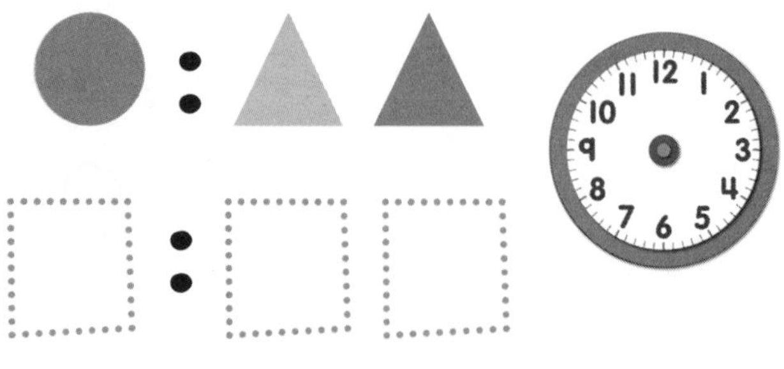

SHAPE MASTER

Skill: Dividing Shapes

Cut out the red squares. Then, cut them into smaller pieces that match the blue shapes.

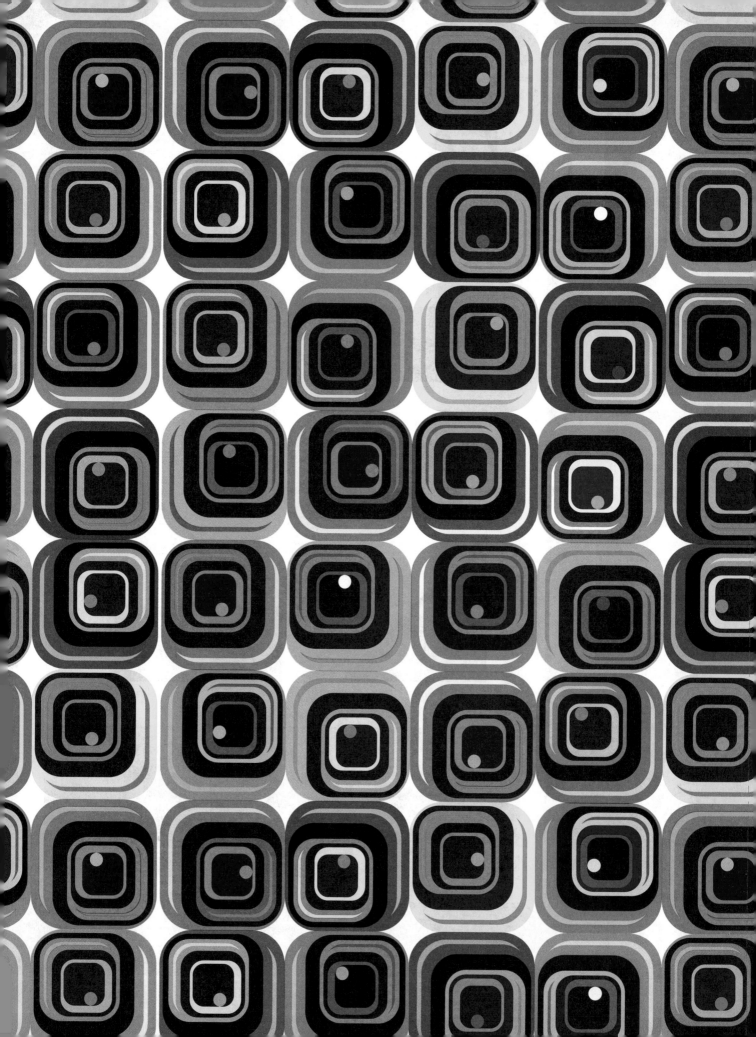

On the Lookout!

Skills: Addition, Subtraction, Counting by Tens

Look at each number. If it is followed by a plus sign (+), add 10. If it is followed by a minus sign (–), subtract 10. Then, circle each answer going across or down in the puzzle.

32+
63–
44+
21+
97–
78–
29–
36+
87–
8+

3	4	7	4	2
1	6	0	1	9
2	5	3	8	5
7	4	9	3	2
7	3	6	8	7

STORY STUMPERS

Read each story. Use the pictures to help you find the answer.

Skill: Word Problems

20 bees buzzed in the garden. Then, 12 bees flew away. Next, 7 bees came back. How many bees are in the garden now?

☐ **bees**

12 chickens pecked in the barnyard. 5 cows rested in the barnyard, too. Then, 3 cows left. 5 chickens followed them. How many animals were left in the barnyard?

☐ **animals**

IT FITS!

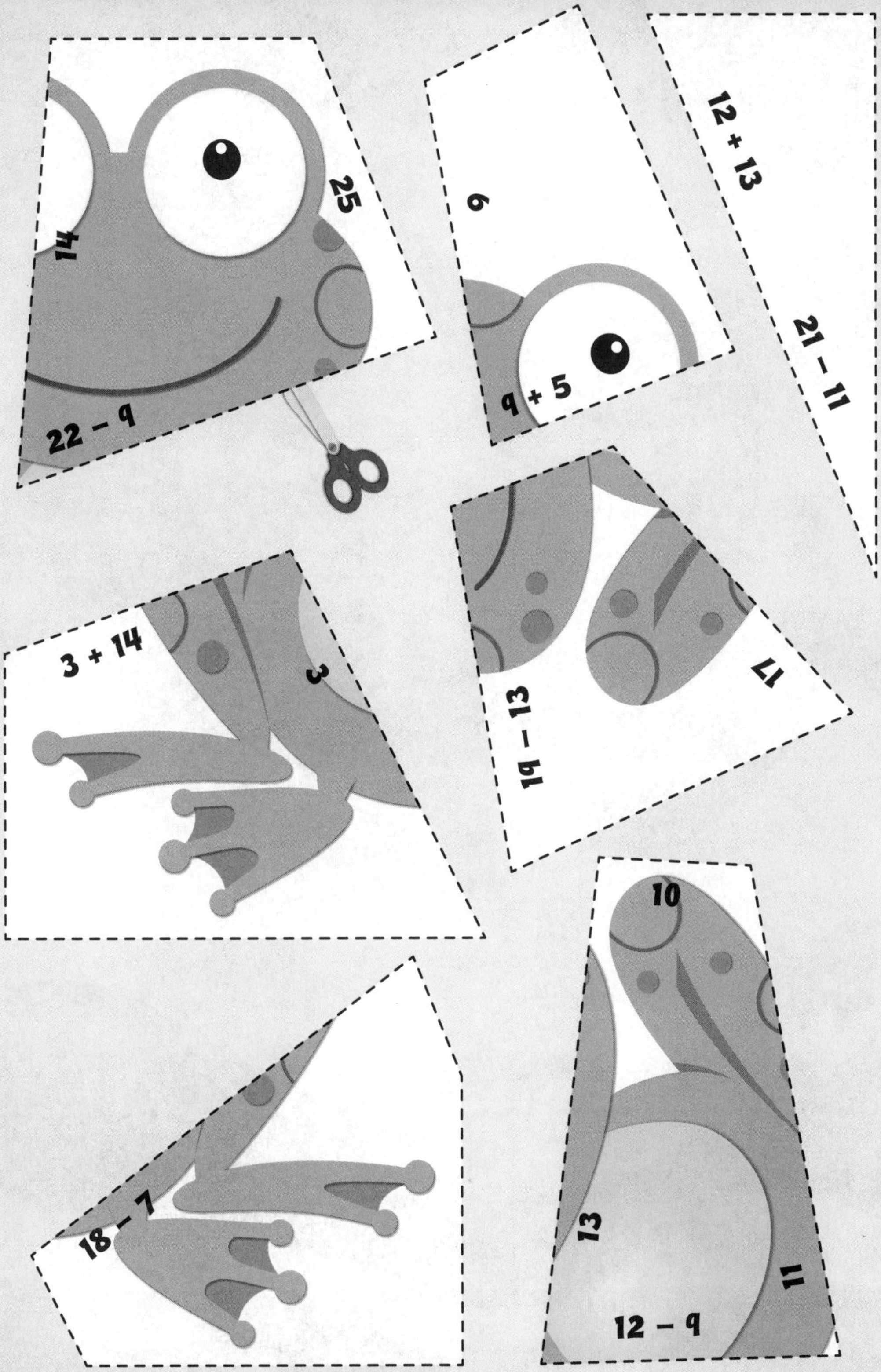

Skills: Addition, Subtraction

Cut out the puzzle pieces. Fit them together to make a picture. When you are done, each problem will be next to its answer.

Shortest (2 inches)	Short (3 inches)	Long (4 inches)	Longest (5 inches)

A Show of Hands

Skills: Measuring Length, Comparing Length

Cut out the worms. Then, find something inside or outside that is about the same length as each worm. Draw what you measured, or write its name, in each space.

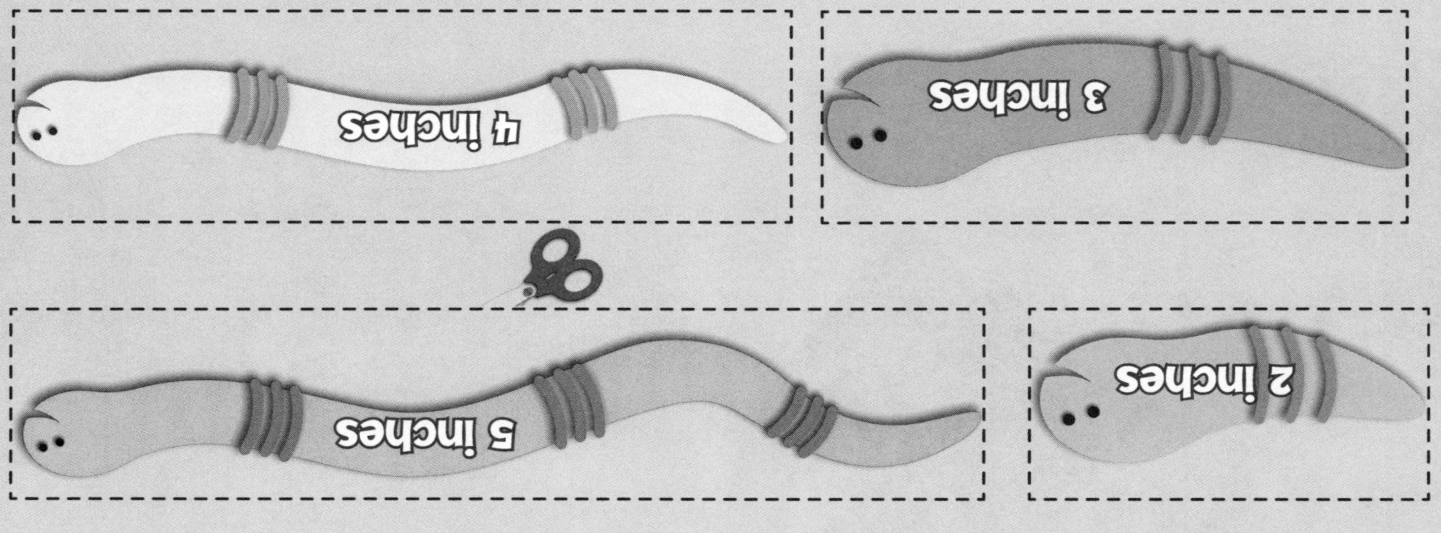

GUESS AGAIN

Use the clues to find each secret two-digit number.

It is more than 20.

It is less than 30.

Add its digits together, and you get 7.

Secret Number:

Tens | Ones

It is less than 50.

It is more than 45.

Add its digits together, and you get 11.

Secret Number:

Tens | Ones

Skills: Comparing Numbers, Addition, Place Value

It is less than 42.

It is more than 37.

Add its digits together, and you get 4.

Secret Number:

Tens | Ones

It is more than 55.

It is less than 60.

Add its digits together, and you get 13.

Secret Number:

Tens | Ones

PATTERN POWER

Skills: Addition, Subtraction, Counting by Tens

Add 12.

10	22				

Add 8.

9	17				

Subtract 20.

120	100				

Subtract 10.

84	74				

Read the rule for each pattern. Then, fill in the next four numbers.

Skill: Working with Data

Topp's Toy Store has a lot of bears! Count the bears of each color. Write the number at the bottom of the page after the equal sign. Then, circle the colored bear that has the largest group.

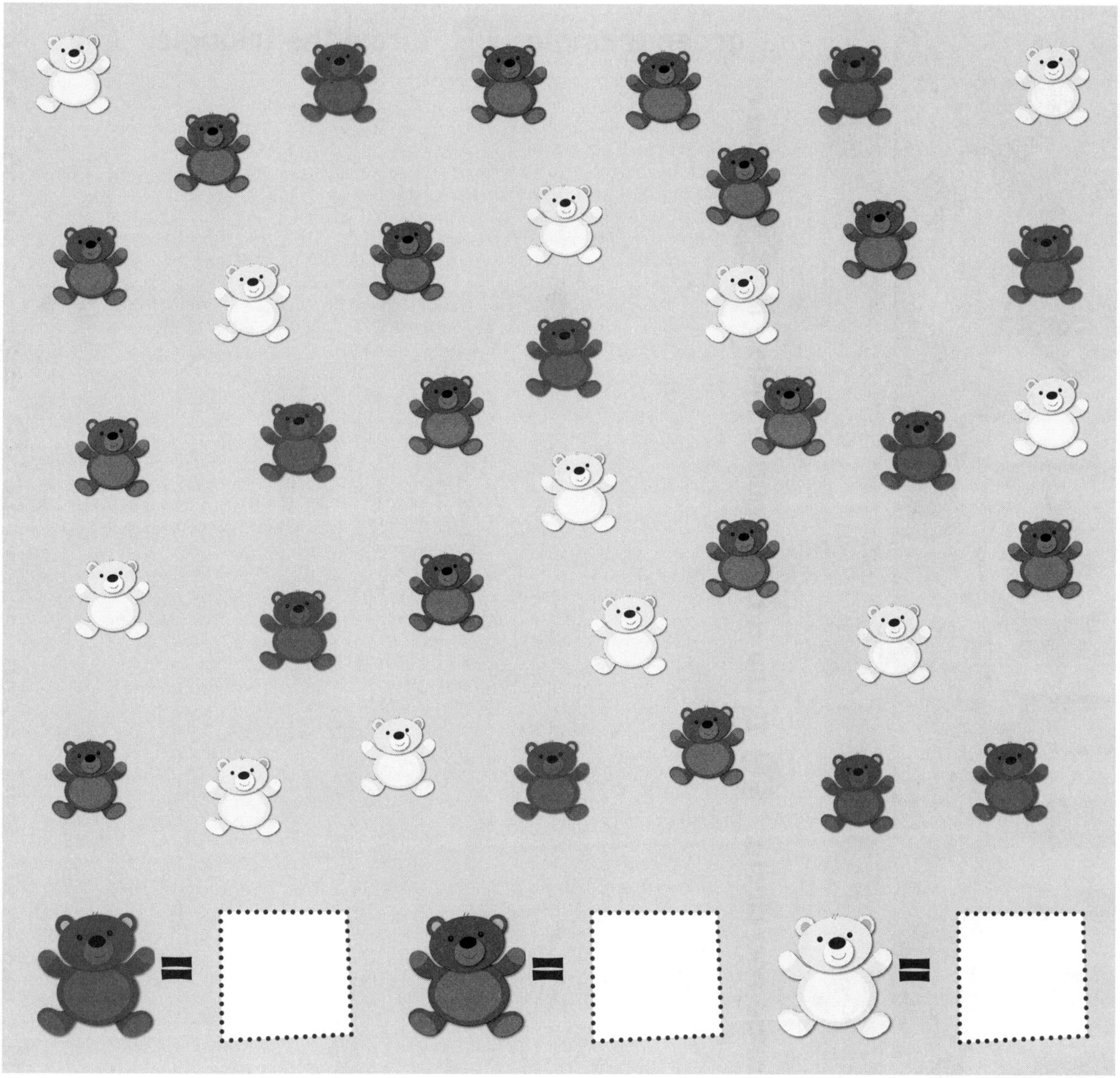

Picture Perfect!

QUICK DRAW

Follow the directions. What does your drawing look like? Have a friend follow the directions, too. Then, compare the two drawings.

Skill: Drawing Shapes

1. Draw a large red circle.
2. Draw a blue square inside it.
3. Draw a green triangle.
4. Circle the triangle.
5. Draw a yellow triangle.
6. Write your name inside the circle.
7. Draw a purple rectangle around a shape you already made.

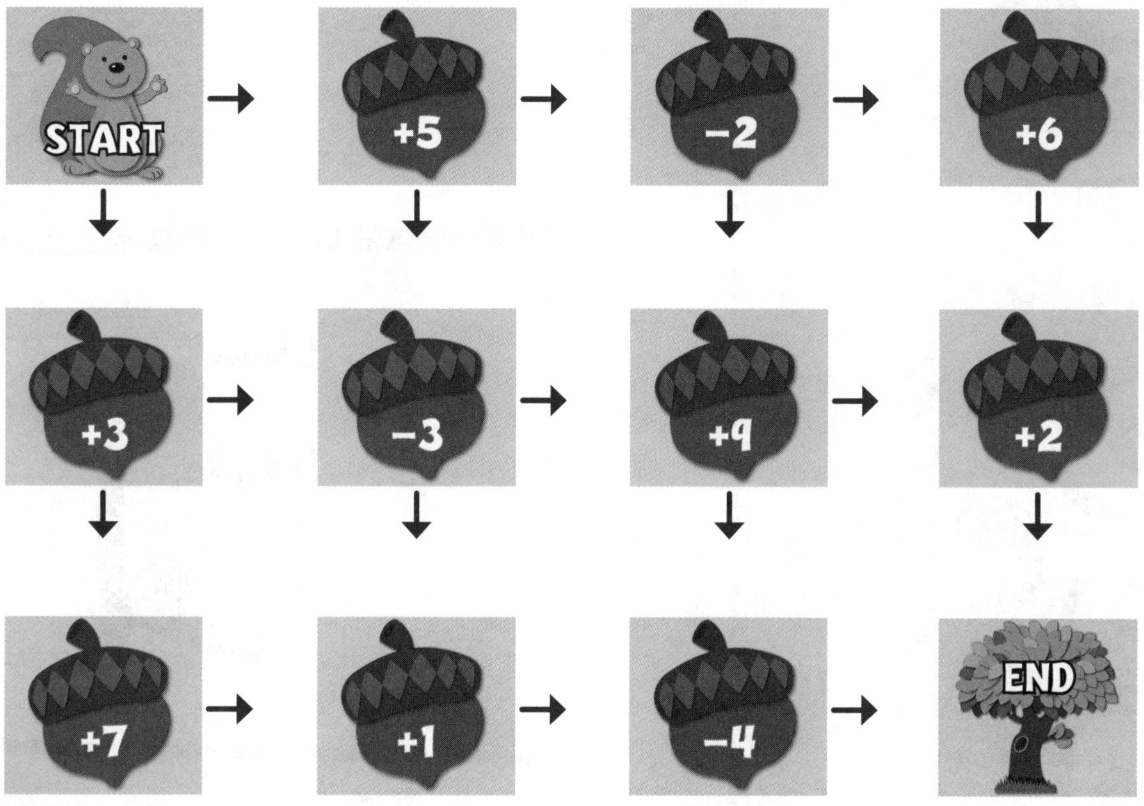

Start with 0. Follow the arrows and perform each operation. Keep a running total. Can you end with 8? There is only one correct path.

Math path

Magic Square

Use the code to add up the yummy rows and columns. Write the sums in the blanks.

 = 10 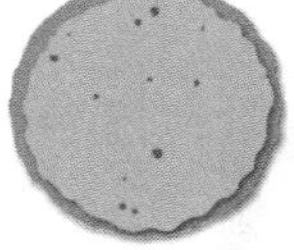 = 30  = 20  = 40

Skills: Addition, Counting by Tens

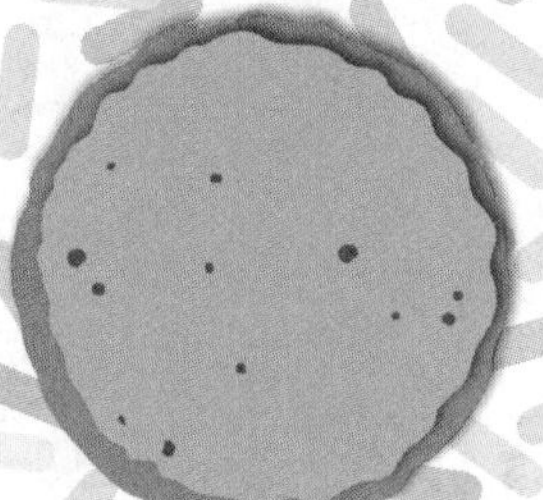

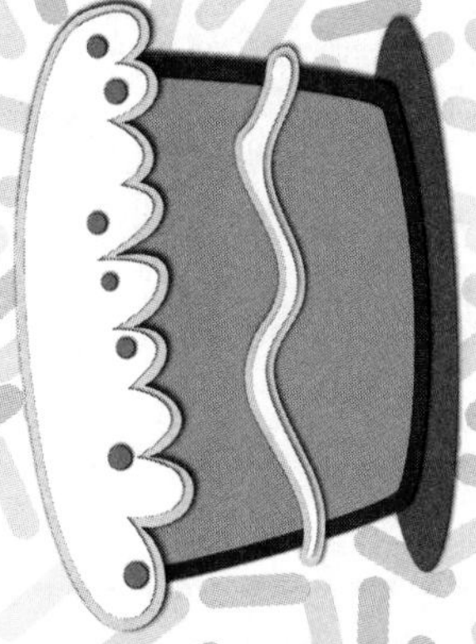

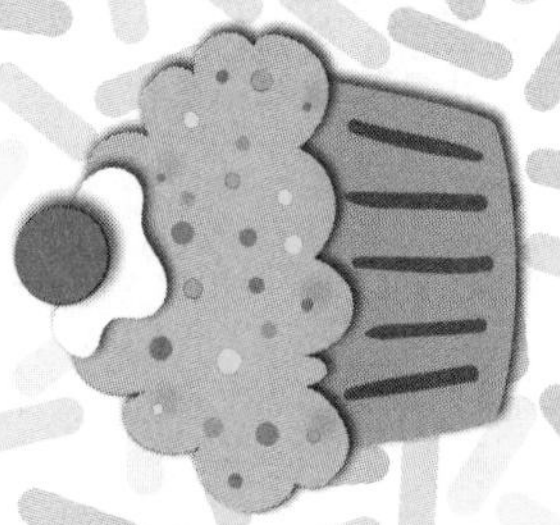

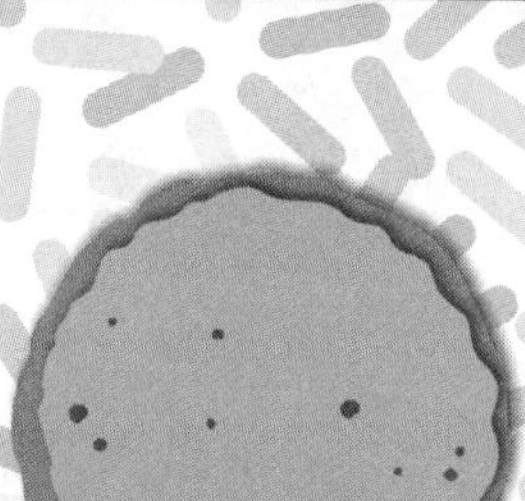

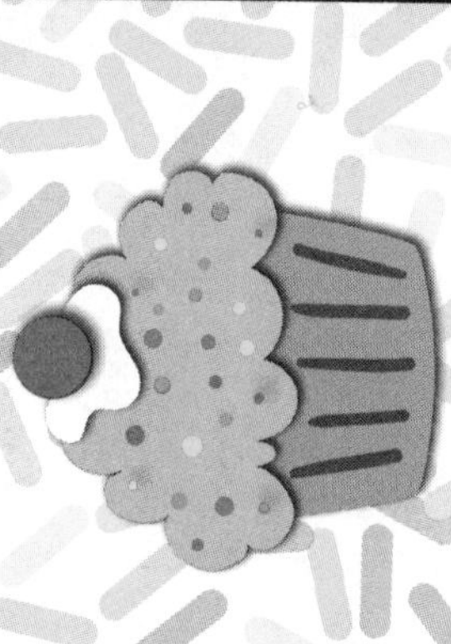

e(quation) sen+sation

Skills: Counting by Tens, Place Value

Use the code to write each problem using numbers. Then, solve.

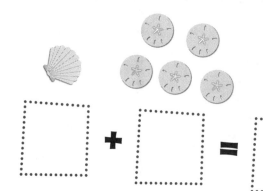

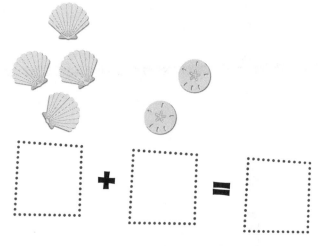

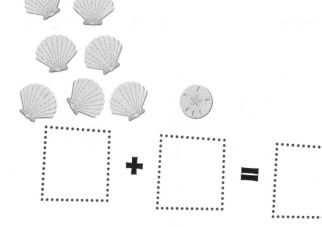

 = 10  = 1

___ + ___ = ___

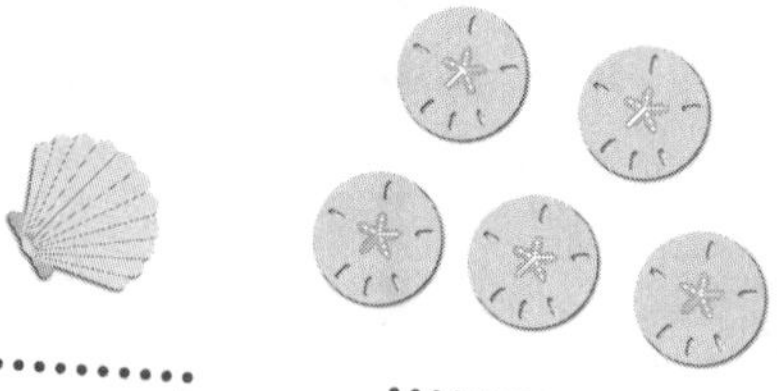

___ + ___ = ___

___ + ___ = ___

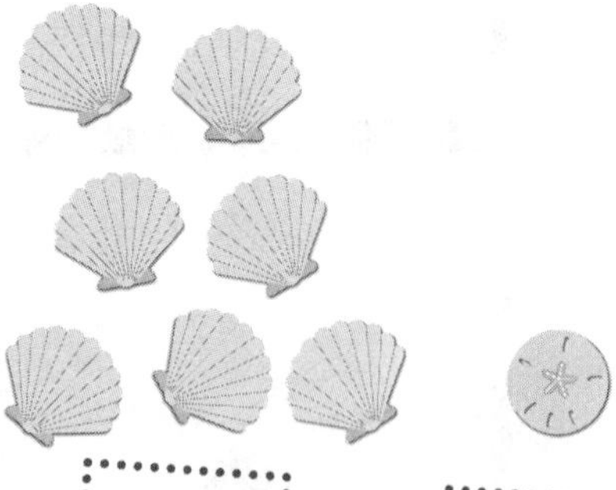

___ + ___ = ___

PATTERN POWER

Skill: Telling Time

The times shown by the clocks in each row form a pattern. Draw hands on the last clock to complete the pattern.

STORY STUMPERS

Read each story. Use the pictures to help you find the answer.

Skill: Word Problems

Players on the Comets soccer team kicked 20 balls on Monday. They kicked 13 on Tuesday. How many more did they kick on Monday?

☐ balls

Mr. Lee packed 8 turkey sandwiches, 5 ham sandwiches, and 4 veggie sandwiches. 15 sandwiches were eaten at the picnic. How many were left?

☐ sandwiches

MASTER SHAPE

Skills: Measuring Length, Understanding Shapes

Cut out the squares. Each is one inch tall and one inch wide. Glue or tape the squares together to make a rectangle. Count the squares to measure your rectangle in inches.

rectangle

☐ inches tall ☐ inches wide

DARE TO DECODE

Skill: Addition

Each shape stands for a digit from 0 to 8. Look at the number sentences written in code. Use what you know about adding doubles to crack the code. Write a digit above each shape.

Code Key

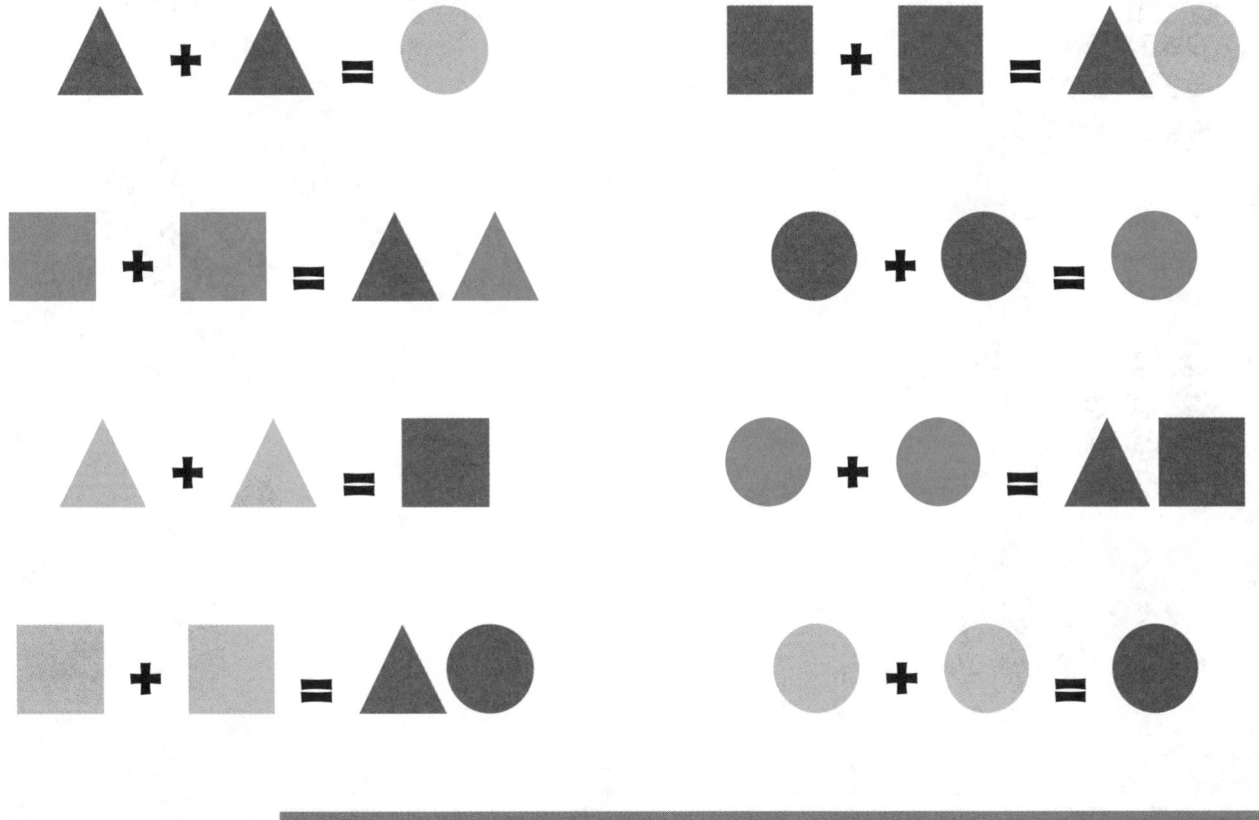

Skill: Subtraction

NUMBER CROSS

Across

1. 

4. 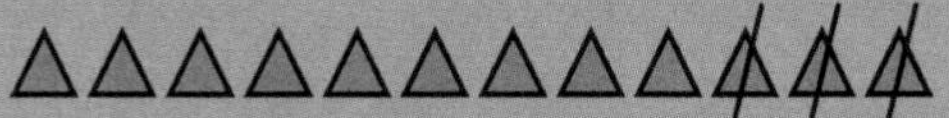

5.

7.

8.

Down

1.

2. 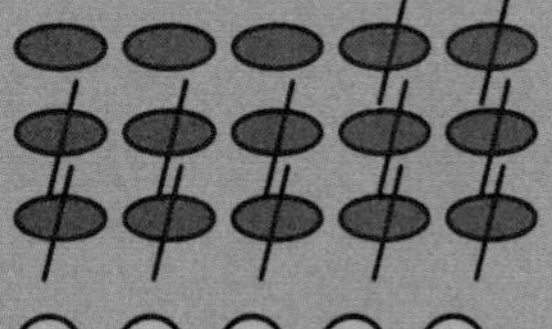

3. 

6. 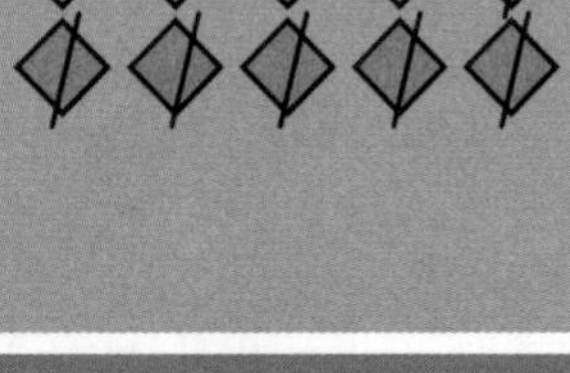

Think of a subtraction number sentence to describe each group of shapes. Write it in the puzzle. One is done for you.

Solve the problems. Then, draw a line to connect the dots between problems that have the same answer. Write the name of the shape you made.

35 + 40 = ____ 45 − 20 = ____ 35 + 20 = ____ 16 + 9 = ____

20 + 30 = ____ 65 − 30 = ____ 65 − 10 = ____ 80 − 30 = ____

27 + 8 = ____ 95 − 20 = ____

On THE DOT

Skills: Addition, Subtraction

35 + 40

65 − 10

20 + 30

27 + 8

45 − 20

16 + 9

shape:

65 − 30

80 − 30

35 + 20

95 − 20

____

GUESS AGAIN

Use the clues to find each secret two-digit number.

It is between 50 and 70.

Add its digits together, and you get 11.

The first digit is greater than the second digit.

Secret Number:

Tens	Ones

It is between 20 and 40.

Add its digits together, and you get 8.

The difference between the digits is 2.

Secret Number:

Tens	Ones

Skills: Comparing Numbers, Place Value

It is between 60 and 80.

Add its digits together, and you get 13.

The first digit is greater than the second digit.

Secret Number:

Tens	Ones

It is between 10 and 30.

Add its digits together, and you get 8.

The difference between the two digits is 6.

Secret Number:

Tens	Ones

IT FITS!

Each side is ☐ inches long.

Skills: Measuring Length, Understanding Shapes

Cut out the puzzle pieces. Fit them together to make a square. When you are done, use a ruler to measure the sides in inches. How long is each side?

On the Lookout!

Skills: Addition, Subtraction

Addition and subtraction number sentences are hidden in the puzzle. Find and circle 11 number sentences that are true.

8	–	3	=	7	+	2	=	9
+	5	+	10	=	15	–	6	+
4	+	9	–	8	=	1	–	0
=	6	+	4	=	9	=	3	=
12	=	1	=	5	+	1	=	7
–	3	=	6	+	5	=	3	+
3	–	12	+	7	=	19	–	8
=	1	+	3	=	14	+	2	=
9	+	11	–	7	=	4	–	15

Sort the butterflies into two groups. Write the number in each group. Next, sort the butterflies in a different way. Now how many are in each group?

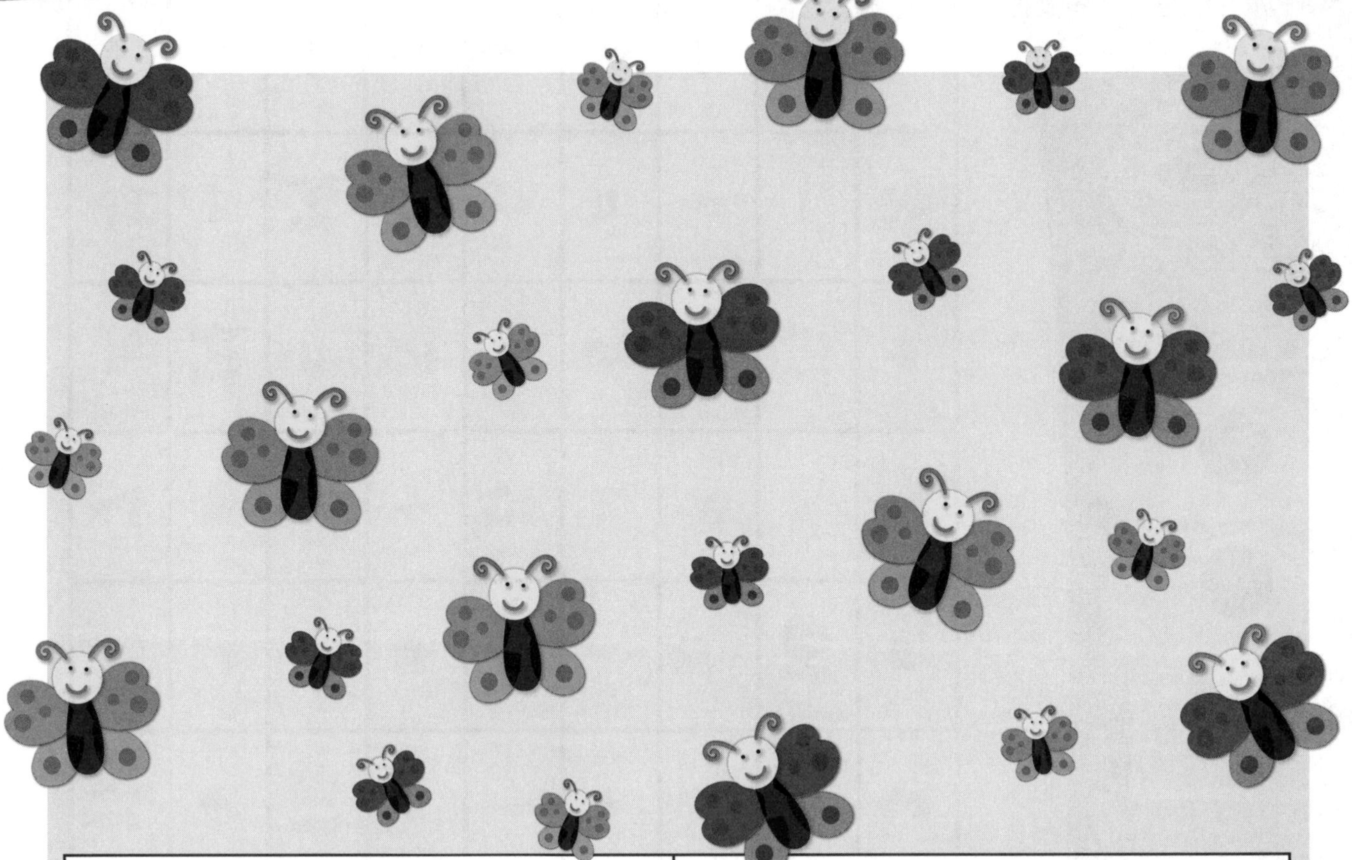

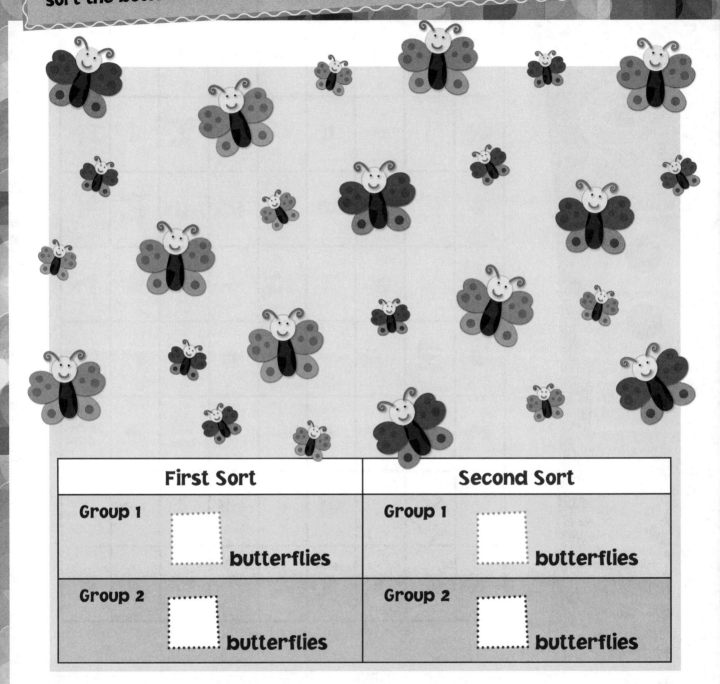

First Sort	Second Sort
Group 1 ☐ butterflies	Group 1 ☐ butterflies
Group 2 ☐ butterflies	Group 2 ☐ butterflies

Picture Perfect!

QUICK DRAW

Draw lines to divide the rectangle into equal fourths. Color each quarter with one of these patterns: stripes, polka dots, swirls, and zigzags.

Skill: Dividing Shapes

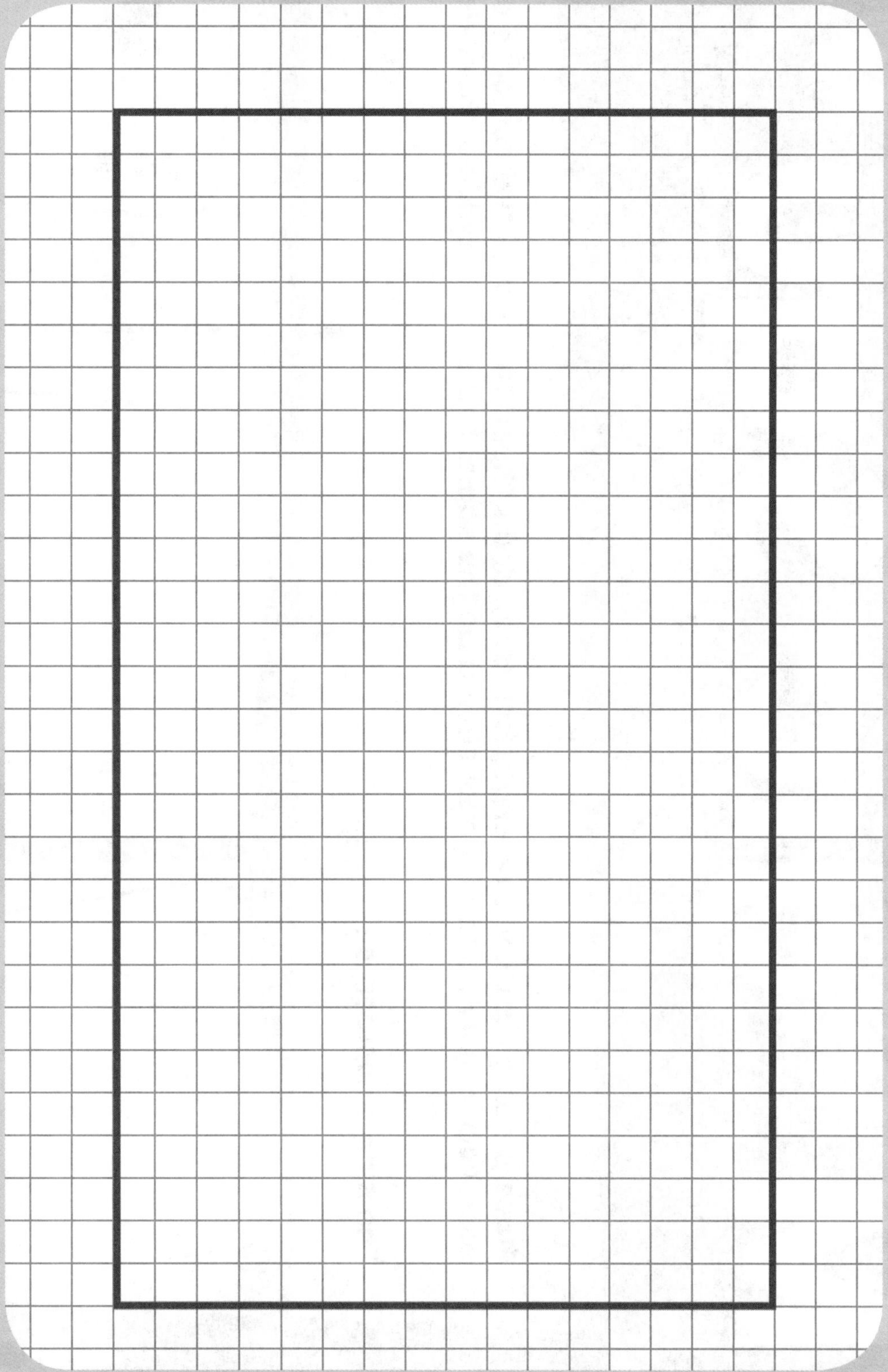

Magic Square

Place playing cards in the empty boxes, or draw them. The sum of the numbers on the cards in each row, column, and diagonal should be the same. This is the magic number. Write it below.

The magic number is ____ .

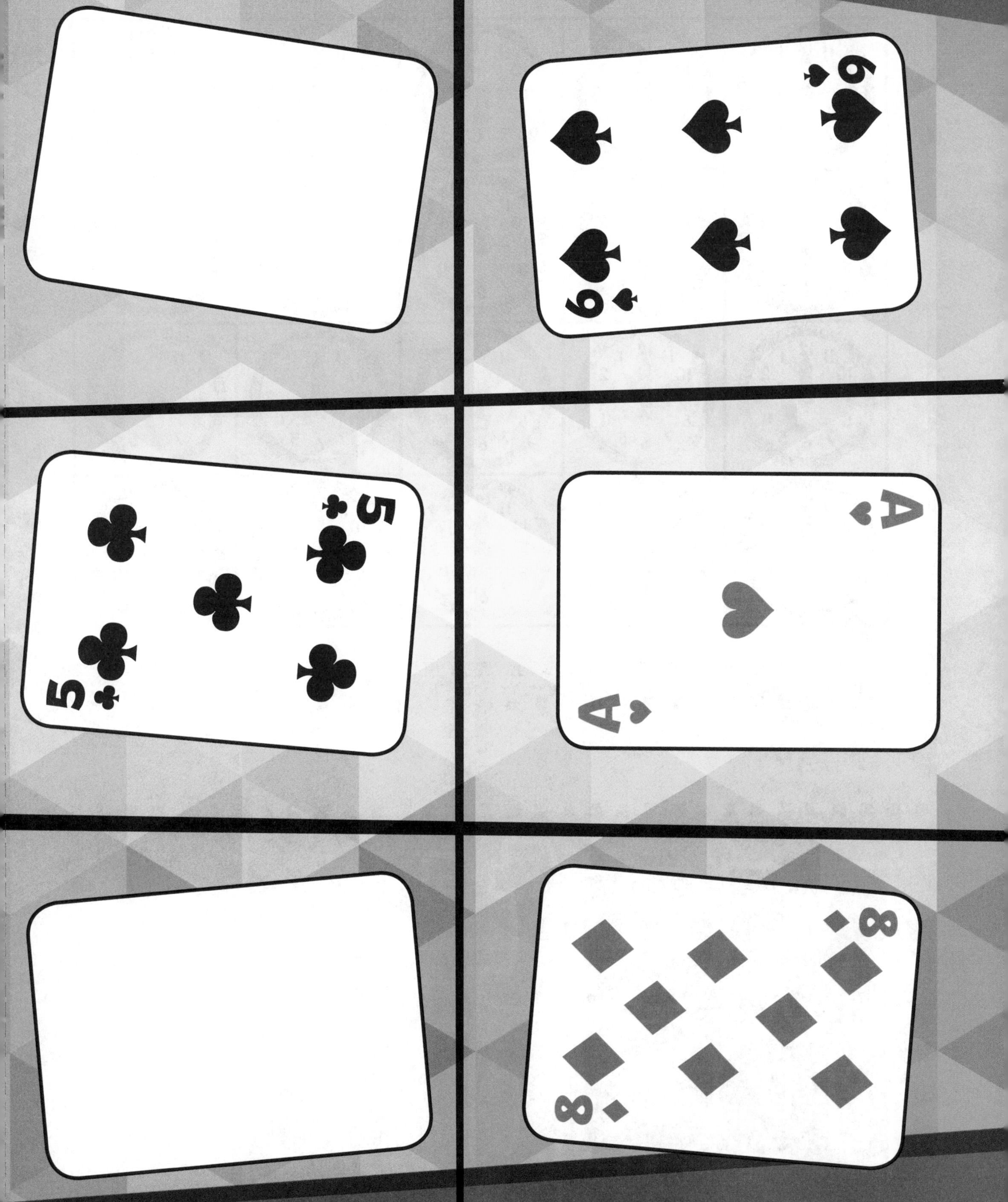
6
5
A
8

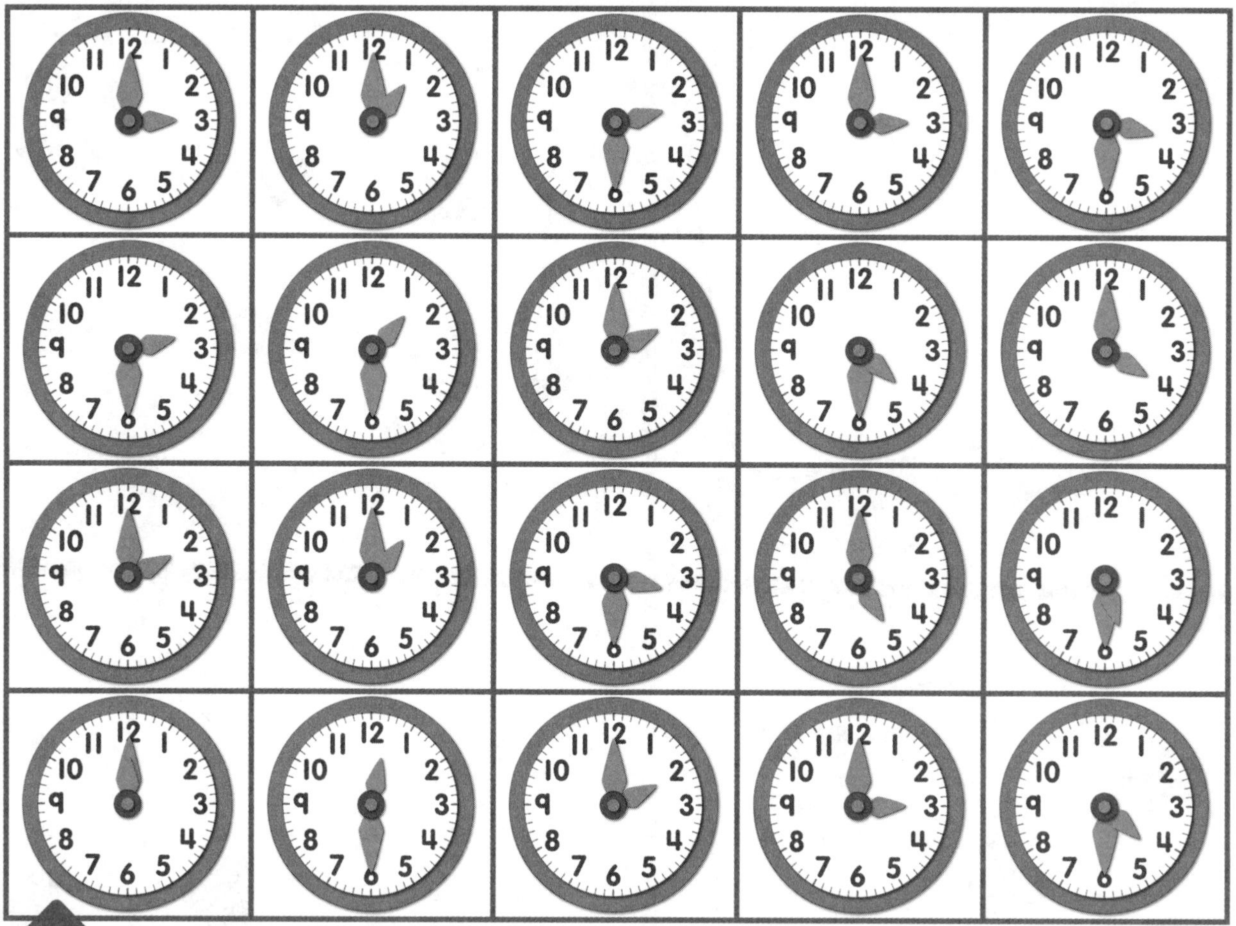

Start at 12:00. Move from clock to clock, adding 30 minutes each time. Circle the last clock in the path.

Math path

A Show of Hands

Skills: Comparing Numbers, Place Value

Cut out each two-digit number. Place all of the numbers face-down. Then, choose one or more games to play with your cards.

21	92
16	35
58	12
63	74
36	47
85	29
53	61

Games to Play

Game #1: Set a timer. Turn over the cards. Put the numbers in order from least to greatest. How long did it take? Play again. Can you beat your first time?

Game #2: Set a timer. Turn over the cards. Put the numbers in order from greatest to least. How long did it take? Play again. Can you beat your first time?

Game #3: Turn over two cards at a time. Do both numbers have the same digits? If they do, keep the cards and turn over two more.

PATTERN POWER

Skill: Addition

8		22	29		43
11	21			51	61
	28	36		52	
	55		65	70	

Find the pattern in each row. Write the missing numbers.

e(quation) sen+sation

Skills: Addition, Subtraction

The number sentences are missing their signs. Write + or – in each flower to make the sentence true.

1. 8 ☐ 4 ☐ 1 = 11
2. 2 ☐ 7 ☐ 3 = 12
3. 14 ☐ 10 ☐ 1 = 3
4. 2 ☐ 8 ☐ 3 = 7
5. 12 ☐ 6 ☐ 3 = 9
6. 15 ☐ 7 ☐ 5 = 13

STORY STUMPERS

Read each story problem. Draw lines to show the answers.

Skills: Comparing Length, Word Problems

Molly's ribbon is longer than Nina's. Jack's ribbon is the shortest. Match each ribbon to its owner's name.

Jack

Nina

Molly

Lily's pencil is shorter than Lucy's. Henry's pencil is shorter than Lily's. Match each pencil to its owner's name.

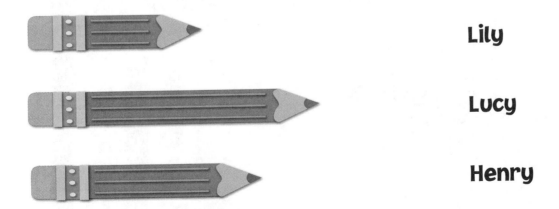

Lily

Lucy

Henry

Skills: Addition, Subtraction, Counting by Tens

NUMBER CROSS

Across

2. 95+
4. 68–
5. 86–
7. 2+
8. 21+
10. 83+
12. 30–
13. 54+
15. 57–
16. 100+

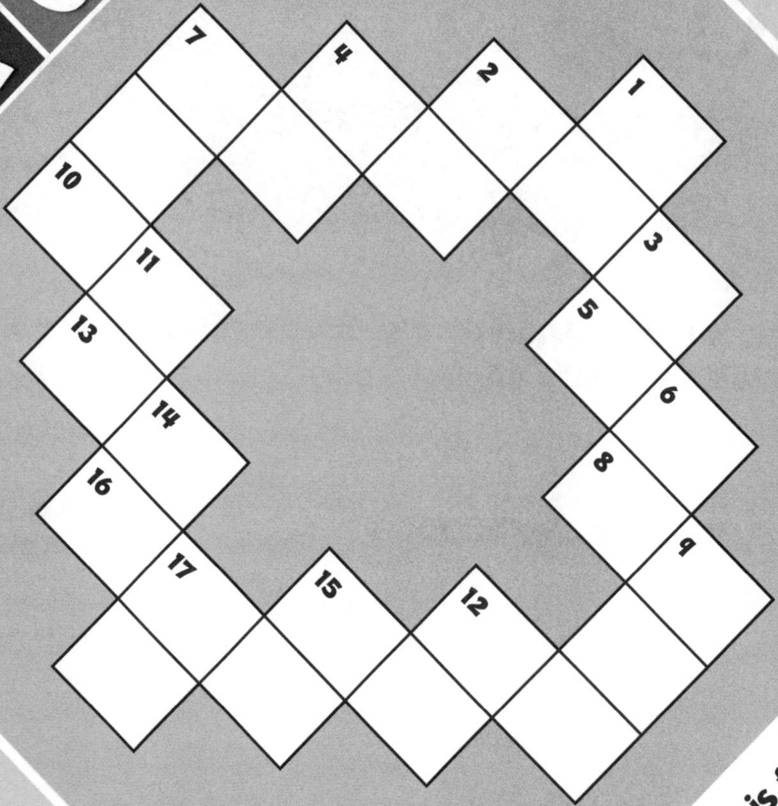

Down

1. 50–
2. 8+
3. 67–
4. 42+
6. 73–
7. 99+
9. 90+
11. 46–
12. 37–
14. 31+
15. 50–
17. 27–

Look at each number. If it is followed by a plus sign (+), add 10. If it is followed by a minus sign (–), subtract 10. Then, write the new number in the puzzle.

MASTER SHAPE

Skill: Understanding Shapes

How many different shapes do you see? Count each kind of shape. Write the total.

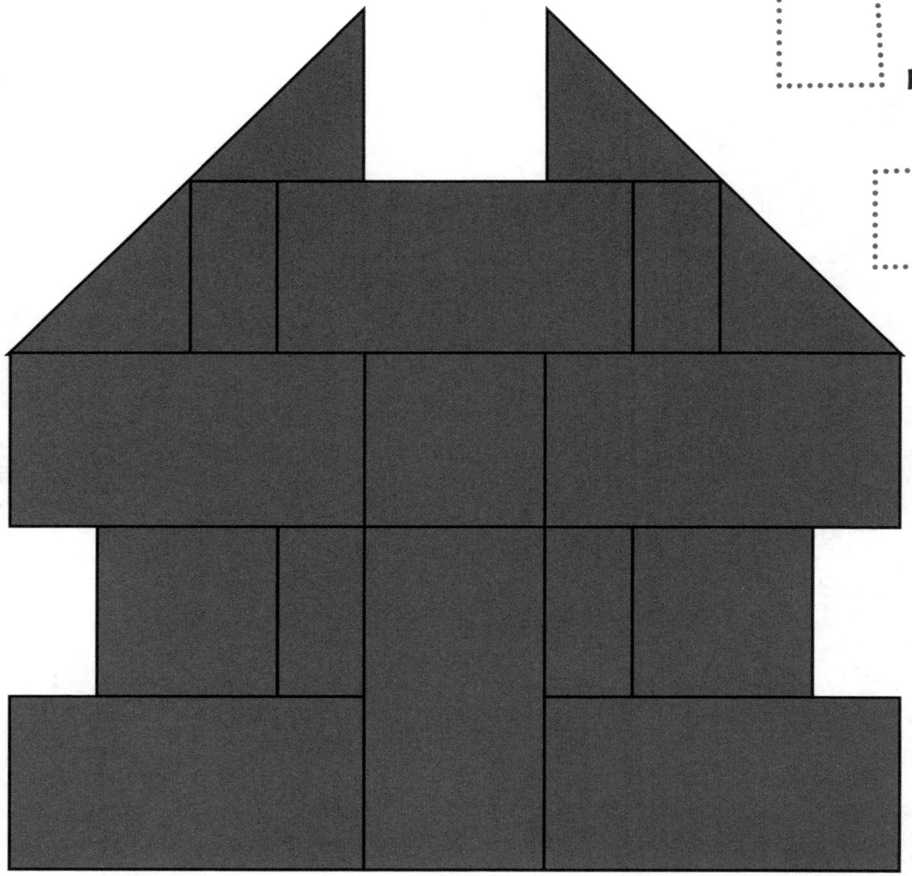

☐ rectangles

☐ triangles

☐ squares

DARE TO DECODE

Skill: Addition

Use the key to write the numbers in the addition problems. Solve the problems. Then, write your answers in code under the problem numbers to find a secret message.

Code Key

0	1	2	3	4	5	6	7	8	9
G	E	S	I	L	N	F	A	U	R

1. SE + SG = ☐

   ☐ + ☐ = ☐

2. AS + A = ☐

   ☐ + ☐ = ☐

3. SI + IG = ☐

   ☐ + ☐ = ☐

4. LE + R = ☐

   ☐ + ☐ = ☐

5. ER + A = ☐

   ☐ + ☐ = ☐

6. IN + NG = ☐

   ☐ + ☐ = ☐

1	2	3	4	5	6
_ _	_ _	_ _	_ _	, _ _	_ _

IT FITS!

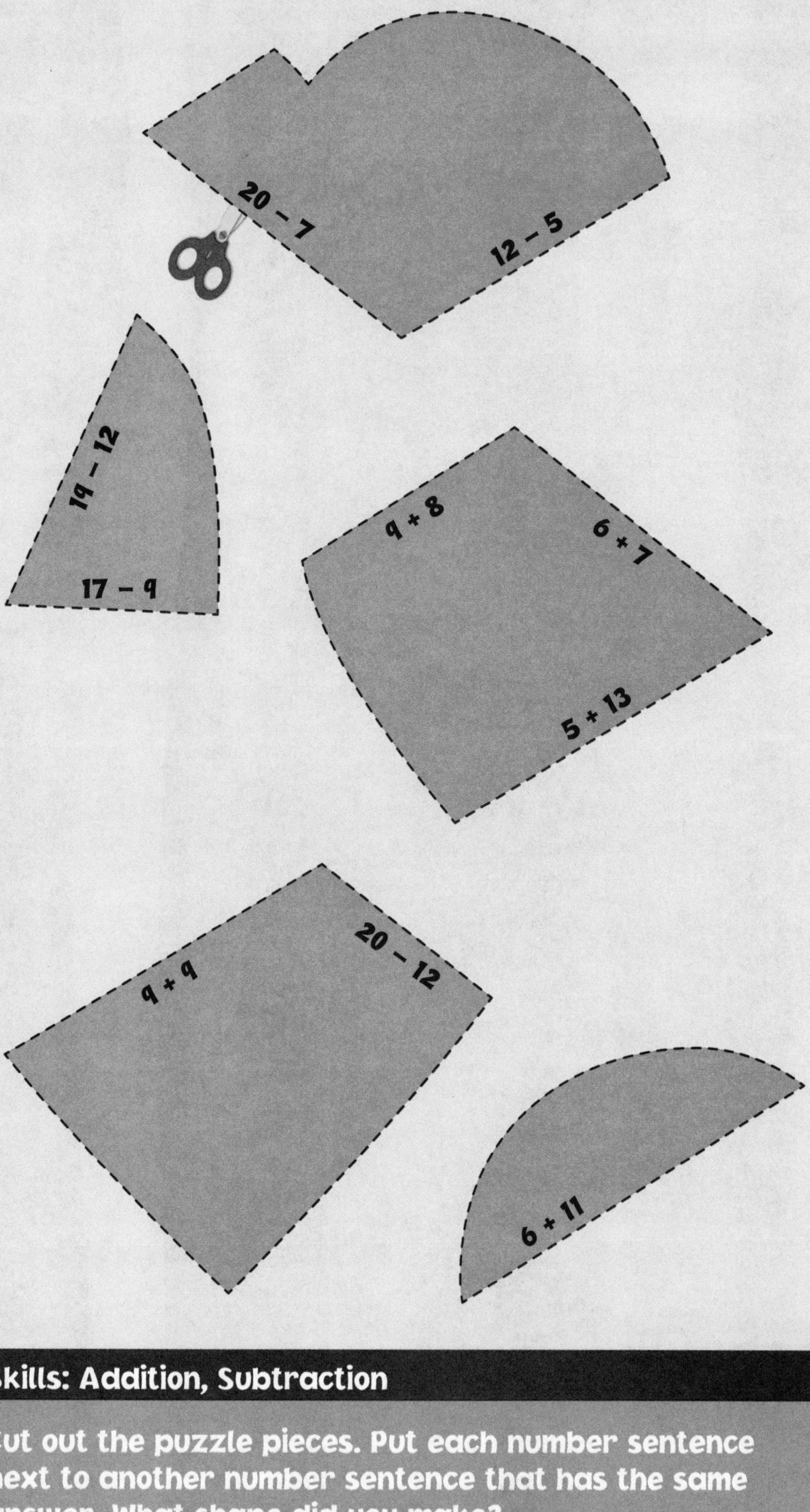

Skills: Addition, Subtraction

Cut out the puzzle pieces. Put each number sentence next to another number sentence that has the same answer. What shape did you make?

Guess Again

Use the clues to find each secret two-digit number.

It is more than 83.

It is less than 92.

Add its digits together, and you get 12.

Secret Number:

Tens Ones

It is less than 39.

It is more than 29.

The difference between its digits is 4.

Secret Number:

Tens Ones

Skills: Comparing Numbers, Place Value

It is less than 79.

It is more than 69.

The difference between its digits is 0.

Secret Number:

Tens Ones

It is more than 42.

It is less than 55.

Add its digits together, and you get 5.

Secret Number:

Tens Ones

ON THE DOT

Skills: Addition, Counting by Tens

Start at the smallest number. Add 10 each time as you connect the dots.

What kind of vehicle did you make? Circle the answer.

race car	sailboat
train	truck

77 • • 107

87 • 67 • • 17 • 97

57 • • 27

47 • • 37

QUICK DRAW

Use a ruler to draw a square. Make each side two inches long. Use a ruler to draw a triangle. Make one side three inches long. Color and decorate the shapes.

Skills: Drawing Shapes, Measuring Length

square

triangle

Magic Square

Use the code to find the total in each square. Then, write the sum of the numbers in each row and column.

 = 10  = 1

Follow the directions to divide each shape into equal pieces.

Divide the shape in half to make 2 equal triangles.

Divide the shape in half to make 2 equal squares.

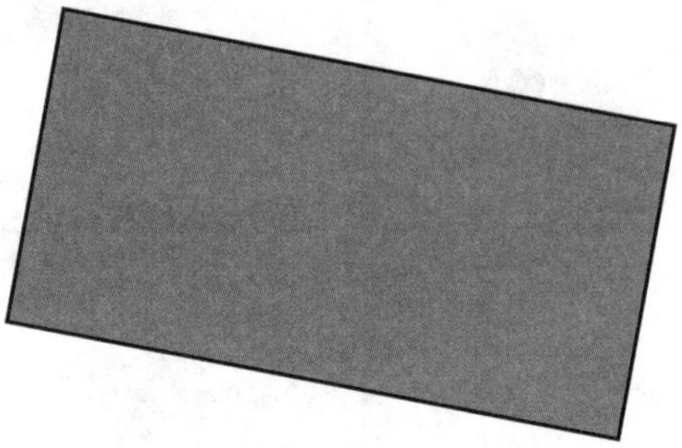

Divide the shape into fourths to make 4 equal triangles.

Divide the shape into fourths to make 4 equal squares.

Picture Perfect!

A Show of Hands

Skill: Telling Time

Cut out each clock face. Glue or tape it onto the circle that shows the same time.

10:30

1:30

2:00

8:00

3:30

12:30

11:00

6:30

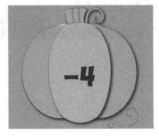

−3	+7	−2	END
+5	−4	+6	−10
START	+11	+2	+3

Start with 0. Perform each operation. Keep a running total. Can you end with 8? There is only one correct path.

Math path

PATTERN POWER

Skills: Addition, Subtraction

102	☐	62	42	☐	2
12	23	☐	45	56	☐
☐	87	77	☐	57	☐
☐	32	☐	40	44	☐

Find the pattern in each row. Fill in the missing numbers.

LANGUAGE ARTS

Skill: Adjectives

In Search Of

Circle the adjective in each phrase. Then, find the adjectives in the puzzle. Look closely! The words may be hidden backward or diagonally.

the tall girl
the silly clown
the slow snail
the red ball
the hot sun
six cats

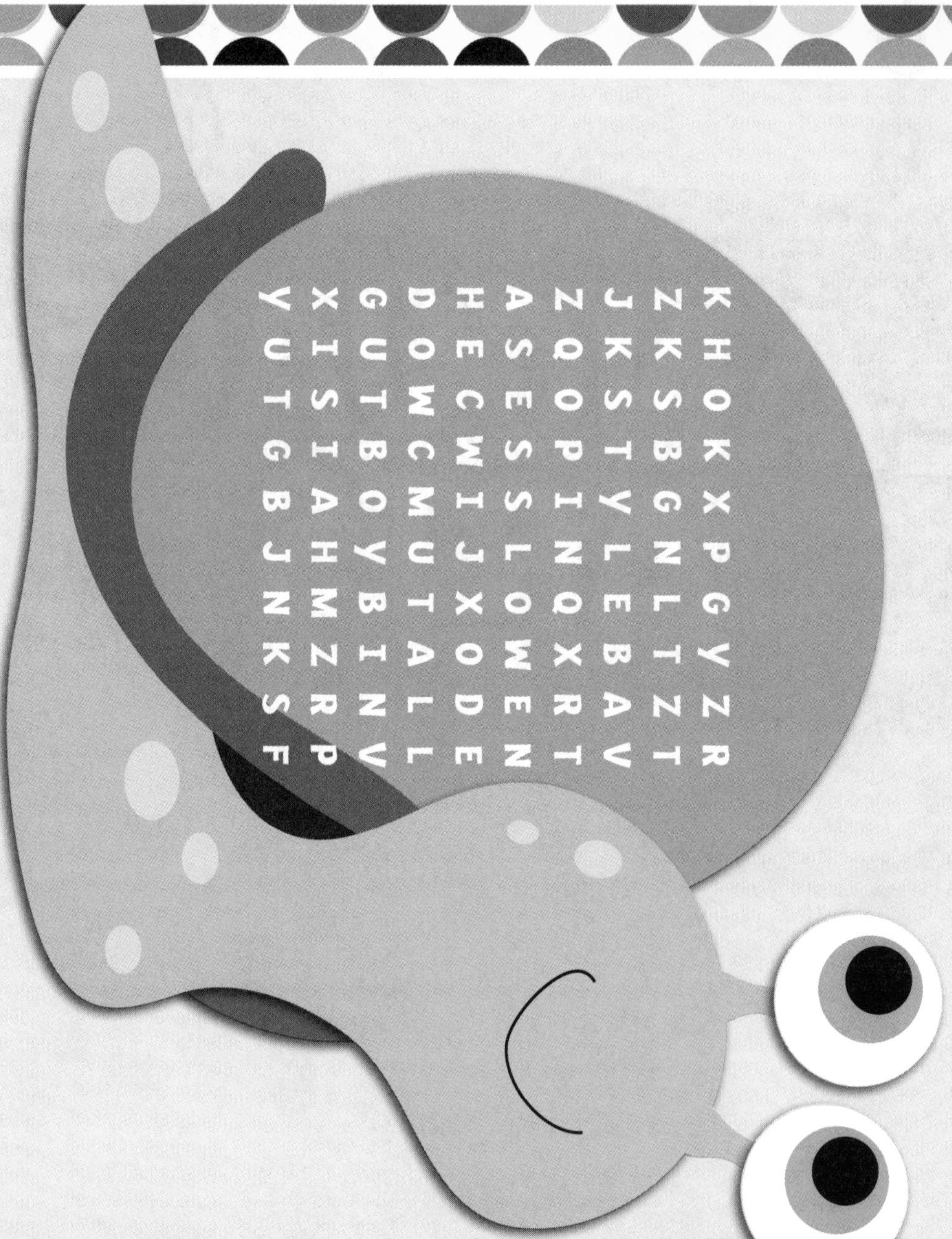

Skill: Categories

Cut out the pictures. Read the words. Glue or tape pictures of pond animals onto the pond. If the animal is not found at a pond, do not put it in the picture.

Picture This!

JUMBLED UP

Skill: Nouns

Nouns name people, places, and things. Unscramble each noun. Then, draw lines to match the words and pictures.

rkfo

hreso

igrl

ahdn

atsr

tere

Sudoku for You

____	c	____
t	____	____
____	____	a

Skills:
Handwriting, Spelling

Write letters in the boxes so that each row and column has the letters to spell  . Do not use any letter more than once in the same row or column.

Skill: Writing Sentences

Sentence Scramble

Draw a line to connect the words and form a sentence. Write the sentence on the lines.

____

____

CODE BREAKER

Skill: Vowel Sounds

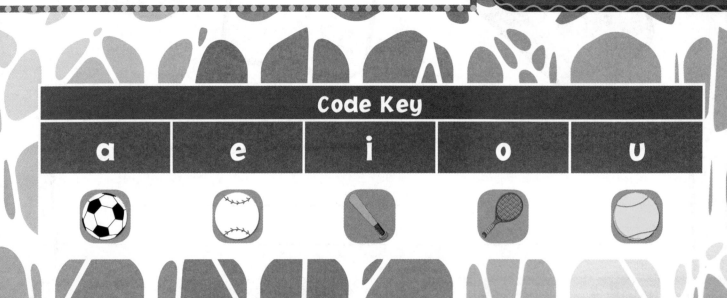

All the vowel letters in the words are written in code. Use the code to write the words. Circle all the words with long vowel sounds.

1. k  t  =

2. m   n =

3. st  mp =

4. p  st =

5. c  t  =

6. p  g =

Code Key

a	e	i	o	u

MIRROR

Skills: Verbs, Spelling

1. bang   banged .... ○
2. dance   danced .... ○
3. cry   cryed .... ○
4. play   played .... ○
5. chew   chewed .... ○
6. stop   stoped .... ○

Read each verb. Then, hold the page up to a mirror to read the word beside it. If the past-tense form of the verb is spelled correctly, draw a happy face in the circle (☺). If it is not spelled correctly, draw a sad face (☹).

Write a sentence with a four-letter noun and a four-letter verb.

____

Use the letters in "tub" to make a conjunction. Use it in a sentence.

____

Use letters from "craft" to make a noun and an adjective. Use them in a sentence.

____

Write a sentence with the conjunction "and" and a three-letter adjective.

____

How good are you at following directions? Write the sentences described to find out! Begin each sentence with a capital letter. End with an end mark.

Skills: Conjunctions, Writing Sentences

QUIZ WHIZ

JUMBLED UP

Skills: Spelling, Handwriting

How many words can you make from the letters in "ladybug"? Write them on the lines.

ladybug

RIDDLE ME

Use the clues to spell a word with a common prefix. On the line, write the base word.

Skills: Prefixes, Base Words

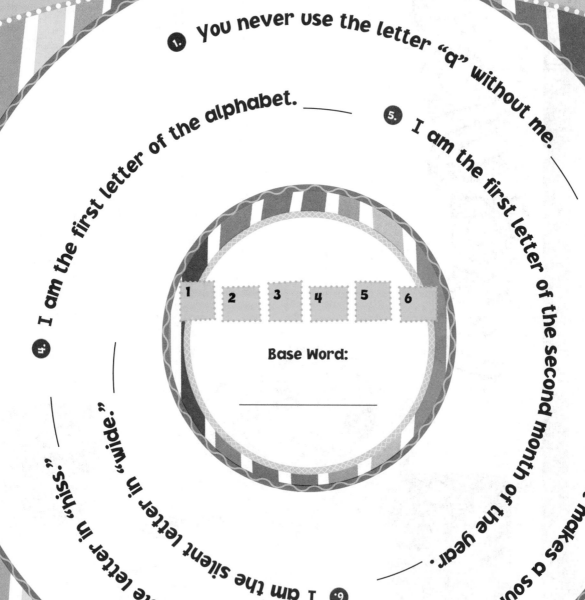

1. You never use the letter "q" without me. ____
2. I am the first letter that makes a sound in "knife." ____
3. I am the double letter in "hiss." ____
4. I am the first letter of the alphabet. ____
5. I am the first letter of the second month of the year. ____
6. I am the silent letter in "wide." ____

1	2	3	4	5	6

Base Word: ____________

ALPHA-CHALLENGE

Skills: Syllables, Vowel Sounds

Look at the two-syllable word that fits each topic. Circle at least one vowel letter in each syllable. Then, write a one-syllable word that fits each topic. Circle at least one vowel letter in each word you write.

Topic	One-Syllable Word	Two-Syllable Word
Animal		chick•en = chicken
Fruit		ap•ple = apple
Boy Name		Ja•son = Jason
Girl Name		Ri•ta = Rita
Clothing		rain•coat = raincoat
Toy		glid•er = glider
Shape		rhom•bus = rhombus
Color		pur•ple = purple

MAZE CRAZE

Skills: Prepositions, Writing Sentences

Help the pirate find the treasure. Make a path by coloring each space that has a preposition. Then, choose one preposition you colored. Use it to write a sentence on the lines.

for	she	moon	swim	red	they
from	ball	him	fell	rug	bed
in	girl	pretty	to	at	under
at	over	by	of	bunny	into
table	bug	it	six	hit	for
he	fan	kite	I	jump	with

MIRROR

Skill: Nouns and Verbs

1. Ella and Lex walks to school.

2. The frog jumps in the pond.

3. I will be late today.

4. Cam play ball.

5. Mom mows the lawn.

6. We pushes the baby in her stroller.

Hold up the page to a mirror to read each sentence. If the verb in the sentence matches the noun, circle the thumbs-up sign (👍). If the verb does not match the noun, circle the thumbs-down sign (👎).

PREST-O CHANGE-O!

Skills: Verbs, Handwriting

How can you change the present into the past? One letter at a time! Write a word to match each clue. Each word should be the same as the word above it except for one changed letter. Watch the verb change from the present tense to the past tense like magic!

s i t

___ i t

h ___ t

___ o t

p ___ t

___ a t

s a t

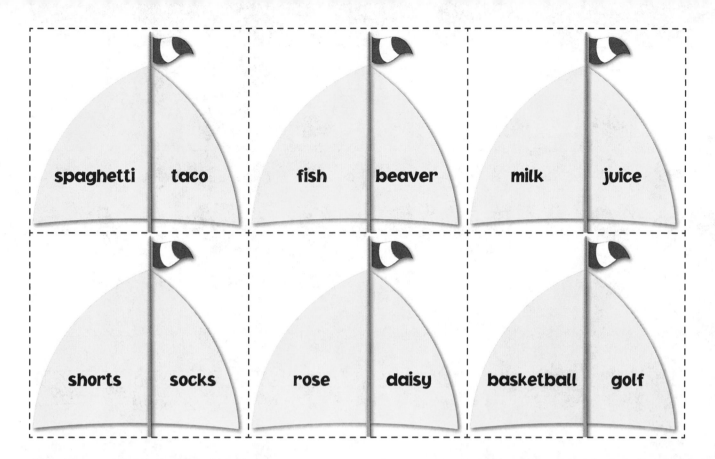

spaghetti / taco	fish / beaver	milk / juice
shorts / socks	rose / daisy	basketball / golf

Skill: Categories

IN PIECES

Cut out the pieces. Match the words on each sail to a category on a boat.

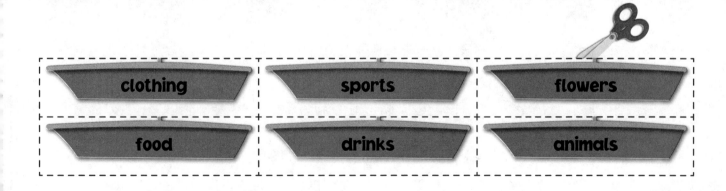

clothing	sports	flowers
food	drinks	animals

RIDDLE ME

Write a letter for each clue. Put the letters together to answer the riddle.

Skills: Spelling, Context Clues

1. The first letter is in 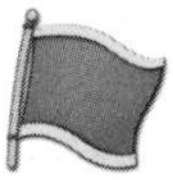 and in .

2. The second letter is in  but not in 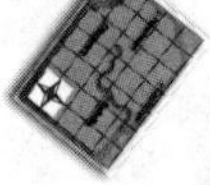.

3. The third letter is doubled at the end of 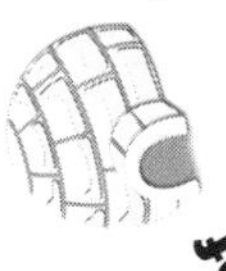.

4. The fourth letter is in  but not in .

5. The fifth letter is in  but not in .

I might honk at you,
but I am not a car.
I am a . . .

Answer:

1	2	3	4	5

Sudoku for You

	e	
		s
h		

Skills: Pronouns, Handwriting

Write letters in the boxes so that each row and column has the letters to spell a pronoun that could take the place of "Hannah" in the sentence. Do not use any letter more than once in the same row or column.

<u>Hannah</u> kicked the soccer ball.

In Search Of

Skill: Writing Sentences

In each row of the puzzle, cross out the letter that appears most often. The rest of the letters will spell a word. Write the word at the end of each row. Then, use all the words to write a question. Do not forget to write a question mark at the end of your sentence. Write a sentence that answers the question you wrote.

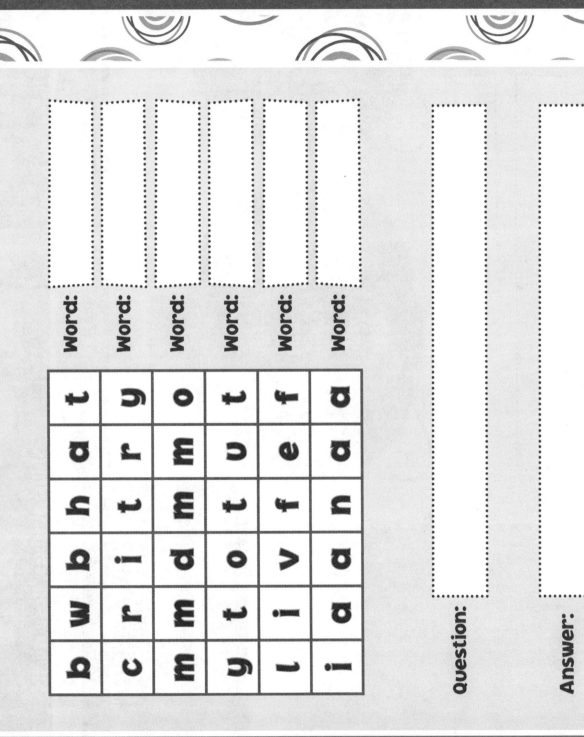

b	w	b	h	a	t	Word:
c	r	i	t	r	y	Word:
m	m	d	m	m	o	Word:
y	t	o	t	u	t	Word:
l	i	v	f	e	f	Word:
i	a	a	n	a	a	Word:

Question:

Answer:

JUMBLED UP

Skills: Suffixes, Base Words

Match base words from the pumpkin on the left with suffixes from the pumpkin on the right. Write the new words you made.

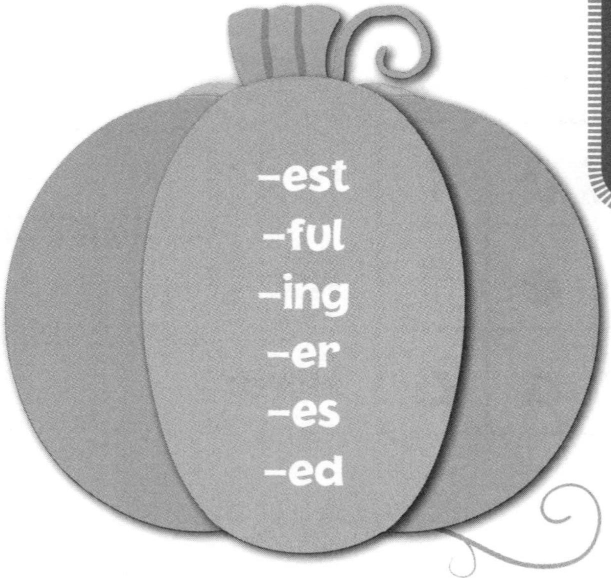

CODE BREAKER

Skill: Using Capital Letters

Use the code to find the names of days and months. Begin each word with a capital letter.

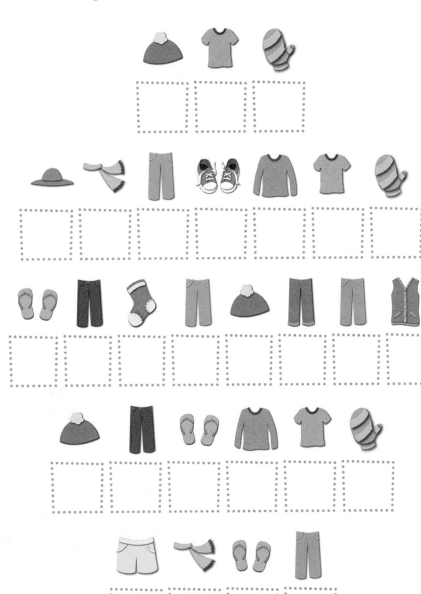

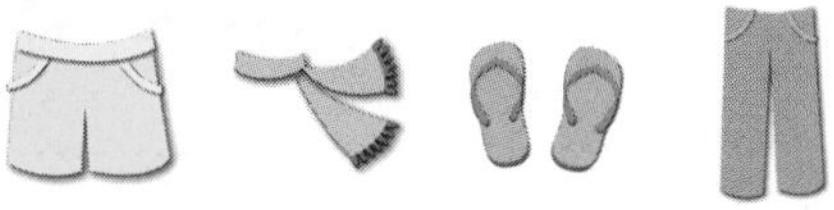

Code Key

a	b	d	e	j	m	n	o	r	s	t	u	v	y

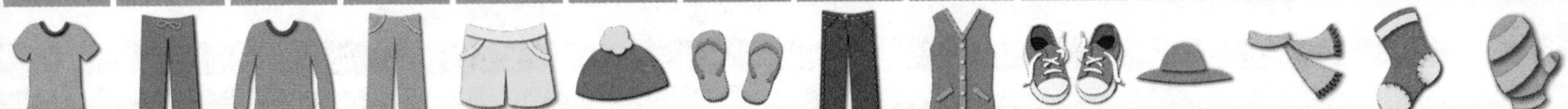

Skill: Writing Sentences

Use the words beside the pictures to form simple and compound sentences.

 ant  an apple 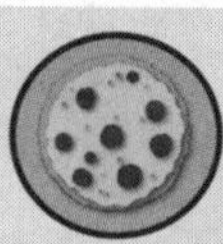 a cookie

Simple Sentence:

A happy __________ found __________ on the picnic blanket.

 a fish  a seashell  the boat

Compound Sentence:

I saw __________ jump near __________,

and I found __________ on the beach.

 cat 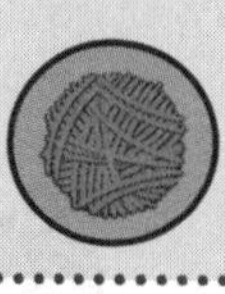 yarn 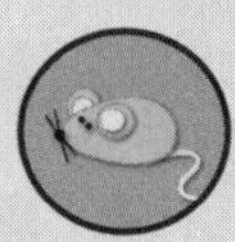 a toy mouse

Simple Sentence:

My __________ plays with __________.

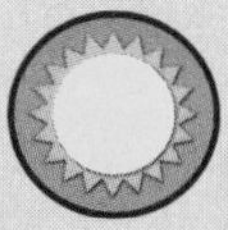 sunny 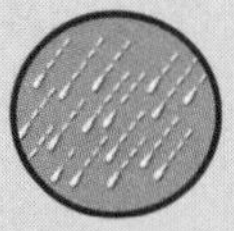 rainy  cloudy

Compound Sentence:

Is it __________ today, or is it __________?

Picture This!

Skills: Vowel Sounds, Spelling

GO ACROSS

The word in each clue has a long vowel sound. Unscramble the underlined letters to write a word in the puzzle that has a short vowel sound.

1. 
plane

2. 
globe

3. 
rain

4. 
nose

5. 
kite

6. 
beads

7. 
grapes

Where could you grow flowers? Write the circled letters in order to find the answer.

in a ___ ___ ___ ___ ___ ___ ___

RIDDLE ME

Write the word that completes each hink pink.

Skills: Context Clues, Spelling

A hink pink is a pair of rhyming words that answer a riddle.

Example: fat cat

1. What is a huge hog? a big ________
2. What is an unhappy father? a ________ dad
3. What is a large branch? a ________ twig
4. What is a rabbit that tells jokes? a funny ________
5. What is a clean road? a neat ________
6. What is a cozy insect? a ________ bug

Write a sentence using the word ending in silent e.

____

Write a sentence using the word that ends with a vowel sound.

____

Write a sentence using the word with a long a sound.

____

Write a sentence using the word with a short i sound.

____

Read each direction. Write a sentence using a word from the box. Cross out each word as you use it. Write the two words that are left over: ______________ ______________

Word Box

short	bring
mail	tall
horse	silly

Skills: Writing Sentences, Vowel Sounds

QUIZ WHIZ

MAZE CRAZE

Skills: Articles, Writing Sentences

Articles are small words (such as "the," "an," and "a") that come before a noun. Help the monkey find a path to the banana. Color each space that has an article. Then, choose two articles from the puzzle. Use them to write a sentence on the lines.

a	an	the	an	what	she
with	pen	ring	the	cup	too
smile	but	gate	a	to	push
it	cut	fan	an	catch	and
rug	from	pool	the	me	I
beg	safe	in	a	the	an

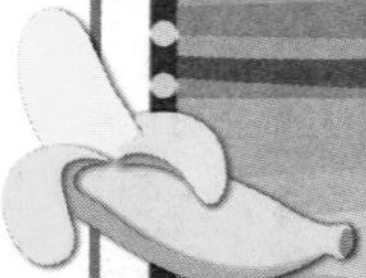

CODE BREAKER

Skill: Handwriting

Use the code to answer the questions.

1. What letter comes after "U"? ________

2. What letter comes between "J" and "H"? ________

3. Write the uppercase form of the letter that comes between "D" and "e." ________

4. What letter comes before "M"? ________

5. What is the third letter after "p"? ________

6. What letter comes between "c" and "i"? ________

Code Key

p	D	n	e	B	t	h	a	l	U	F	v	M	c	b	i	J	t	H

In Search Of

Read each present-tense verb. Find and circle its past-tense form in the puzzle. For example, if the word shown is "kick," search for "kicked" in the puzzle. Look carefully! Words may be hidden backward or diagonally.

- work
- ask
- bake
- drop
- hug
- pinch
- wash

Skill: Verbs

A	S	K	E	D	N	B	P	W	G
T	O	B	D	N	D	C	I	O	U
G	B	E	M	Y	Z	N	N	R	H
D	R	O	P	P	E	D	C	K	E
W	W	O	E	D	B	S	H	E	U
O	A	K	U	A	E	Q	E	D	W
X	E	S	K	R	G	G	D	K	V
R	S	E	H	E	O	T	G	B	P
I	D	J	Q	E	E	J	F	U	S
N	R	G	T	D	D	W	G	P	H

PRESTO-CHANGE-O!

Skills: Vowel Sounds, Handwriting, Spelling

How can you change a cat into a dog? One letter at a time! Write a short vowel word to match each clue. Each word should be the same as the word above it except for one changed letter.

c a t

c a ___

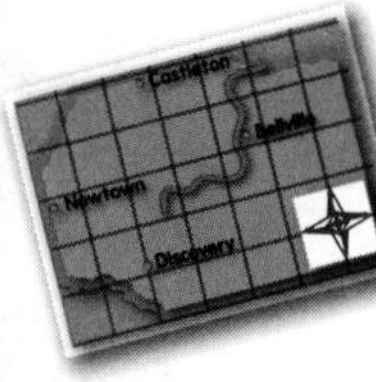

___ a p

m ___ p

___ o p

p o ___

___ o t

d o g

Skill: Writing Sentences

Sentence Scramble

Draw a line to connect the orange words to make a question. Draw a line to connect the green words to make a command. Write the sentences on the lines. End the question with a question mark (?). End the command with an exclamation mark (!).

that

for

Have

seen

you

Watch

boots

snake

out

my

JUMBLED UP

Skill: Writing Sentences

A compound sentence tells two ideas. It contains a joining word such as "and" or "but." Cut out the tiles. Arrange them to make a compound sentence. Write the sentence on the lines.

at is al

l whi

my ca

Max's c

ripes.

t has st

te, but

Sudoku for You

		y	
	a		p
l			
		p	

Skills: Verbs, Handwriting

Write letters in the boxes so that each row and column has the letters to spell the verb that is missing from the second sentence. Do not use any letter more than once in the same row or column.

Yesterday, we played.

Today, we ________.

WORD MATH

Skill: Consonant Blends

Solve each word puzzle. Circle a consonant blend or consonant team in each word you write.

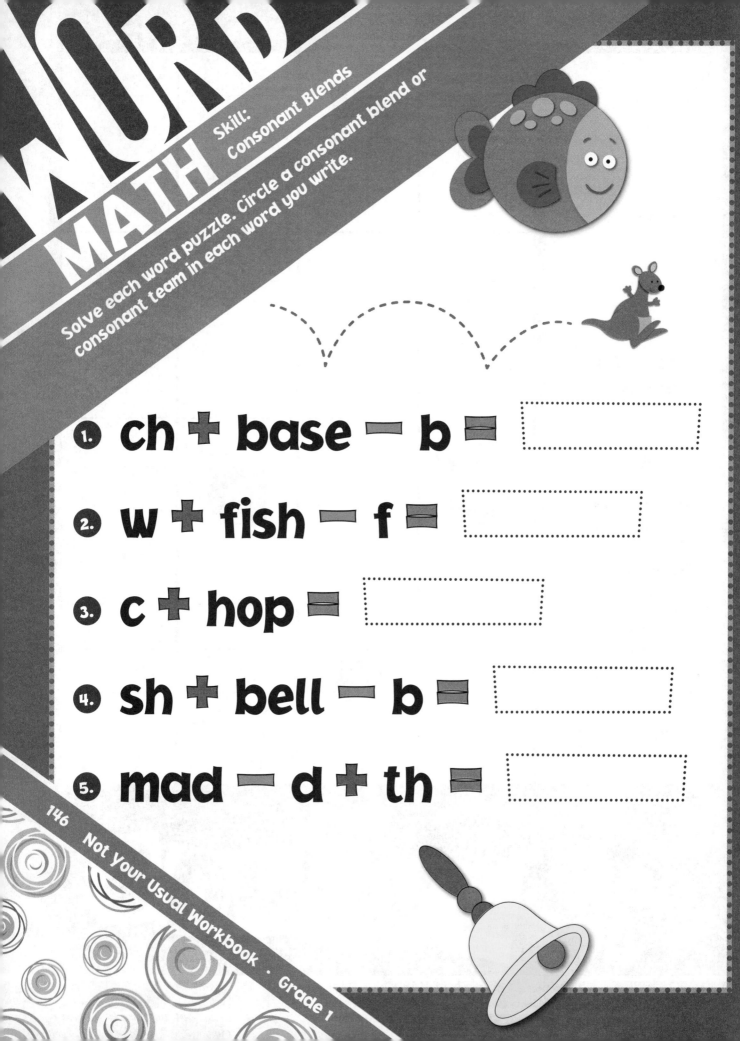

1. ch + base − b = ______
2. w + fish − f = ______
3. c + hop = ______
4. sh + bell − b = ______
5. mad − d + th = ______

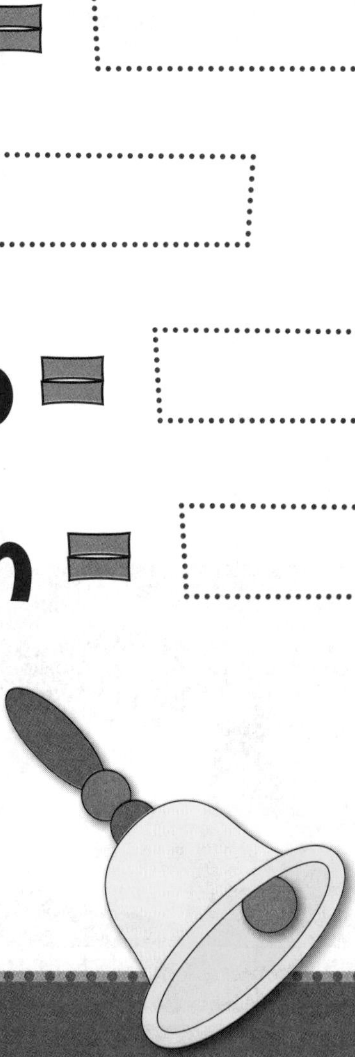

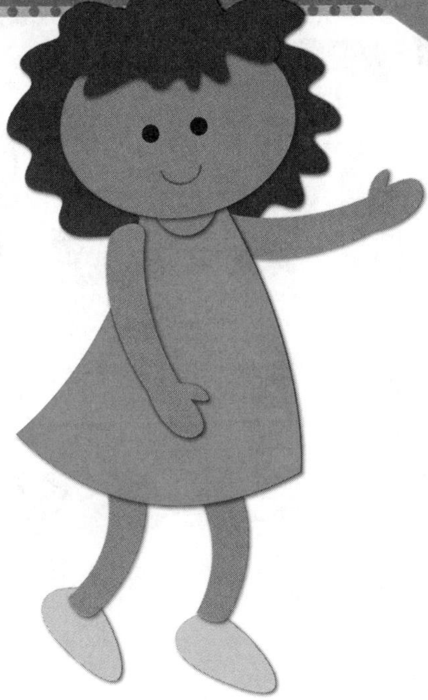

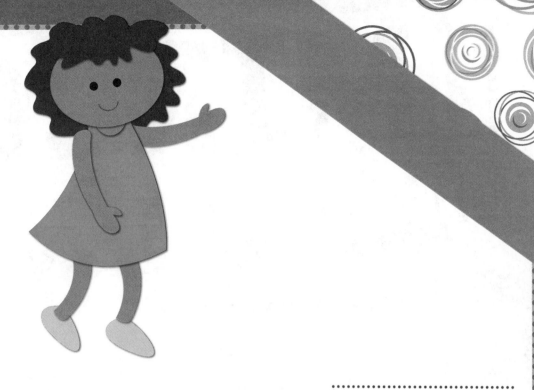

6. ch + dress − dr = ☐

7. took − k + th = ☐

8. th + twin − tw = ☐

9. sh + brake − br = ☐

10. wh + feel − f = ☐

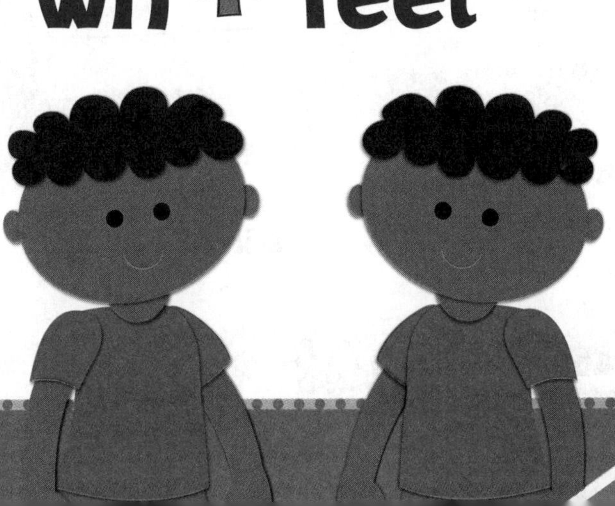

Skill: Using Commas

MIRROR

1. pens markers and glue

2. a dog a cat and a hamster

3. Mom Dad Andy and me

4. the bee the ant and the frog

5. eggs milk butter and bread

6. a game a doll and two balls

In a list, write a comma (,) after each item before the word "and." Hold the page up to a mirror to read each phrase. Then, write it on the line. Add commas where they are needed.

ALPHA-CHALLENGE

Skill: Nouns

Common nouns name types of people, places, and things. Proper nouns name specific people, places, and things. When you write a proper noun, begin each important word with a capital letter. Write nouns to complete the chart.

Nouns

Common Noun	Proper Nouns
man	Mr. Woods
girl	
street	
	Rockland Public Library
	Atlantic Ocean
state	
	The Cat in the Hat
pet	
	St. Ann Hospital

1. Q: What is "brighter"?

A: It is a word that means "more bright."

2. Q: ______________________________

A: It is a word that means "fill again."

3. Q: ______________________________

A: It is a word that means "most tall."

4. Q: ______________________________

A: It is a word that means "full of joy."

5. Q: ______________________________

A: It is a word that means "not able."

Write a question to match each answer. Your question should use a word from the word box. The first one is done for you.

Word Box

unable
tallest
joyful
refill
brighter

QUIZ WHIZ

Skills: Prefixes, Suffixes

Skill: Vowel Sounds

IN PIECES

Cut out the pieces. Decide whether each word has a short vowel sound or a long vowel sound. Use the pieces to make two trains.

Skill: Handwriting

Look at each letter below. Does it have straight lines, curvy lines, or both? Write the letters in the Venn diagram.

h A S R d H p I t O x z U W B C M f

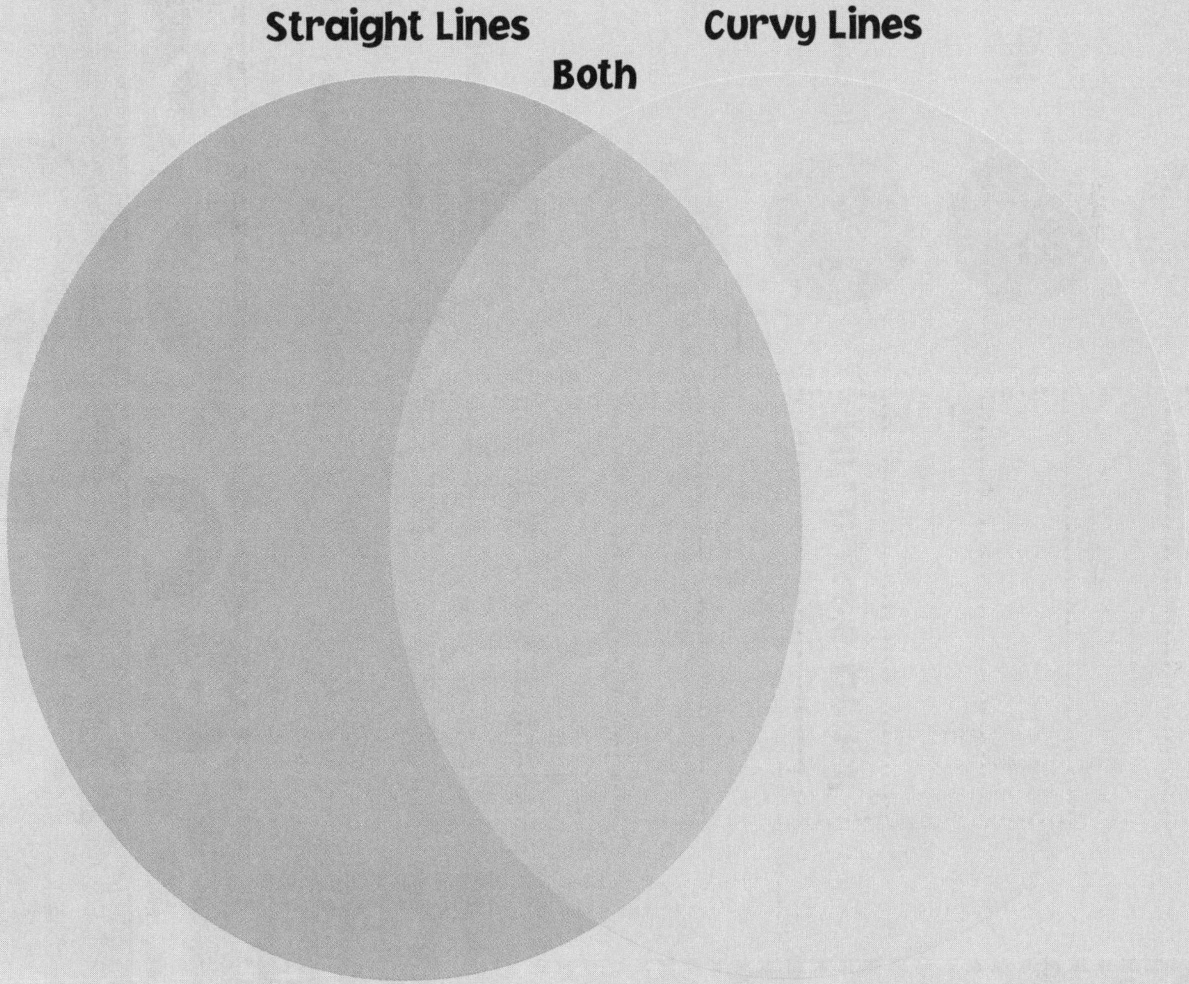

Picture This!

JUMBLED UP

Skill: Nouns

Draw a line to match each owner with something that is owned. Combine the words to write a phrase. The first one is done for you.

Who Owns It?		What Is Owned?		
Lena's		bone		
Mom's		car		
Mac's		pencil	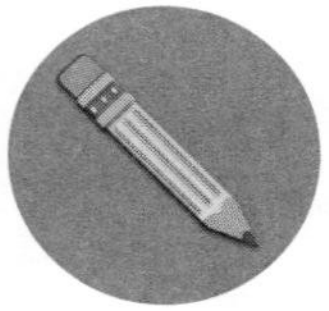	Mr. Duke's pencil
Mr. Duke's		gift		
Tucker's		hat		

In Search Of

Skill: Prepositions

Circle the preposition in each phrase. Then, find the prepositions in the puzzle.

in the pool	from the girl	under the bed	for my mom
by the car	with the cheese	over the tree	at Lola's house

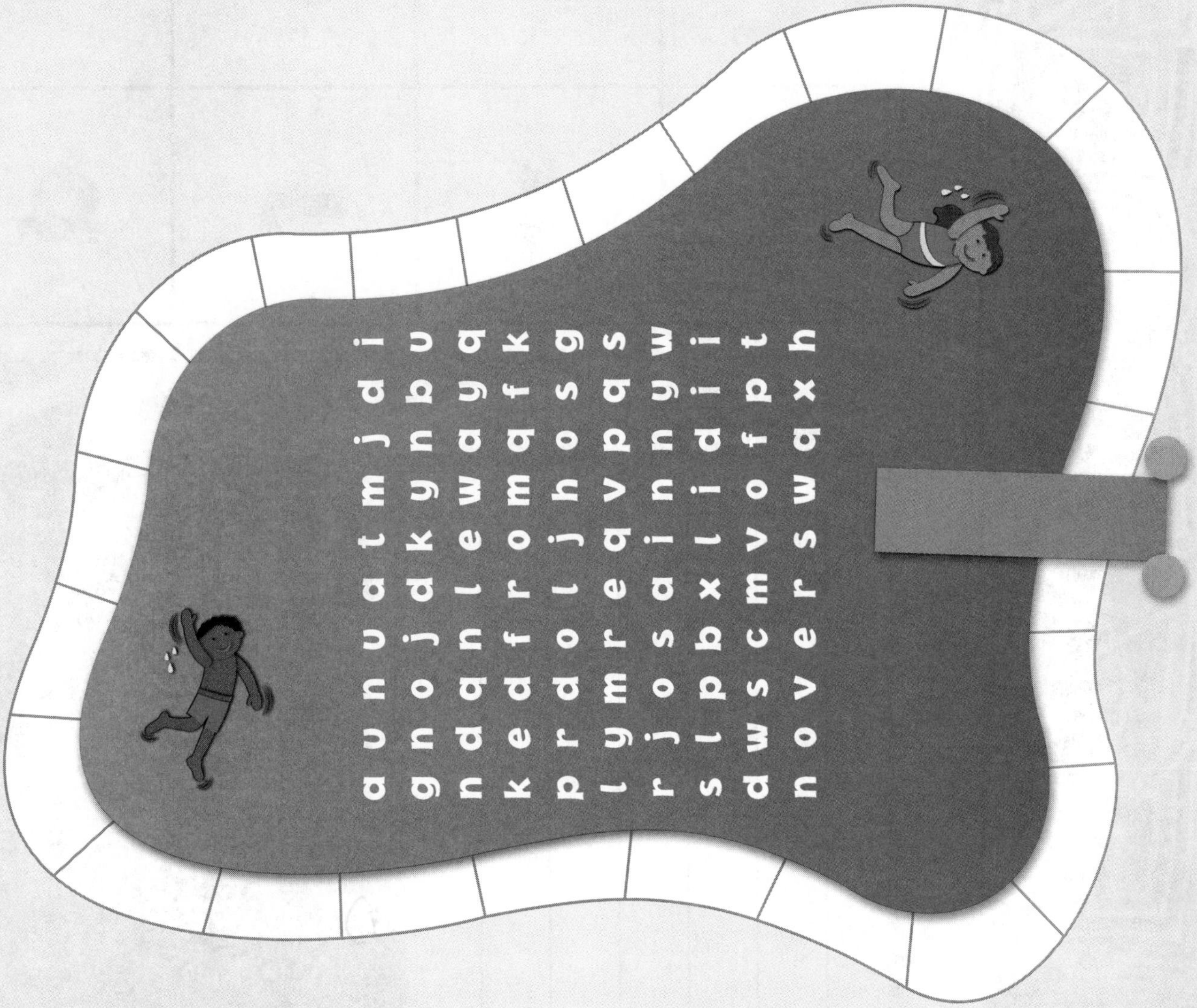

a	u	n	u	a	t	m	j	d	i
g	n	o	j	d	k	y	n	b	u
n	d	q	n	l	e	w	a	y	q
k	e	d	f	r	o	m	q	f	k
p	r	d	o	l	j	h	o	s	g
l	y	m	r	e	q	v	p	q	s
r	j	o	s	a	i	n	n	y	w
s	l	p	b	x	l	i	d	i	i
d	w	s	c	m	v	o	f	p	t
n	o	v	e	r	s	w	q	x	h

MAZE CRAZE

Skill: Conjunctions

Conjunctions are joining words. Some conjunctions are "and," "but," "or," "so," "for," and "yet." Use the letters in the boxes to make as many conjunctions as you can. Write them on the lines. You may use letters more than once.

a	y	u	d
l	o	p	f
t	e	n	v
b	c	s	r

____

____

____

____

____

____

Skill: Writing Sentences

Sentence Scramble

Draw a line to connect the words and form a sentence. Write the sentence on the lines. Begin with a capital letter. End with an end mark.

to

loves

carrots

lettuce

and

rabbit

eat

my

Sudoku for You

h		T	
			e
	y	h	

Skills: Pronouns, Handwriting

Write letters in the boxes so that each row and column has the letters to spell a pronoun that could take the place of "Emma and Stevie" in the sentence. Do not use any letter more than once in the same row or column.

Emma and Stevie rode bikes to the lake.

PRESTO-CHANGE-O!

Skills: Spelling, Handwriting

Write words to match the picture clues. Each word ends with "ar." Only the first letters change.

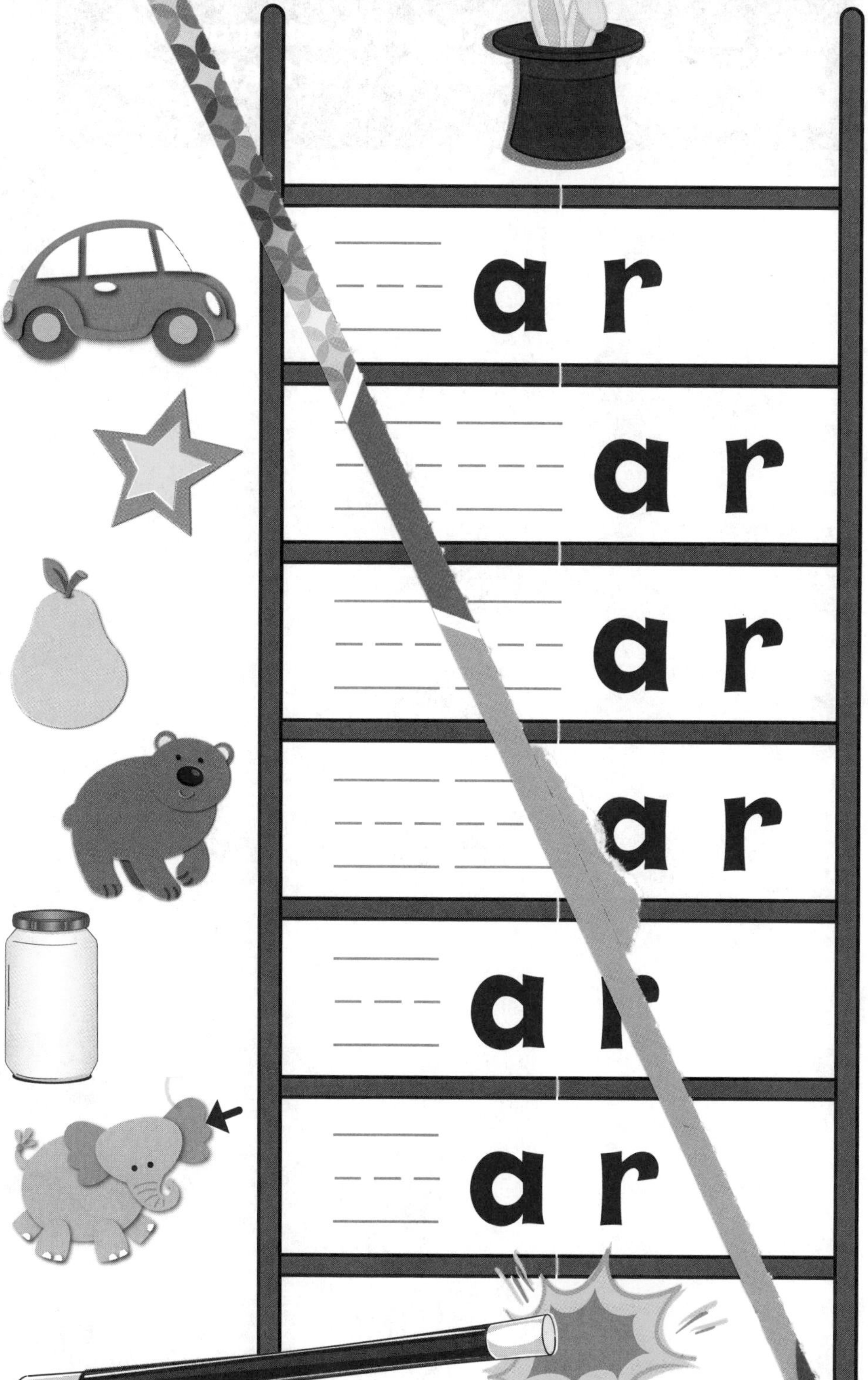

Skill: Consonant Blends

Look at the consonant team in each drawing. On the crayons, write words from the box that contain that sound.

chip	wish	ship
three	lunch	path
sheep	moth	chill

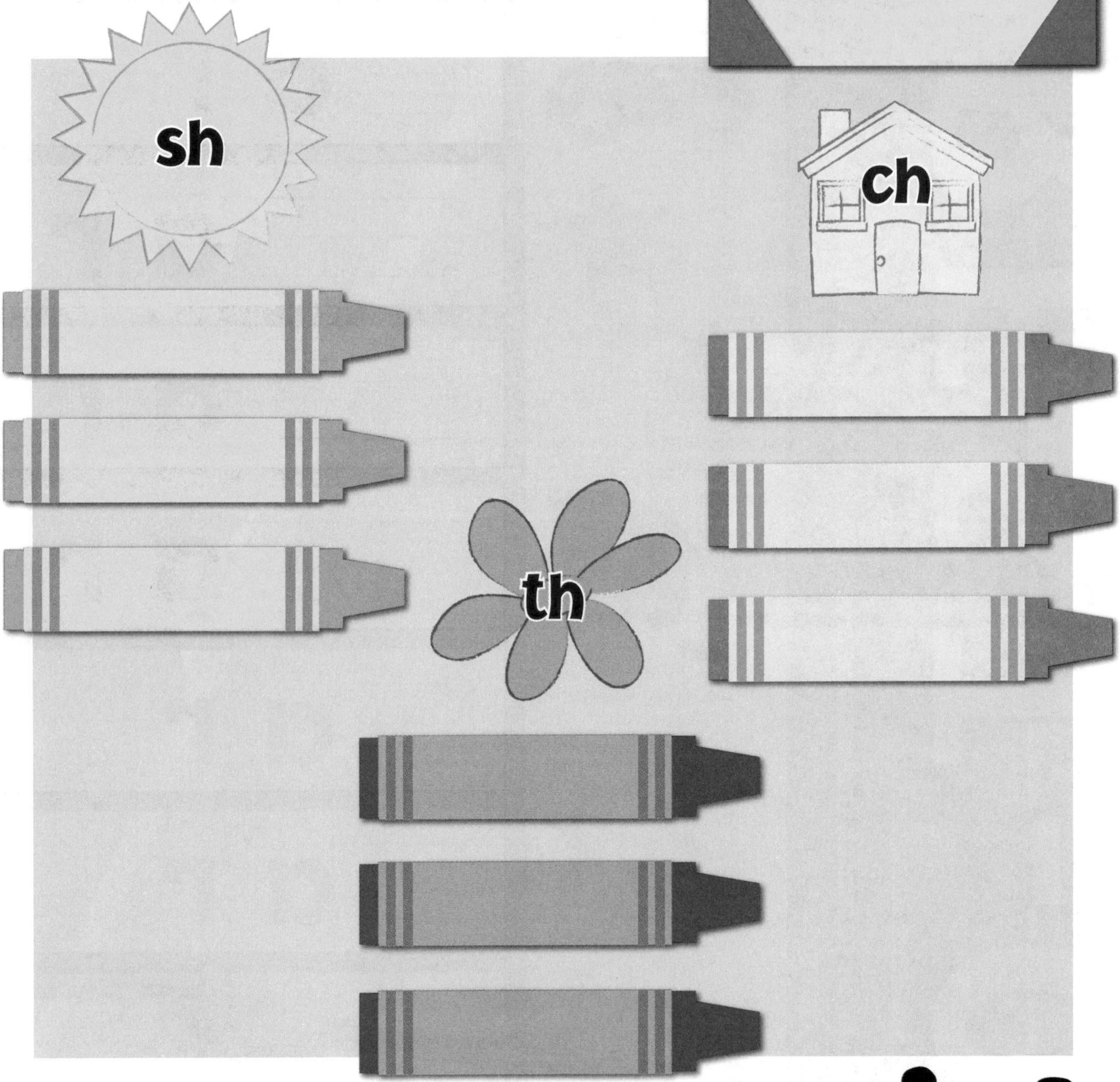

Picture This!

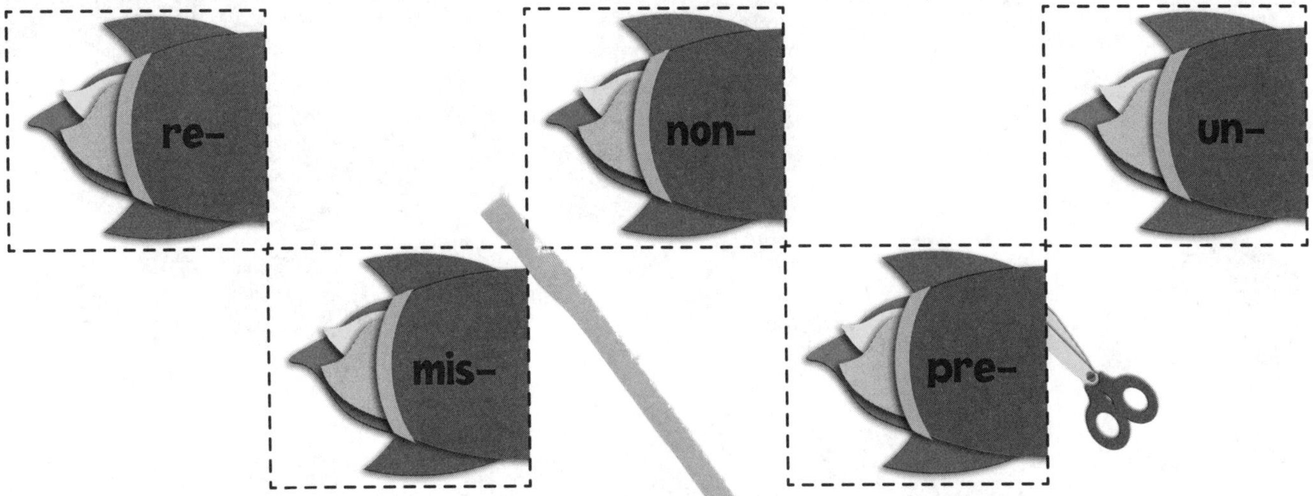

Skills: Prefixes, Base Words

IN PIECES

Cut out the pieces. Match each prefix with a base word to complete the rockets.

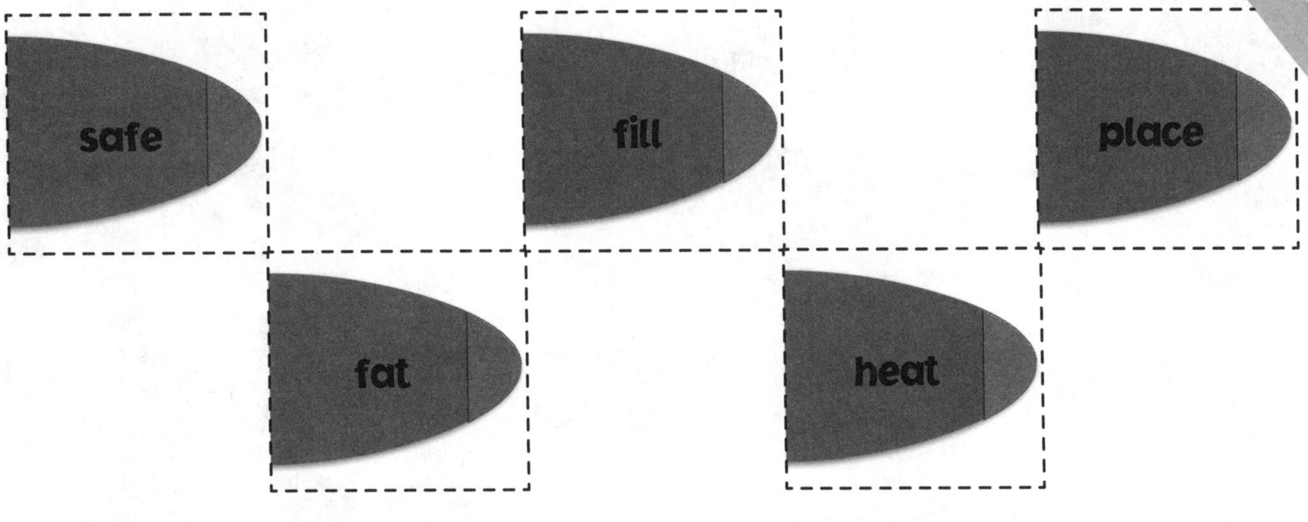

ALPHA-CHALLENGE

Skill: Using Capital Letters

Write a person's name that begins with each letter of the alphabet. Begin each one with a capital letter. Some are given for you.

Names

A	________	N	________
B	Bailey	O	________
C	________	P	________
D	________	Q	________
E	________	R	________
F	________	S	________
G	________	T	________
H	________	U	________
I	________	V	________
J	________	W	Wyatt
K	________	X	________
L	________	Y	________
M	Miguel	Z	________

CODE BREAKER

Skill: Nouns and Verbs

Use the code to write the verb in each sentence. If the noun and verb match, make a check mark (✓) at the end of the sentence. If they do not match, make an X.

1. Li  ______________ the ball. ☐

2. The cats  ______________ at the mouse. ☐

3. My bike  ______________ a flat tire. ☐

4. Will and Nico  ______________ down the street. ☐

5. The chef  ______________ soup for lunch. ☐

Code Key

pounce	lives	makes	kicks	have

MIRROR MIRROR

Skill: Fiction vs. Nonfiction

1. Yoko and her friend made a plan. F NF

2. Ohio is a state in the Midwest. F NF

3. Each bee in the hive has a job to do. F NF

4. First, mix the eggs and milk. F NF

5. The gnome waved at the mouse. F NF

Hold up the page to a mirror to read each sentence. If the sentence would probably be found in a story, circle "F" for "fiction." If the sentence would probably be found in a book that gives information, circle "NF" for "nonfiction."

Write an asking sentence that has two 3-letter words.

Write an exclamation that is five words long.

Write a telling sentence that has a color word in it.

Write a sentence that is a command and has a number word in it.

How good are you at following directions? Write the sentences to find out!

QUIZ WHIZ

Skill: Writing Sentences

JUMBLED UP

Skill: Syllables

Match pairs of syllables to make words. There will be eight two-syllable words in all. Write the words in the blanks.

ger er ball teach stu

ble pen el dent ter

ti tow cil bub base bet

RIDDLE ME

Use the clues to find the letters that spell a base word. Write the base word next to each prefix to complete the riddle. Then, guess the answer to the riddle!

Skills: Prefixes, Base Words, Spelling

1. The first letter of the base word makes the final sound in 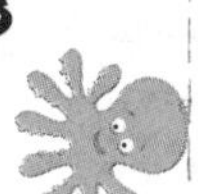. ______

2. The second letter of the base word is the only vowel letter in . ______

3. The third letter of the base word is in  but not in . ______

4. The fourth letter of the base word is the only vowel letter in . ______

You throw
away my out______
and eat my in______. Then,
you eat my out______ and
throw away my in______.

What am I?

☐ ☐ ☐ ☐

Skill: Vocabulary

Look at the words in each list. Their meanings are close but not quite the same. Cut out the words at the bottom of the page. Glue or tape one in each list. Then, color each word to match its list.

peek	trot	drizzle	nibble
look		rain	
	sprint		gobble

pour	stare	eat	run

Picture This!

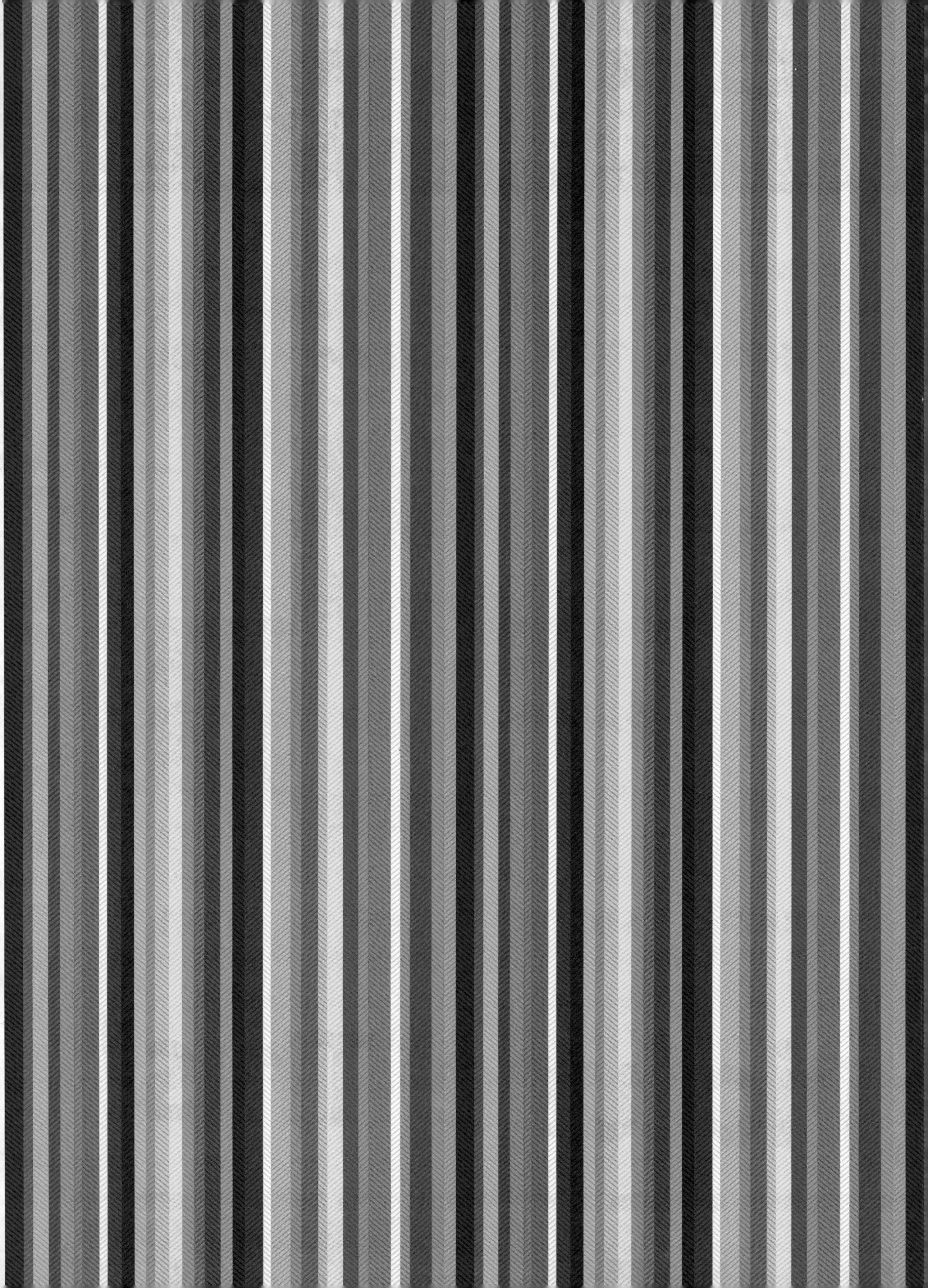

Sudoku for you

		e	
		h	
p			
	l		e

Skills: Verbs, Handwriting

Write letters in the boxes so that each row and column has the letters to spell a verb that completes the sentences. Do not use any letter more than once in the same row or column.

I ________ my family every day.

Yesterday, I ________ed sweep the floor.

Tomorrow I will ________ in the garden.

Sentence Scramble

Draw a line to connect the words and form a sentence. Write the sentence on the lines. Begin with a capital letter. End with an end mark.

the

deer

through

quickly

woods

ran

the

RIDDLE ME

Write the word that completes each hink pink.
Hint: Each word you write will include a consonant team.

Skills: Consonant Blends, Context Clues

1. What is a wiggly hen? a kickin' ________

2. What is a bashful bug? a ________ fly

3. Where do scary fish hang out? at a ________ park

4. What do you call a red fruit with a beard? a hairy ________

5. What do you call adding numbers in the tub? a math ________

6. What do you call a fake horse? a ________ pony

A hink pink is a pair of rhyming words that answer a riddle.

Example: fat cat

I am at the back. I am like a dictionary. Use me to find a meaning. What am I? ____________________

I show something from real life. You might find a caption under me. What am I? ____________________

I am at the start. I am a list. I have page numbers. What am I? ____________________

Find me on the cover. I name a story, book, or article. What am I? ____________________

Answer each riddle with the name of something you might find in a book.

Word Box

table of contents

title

photograph

glossary

QUIZ WHIZ

Skill: Text Features

JUMBLED UP

Skill: Using Commas

Oh, no! Someone bumped the calendar. The dates are all jumbled. Write them correctly. Do not forget to write a comma between the day and the year.

7, 2000 August		January 1958 1,	
2016 4, May		30, November 2020	
29, March 1990		2006 18, April	
31, 1922 July		2009 June 6,	

Skills: Adjectives, Nouns

Read the adjective in each flower. Then, think of nouns that each adjective could describe. Write them on the petals.

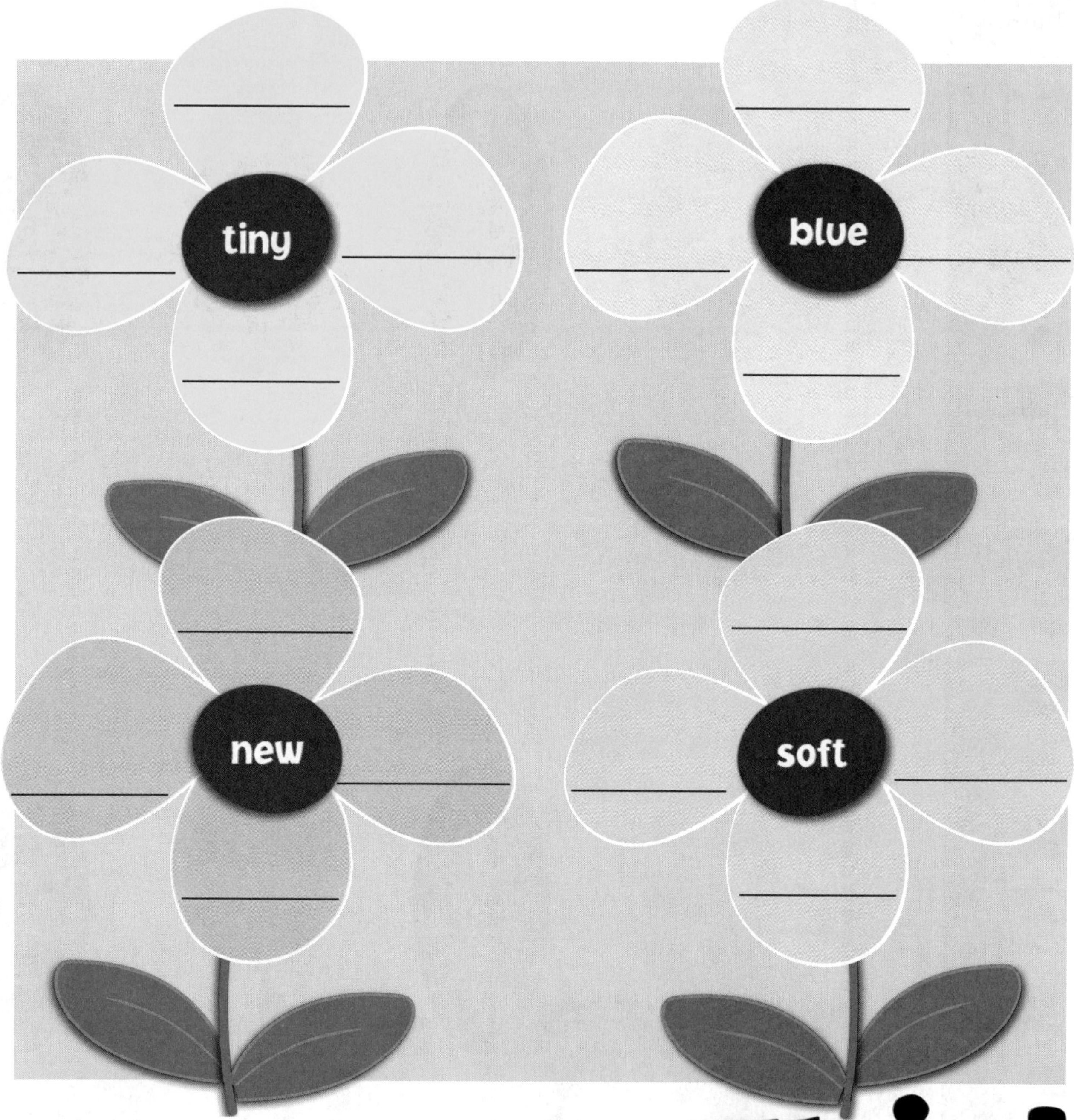

Picture This!

MAZE CRAZE

Skill: Prepositions

Find 11 prepositions hidden in the maze. How will you find them? Cross out the letters of the alphabet in order. Start at the arrow. The letters that are not crossed out form the prepositions. Write them on the lines.

i	n	a	b	c	d	o	n	e	f
g	b	y	h	f	r	o	m	i	j
t	o	k	l	m	o	v	e	r	n
o	p	o	f	q	i	n	t	o	r
w	i	t	h	s	t	u	o	u	t
v	w	u	n	d	e	r	x	y	z

WORD MATH

Skill: Writing Sentences

Decode each sentence. Write it in the blank. Add a period (.), question mark (?), or exclamation mark (!) at the end.

1. 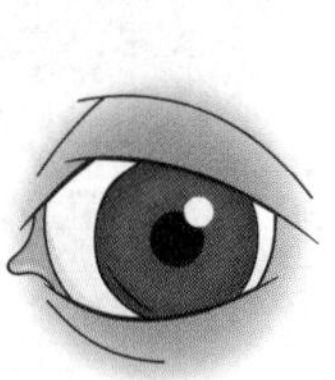 l +  − b 2  in the 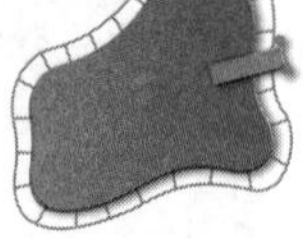

2. The  s +  − h on the 

3. L +  − h shout − sh 4 the 

4. W + 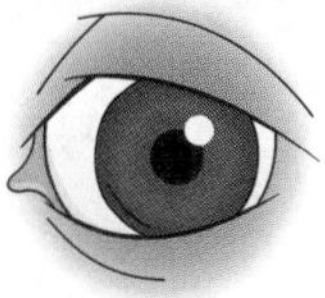 d

\+  − l m + 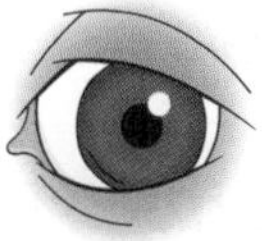 

get a fl +  − b 

5.  shout − sh 4 that

6. Is this n +  − scr

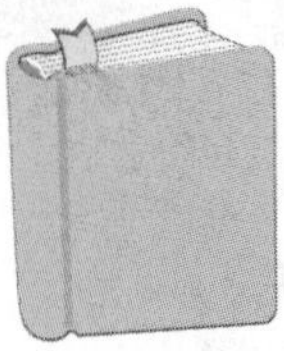 from U

CODE BREAKER

Skill: Handwriting

Use the code to answer the questions.

1. What letter comes after "W"? ______

2. What letter comes between "P" and "g"? ______

3. Write the uppercase form of the letter that comes between "j" and "c." ______

4. What letter comes two letters after "g"? ______

5. What letter comes before "F"? ______

6. What letter is between "e" and "D"? ______

Code Key

H	u	W	F	j	k	c	A	l	L	e	n	D	b	y	P	E	g	x	q

RIDDLE ME

Use the clues to find letters. Put the letters together to make the words in a sentence. Then, circle the answer to the question.

Skill: Point of View

1. This letter sounds like 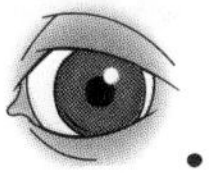 . ______

2. This letter is the first letter of the alphabet. ______

3. This letter is the first letter in the name of the day after Sunday. ______

4. This letter is the first letter in  . ______

5. This letter is the vowel in the middle of 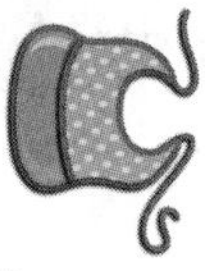 . ______

6. This letter is the last letter in  . ______

Sentence:

______ ______ ______

______ ______ ______.

Who might say this?

CODE BREAKER

Skill: Nouns and Verbs

Use the code to write the verb in each sentence. If the noun and verb match, circle the happy face (☺) at the end of the sentence. If they do not match, circle the sad face (☹).

1. Ivan and I  seven.

2. Ella  rope.

3. The bird  a nest in that tree.

4. They  next door.

5. Anton  the ball.

Code Key

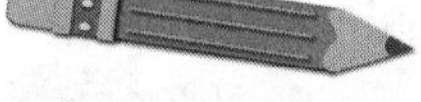				
has	am	live	catch	jumps

Sudoku for You

k			
	i		c
		p	
	k		

Skills: Verbs, Handwriting

Write letters in the boxes so that each row and column has the letters to spell a verb that completes the sentences. Do not use any letter more than once in the same row or column.

Can I ________ a card game to play?

Yesterday, Ned ________ed "Old Maid."

Tomorrow, Ana will ________ "Hearts."

JUMBLED UP

Skill: Vowel Sounds

Use the letters and letter pairs on the moon to make words that have the long a sound. Cross out letters as you use them. Write each long a word on a planet.

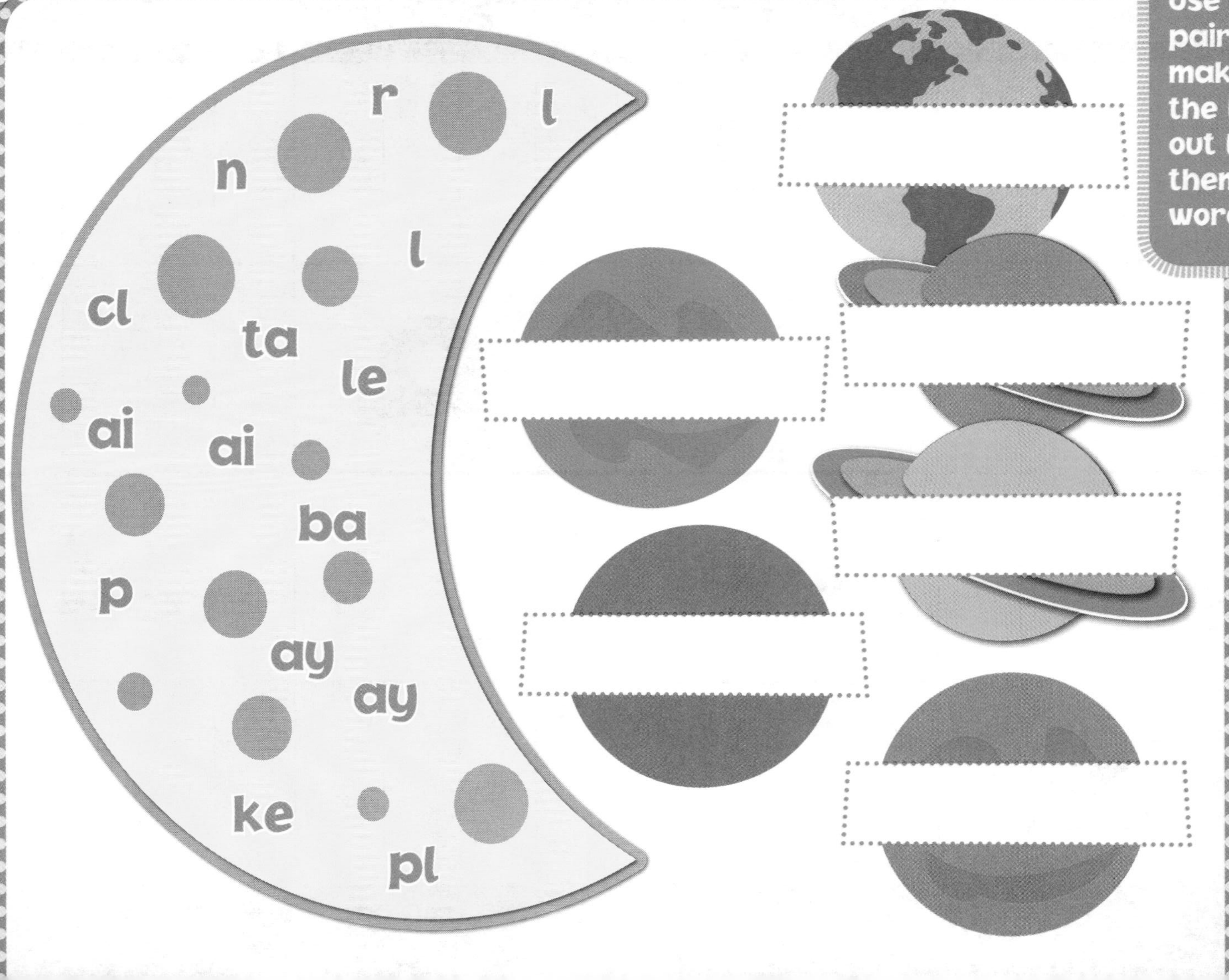

Skill: Writing Sentences

Sentence Scramble

Draw a line to connect the words and form a sentence. Write the sentence on the lines. Begin with a capital letter. End with an end mark.

for

chirp

mother

birds

their

loudly

baby

the

ALPHA-CHALLENGE

Skills: Sensory Words, Adjectives

Think about your five senses. Fill in the chart with adjectives that begin with the letters shown and describe how the things might look, smell, taste, sound, and feel. Some words are given for you.

Thing to Describe	Letter	Adjective to Describe Sight, Smell, Taste, Sound, or Feel
shirt	b	
puppy	s	
playground	c	crowded
dinner	t	
music	l	
sky	d	
flower	r	
carnival ride	f	
frozen treat	i	icy
fish	w	

peach | ask | sad

meet | farm

Skills: Suffixes, Base Words

IN PIECES

Cut out the pieces. Make houses by matching each suffix with a base word.

-es | -ed | -ly

-ing | -er

Skills: Consonant Blends, Spelling

Make as many words as you can with the letters in the box. You may use letters more than once. Each word should have a consonant team such as "sh," "ch," "wh," or "th." Write the words on the lines.

sh	l	p	f
r	o	d	th
a	ch	w	e
n	c	wh	i

____

____

____

____

____

____

____

____

MAZE CRAZE

What 3 animals would you put together to make a new animal?

a chicken,	a monkey,	and a jellyfish

If you went to space, what 3 things would you bring?

		and

Who are the 3 funniest people you know?

		and

What 3 foods are gross?

		and

What 3 jobs would you most like to have?

		and

Answer each question by writing a list of three things. Remember to write a comma (,) after each word before "and." One is done for you.

QUIZ WHIZ

Skill: Using Commas

Skill: Vocabulary

Go Across

What do you need to do each activity?
Write the answers in the puzzle.

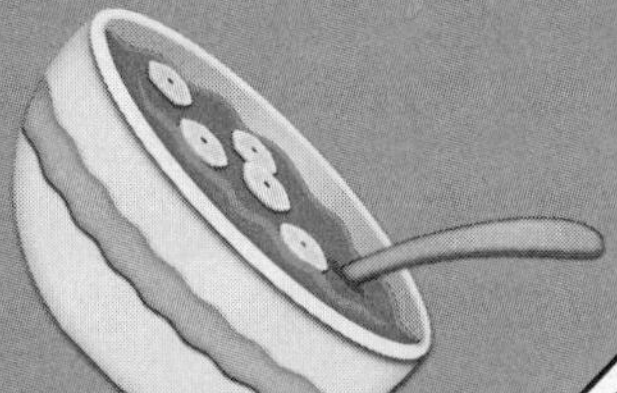

Across

4. cut paper?
5. eat soup?
6. check out a book at the library?
7. clean the floor?

Down

1. color a picture?
2. walk a dog?
3. rest your head?
4. get clean in the tub?
5. mail a letter?

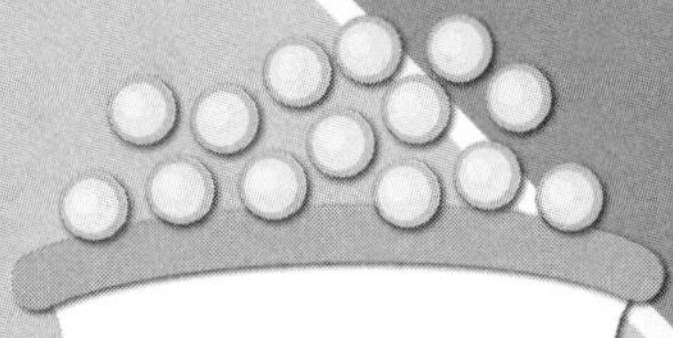

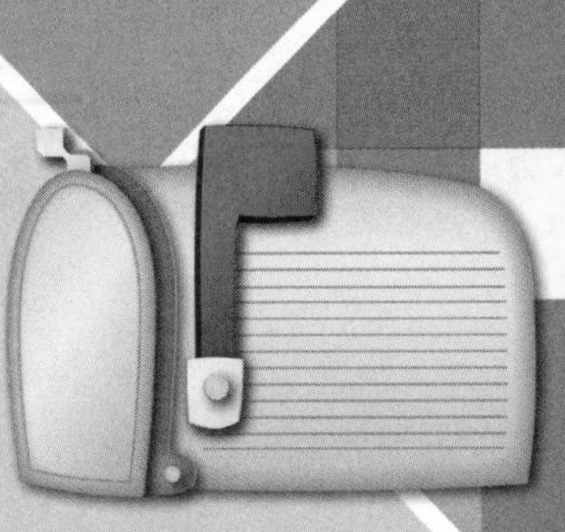

In Search Of

Circle the correctly spelled word in each pair. Then, find it in the puzzle. Look carefully! The words may be hidden backward or diagonally.

mail, mayle

crait, crate

flize, flies

hard, harde

opin, open

yellow, yelo

lewse, loose

rattle, rattul

stikur, sticker

mouse, mowse

Skill: Spelling

S	K	H	M	Q	R	Y	M	S	Q
D	T	D	A	A	J	E	Y	T	F
S	Q	I	T	R	Y	L	Q	C	Y
Q	E	T	C	B	D	L	E	N	L
U	L	I	S	K	E	O	S	O	T
E	A	J	L	S	E	W	O	T	X
O	R	Y	U	F	J	R	O	O	N
E	T	O	M	A	I	L	L	P	G
B	M	H	L	H	A	H	U	E	G
E	T	A	R	C	H	L	P	N	F

Skill: Vowel Sounds

IN PIECES

Cut out the pieces. Match them to make pairs of flip-flops. Each pair should have a vowel sound and a word that contains that sound. For example, you could match "long i" with "fine."

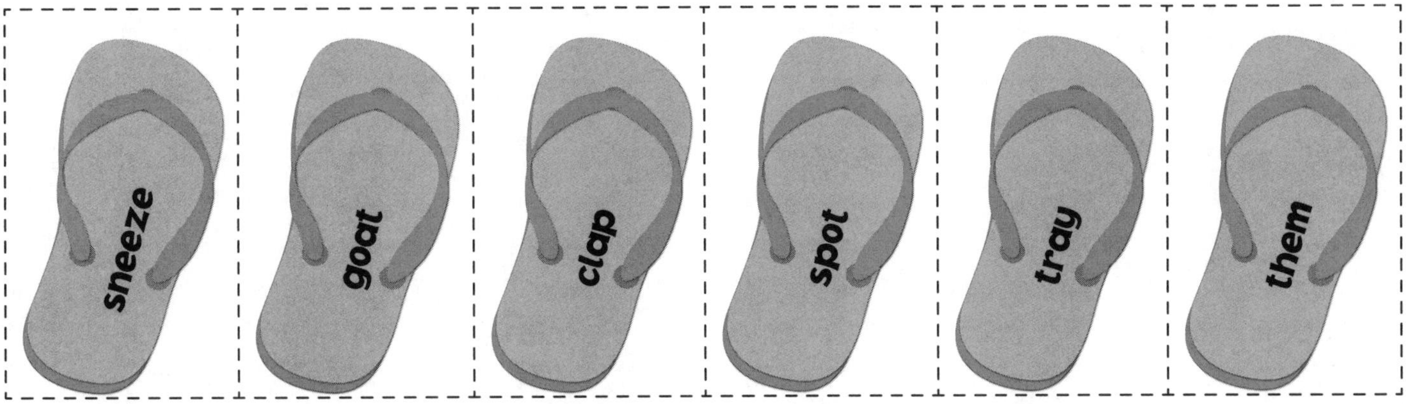

Skills: Writing Sentences, Conjunctions

Sentence Scramble

Draw a line to connect the words and form a sentence. Write the sentence correctly on the lines. It contains two conjunctions, or joining words. Circle them.

WORD MATH

Skill: Using Capital Letters

Solve each riddle to find the name of a famous person. Write the person's name in the blank. Begin each first name and last name with a capital letter.

1. w + salt − s d + this − th + ney = ______ ______

2. babe − b l + pin − p + coln = ______ ______

3. bench − ch fr + bank − b + lin = ______ ______

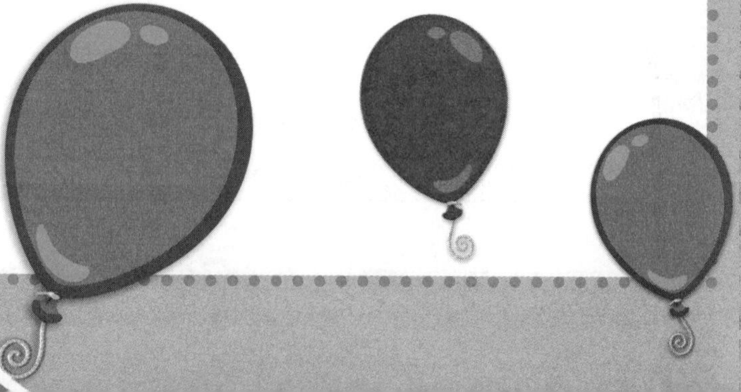

4. rose − e + a

p + lark − l + s

=

5. help − p + en k +

speller − sp =

6. k + sting − st t + shut

− sh =

RIDDLE ME

Use the clues to find letters that complete the name of a famous place. The word you write should begin with a capital letter.

Skills: Vowel Sounds, Using Capital Letters

1. This letter is in  but not in . ____
2. This letter spells the short vowel sound in . ____
3. This letter is in  but not in . ____
4. This letter spells the long e sound at the end of 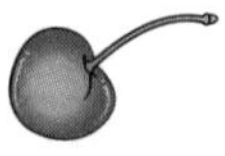. ____
5. This letter spells the short vowel sound in . ____
6. This is the last letter in . ____

What famous American landmark is 277 miles long?

The Grand

1	2	3	4	5	6

PREST-O CHANGE-O!

Skills: Spelling, Handwriting

Write words to match the picture clues. All the words have "ck" in them, but the other letters will change.

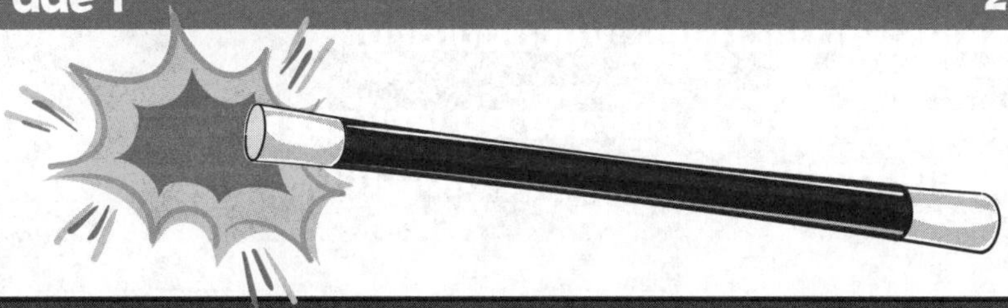

___ ck 

____ ck 

___ ck ___ 

___ ck ___ 

 ____ ck ___

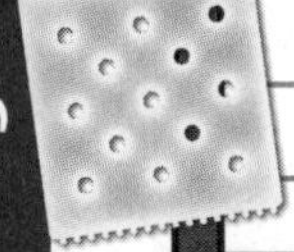 ____ ck ___

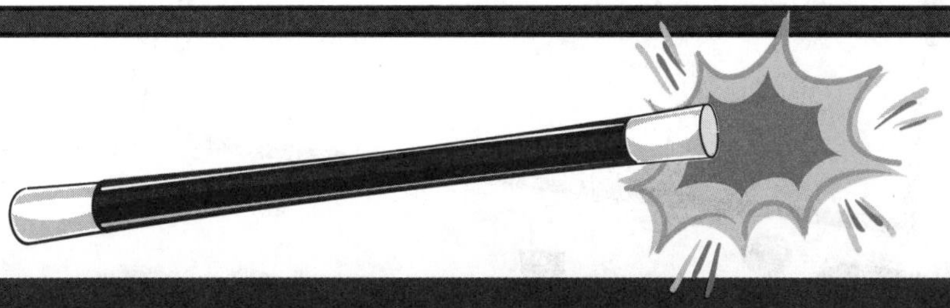

Skills: Adjectives, Vocabulary

Complete each phrase by writing what the adjectives make you think of. Then, draw a picture to match the phrase you made.

cozy, quiet

loud, funny

huge, dark

fuzzy, white

new, speedy

gloomy, gray

Picture This!

ANSWER KEY

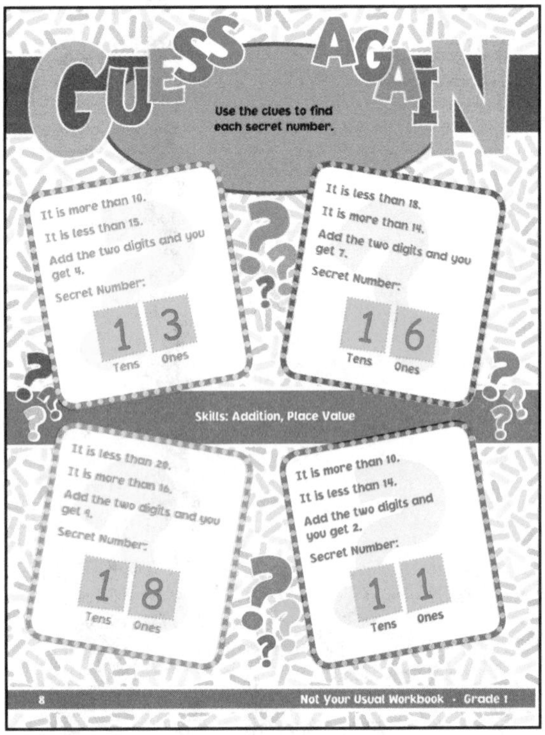
GUESS AGAIN

Use the clues to find each secret number.

It is more than 10.
It is less than 15.
Add the two digits and you get 4.
Secret Number: 1 3
Tens Ones

It is less than 18.
It is more than 14.
Add the two digits and you get 7.
Secret Number: 1 6
Tens Ones

Skills: Addition, Place Value

It is less than 20.
It is more than 16.
Add the two digits and you get 9.
Secret Number: 1 8
Tens Ones

It is more than 10.
It is less than 14.
Add the two digits and you get 2.
Secret Number: 1 1
Tens Ones

8 Not Your Usual Workbook • Grade 1

Page 8

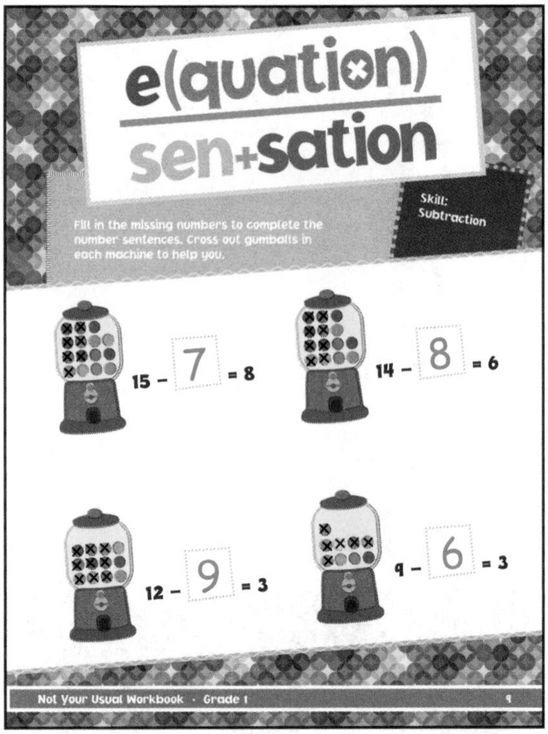
e(quation) sen+sation

Skill: Subtraction

Fill in the missing numbers to complete the number sentences. Cross out gumballs in each machine to help you.

15 − 7 = 8

14 − 8 = 6

12 − 9 = 3

9 − 6 = 3

Not Your Usual Workbook • Grade 1 9

Page 9

PATTERN POWER

Skill: Counting

Find the pattern of dots in each row. Draw dots on the blank domino sides to complete the pattern.

10 Not Your Usual Workbook • Grade 1

Page 10

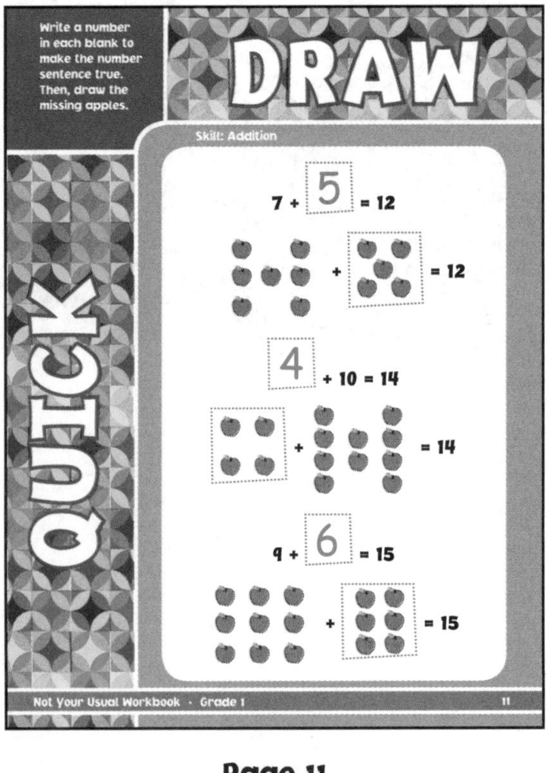
Write a number in each blank to make the number sentence true. Then, draw the missing apples.

QUICK DRAW

Skill: Addition

7 + 5 = 12

+ = 12

4 + 10 = 14

+ = 14

9 + 6 = 15

+ = 15

Not Your Usual Workbook • Grade 1 11

Page 11

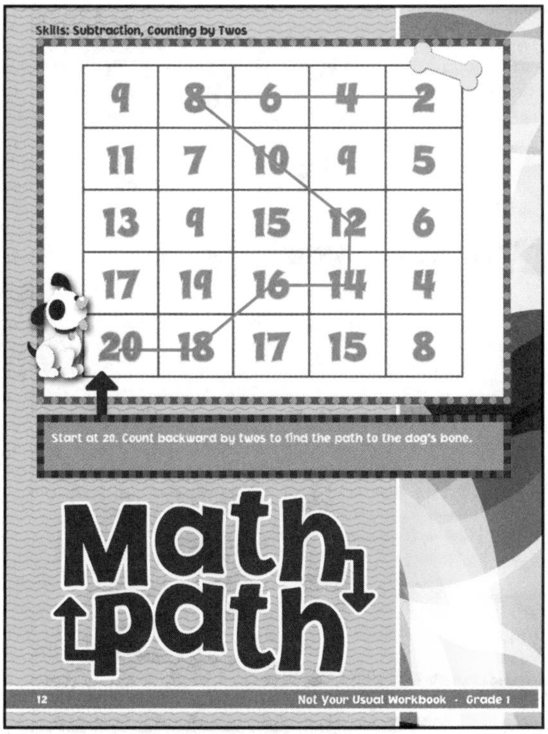

Skills: Subtraction, Counting by Twos
9 8 6 4 2
11 7 10 9 5
13 9 15 12 6
17 19 16 14 4
20 18 17 15 8
Start at 20. Count backward by twos to find the path to the dog's bone.
Math path
12
Not Your Usual Workbook · Grade 1

Page 12

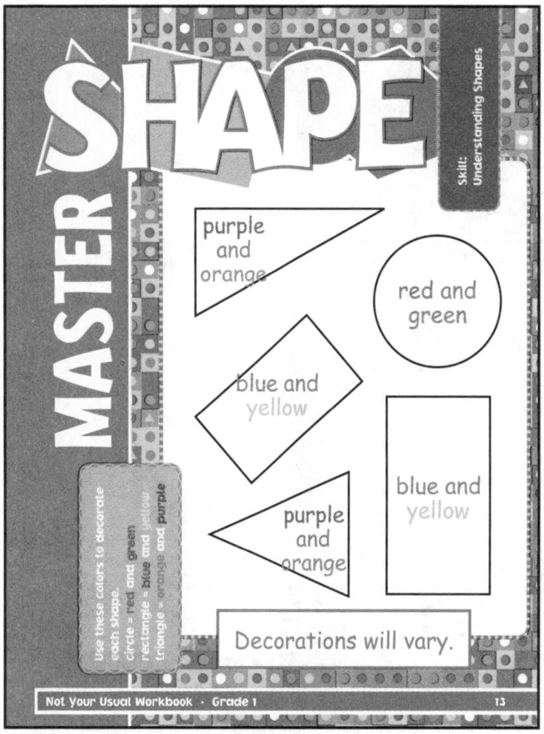

Page 13

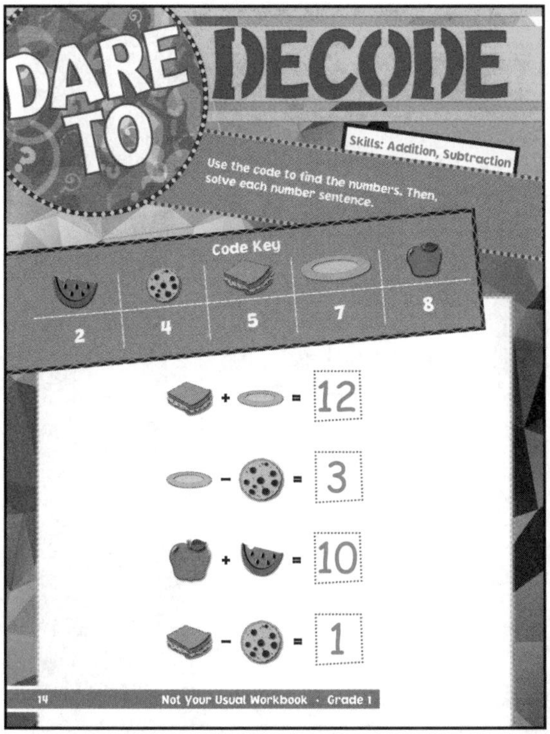

Page 14

Page 15

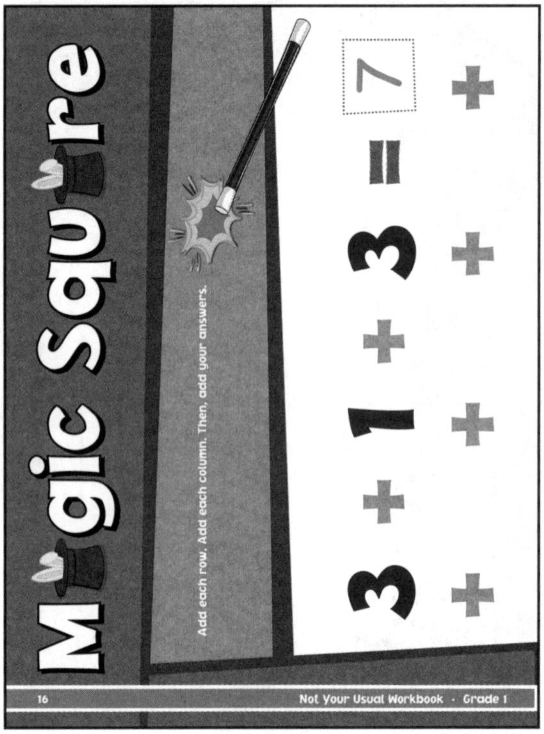

Page 16

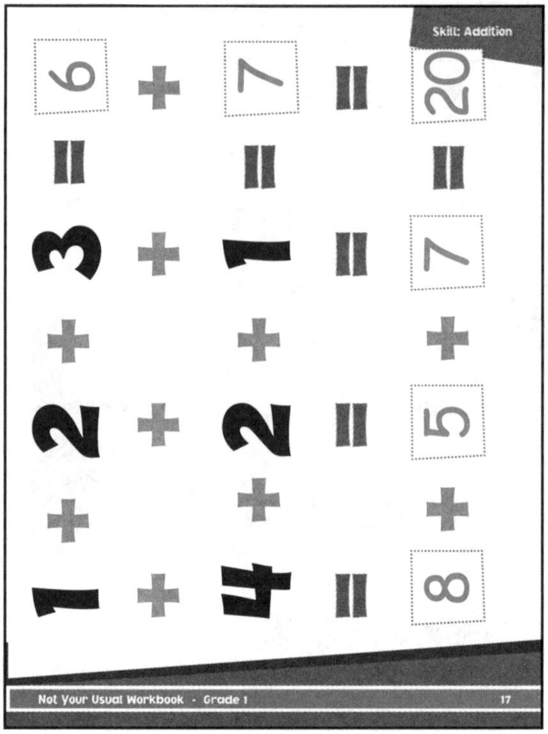

Page 17

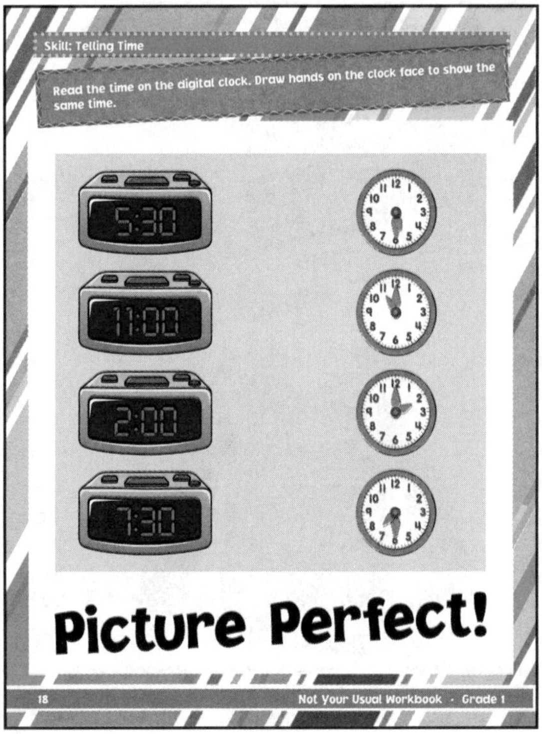

Page 18

Page 19

Skills: Counting, Addition

NUMBER CROSS

Across

4. Start with 2, and then count by twos.

5. Start with 4, and then count by fours.

Down

1. Start with 1, and then count by ones.

2. Start with 3, and then count by threes.

3. Start with 5, and then count by fives.

Read each clue. Write the numbers to fill the spaces in the puzzle.

1 2 3 4 5 / 2 4 6 8 10 / 3 6 9 12 15 / 4 8 12 16 20 / 5 10 15 20 25

20 Not Your Usual Workbook · Grade 1

Page 20

IT FITS!

1 8 | 1 4 | 3 2 | 2 5 | 4 1

one ten, eight ones = 18

three tens, two ones = 32

two tens, five ones = 25

one ten, four ones = 14

four tens, one one = 41

Skills: Counting by Tens, Place Value

Cut out the numbers. Use the clues to fit the pieces together to form two-digit numbers. Then, write the numbers you made.

Not Your Usual Workbook · Grade 1 21

Page 21

STORY STUMPERS

Read each story. Use the pictures to help you find the answer.

Skill: Word Problems

Layla, Dylan, and Charlotte shared 16 jelly beans. Layla ate 5 jelly beans. Dylan ate 6. How many did Charlotte eat?

5 jelly beans

A tank at a pet store held 20 fish. At one o'clock, a man bought 7 fish. At two o'clock, a woman bought 8 fish. How many fish were left?

5 fish

Not Your Usual Workbook · Grade 1 23

Page 23

PATTERN POWER

Skill: Counting by Tens

85 75 65 55 45 35

22 32 42 52 62 72

44 54 64 74 84 94

99 89 79 69 59 49

Find the pattern in each row. Write the missing numbers.

24 Not Your Usual Workbook · Grade 1

Page 24

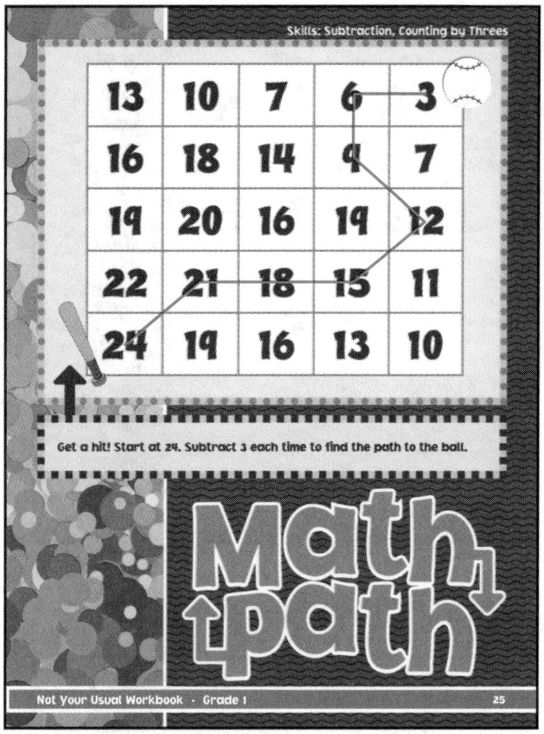

Skills: Subtraction, Counting by Threes
13 10 7 6 3
16 18 14 9 7
19 20 16 19 12
22 21 18 15 11
24 19 16 13 10
Get a hit! Start at 24. Subtract 3 each time to find the path to the ball.
Math path
Not Your Usual Workbook · Grade 1 25

Page 25

Guess Again
Use the clues to find each secret number.
Start with 2.
Add 11.
Subtract 5, and you will find it.
Secret Number:
8
Start with 17.
Subtract 4.
Add 10, and you will find it.
Secret Number:
23
Skills: Addition, Subtraction
Start with 3 more than 5.
Add 5 more.
Subtract 9, and you will find it.
Secret Number:
4
Start with 8 less than 20.
Add 3.
Add 2 more, and you will find it.
Secret Number:
17
26 Not Your Usual Workbook · Grade 1

Page 26

Skill: Working with Data
Cut out the pieces. Glue or tape them in the spaces to make four groups of fruits that are alike.
A Show of Hands
Group 4
Group 3
Group 2
Group 1
Not Your Usual Workbook · Grade 1
27

Page 27

Page 29

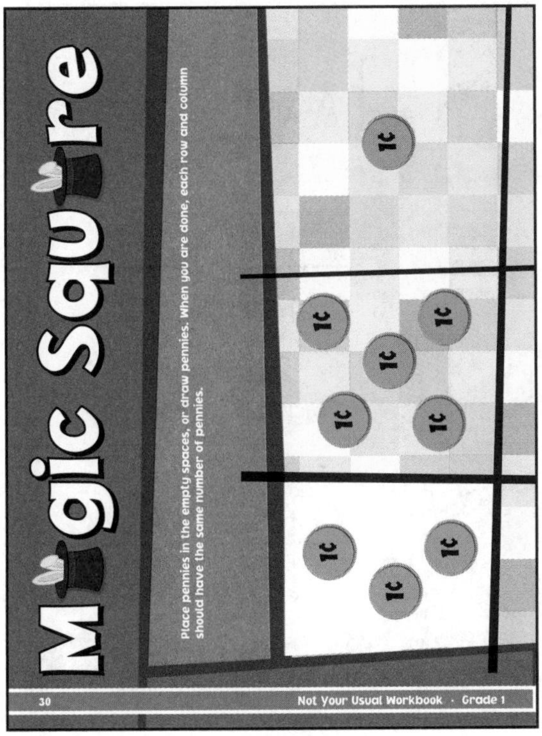

Magic Square
Place pennies in the empty spaces, or draw pennies. When you are done, each row and column should have the same number of pennies.
30
Not Your Usual Workbook · Grade 1

Page 30

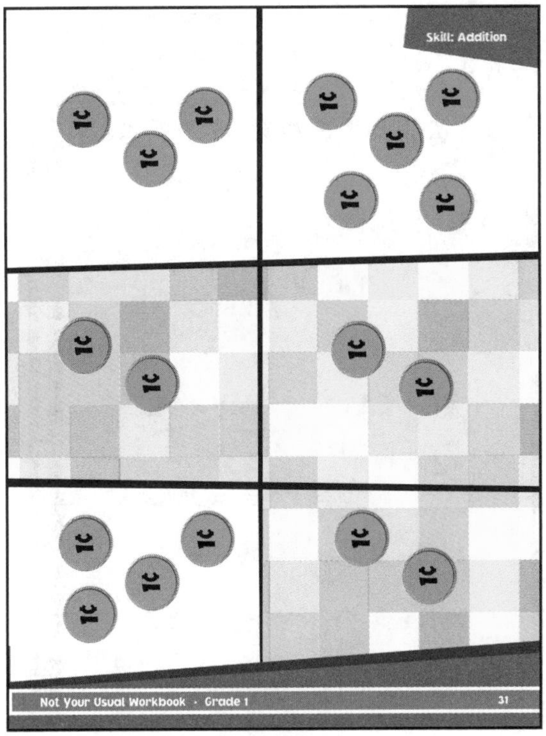

Page 31

Page 32

Page 33

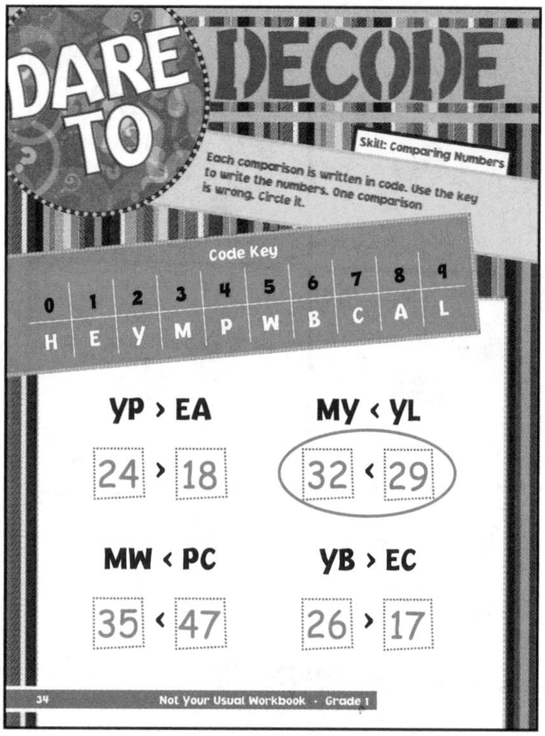
DARE TO DECODE

Skill: Comparing Numbers

Each comparison is written in code. Use the key to write the numbers. One comparison is wrong. Circle it.

Code Key

0	1	2	3	4	5	6	7	8	9
H	E	Y	M	P	W	B	C	A	L

YP > EA
24 > 18

MY < YL
32 < 29

MW < PC
35 < 47

YB > EC
26 > 17

34 Not Your Usual Workbook · Grade 1

Page 34

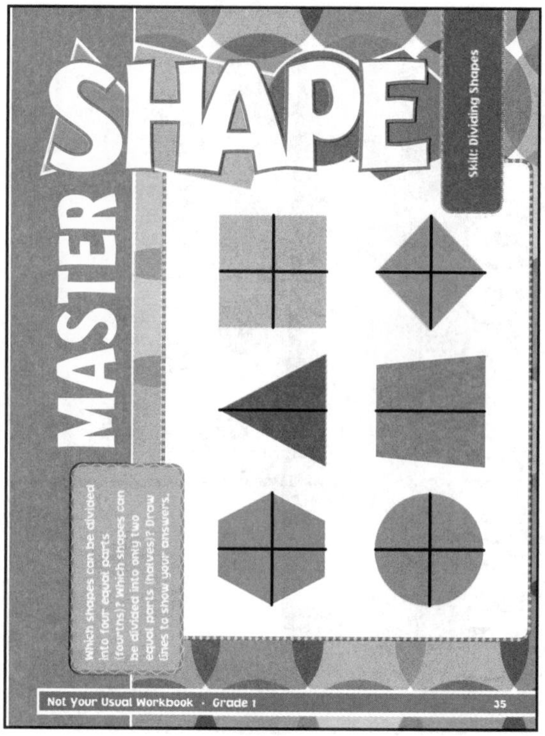
MASTER SHAPE

Skill: Dividing Shapes

Which shapes can be divided into four equal parts (fourths)? Which shapes can be divided into only two equal parts (halves)? Draw lines to show your answers.

Not Your Usual Workbook · Grade 1 35

Page 35

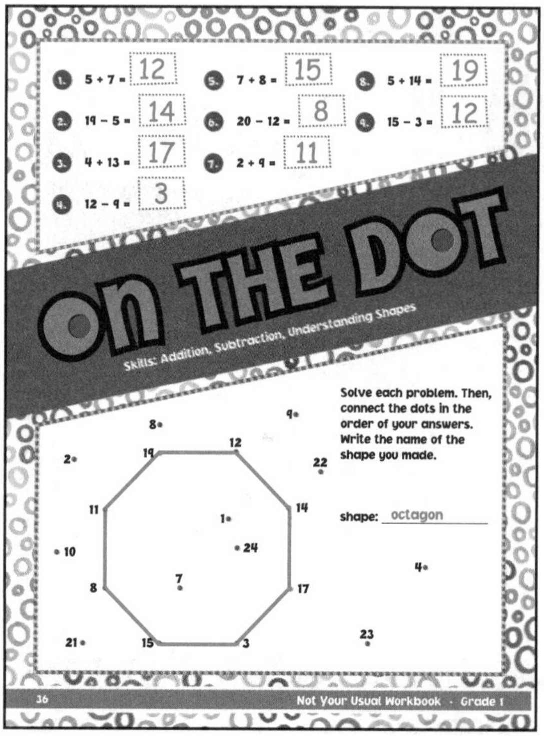
1. 5 + 7 = 12
2. 19 − 5 = 14
3. 4 + 13 = 17
4. 12 − 9 = 3
5. 7 + 8 = 15
6. 20 − 12 = 8
7. 2 + 9 = 11
8. 5 + 14 = 19
9. 15 − 3 = 12

ON THE DOT

Skills: Addition, Subtraction, Understanding Shapes

Solve each problem. Then, connect the dots in the order of your answers. Write the name of the shape you made.

shape: octagon

36 Not Your Usual Workbook · Grade 1

Page 36

On the LOOKout!

Skill: Addition

Find and circle five addition problems in the puzzle. Write + and = to complete each one. The three unused numbers make one more number sentence. Write it in the blanks.

4 + 10 = 14

Not Your Usual Workbook · Grade 1 37

Page 37

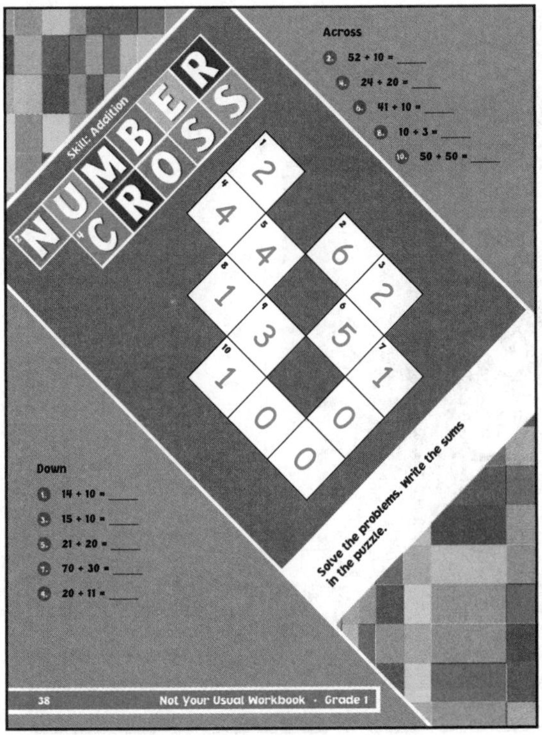
Skill: Addition

NUMBER CROSS

Across

2. 52 + 10 = ____
4. 24 + 20 = ____
6. 41 + 10 = ____
8. 10 + 3 = ____
10. 50 + 50 = ____

Down

1. 14 + 10 = ____
3. 15 + 10 = ____
5. 21 + 20 = ____
7. 70 + 30 = ____
9. 20 + 11 = ____

Solve the problems. Write the sums in the puzzle.

38 Not Your Usual Workbook · Grade 1

Page 38

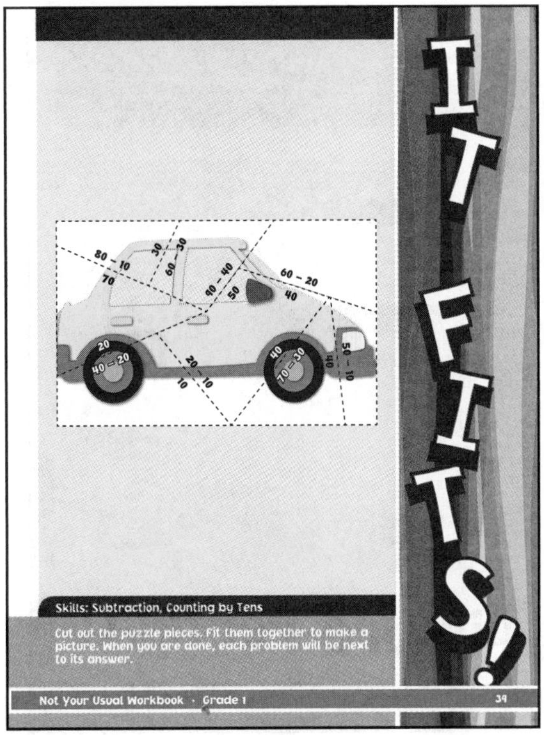
IT FITS!

Skills: Subtraction, Counting by Tens

Cut out the puzzle pieces. Fit them together to make a picture. When you are done, each problem will be next to its answer.

Not Your Usual Workbook · Grade 1 39

Page 39

STORY STUMPERS

Read each story. Use the pictures to help you find the answer.

Skill: Word Problems

Fifteen kids need a ride to the museum. 4 kids can fit in a car. How many cars are needed?

4 cars

A 10¢ is worth 10¢. A 5¢ is worth 5¢. A 1¢ is worth 1¢. Add the coins below. How many cents total?

10¢ 5¢ 1¢ 1¢ 1¢

18 ¢

Not Your Usual Workbook · Grade 1 41

Page 41

PATTERN POWER

Skill: Counting

89	88	87	86	85	84
27	28	29	30	31	32
71	70	69	68	67	66
106	107	108	109	110	111

Look for a pattern in each row. Fill in the missing numbers.

42 Not Your Usual Workbook · Grade 1

Page 42

Skill: Measuring Length
Gather 20 pennies. Put rows of pennies below the pencils. Write how many pennies it took to measure the length of each pencil.
4 pennies
5 pennies
2 pennies
3 pennies
Picture Perfect!
Not Your Usual Workbook · Grade 1
43

Page 43

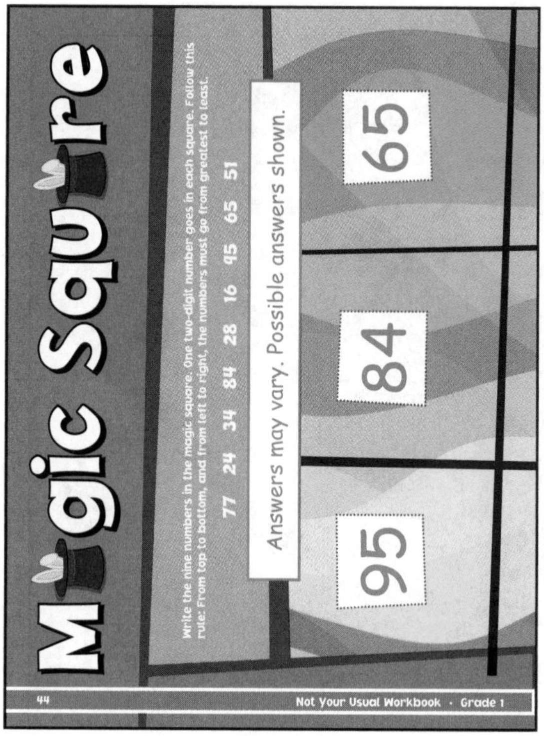

Page 44

Page 45

GUESS AGAIN
Use the clues to guess each secret number.
Start with 22.
Subtract 4.
Subtract 5 more.
Secret Number:
8
Start with 31.
Add 4.
Add 10 more.
Secret Number:
4 5
Skills: Addition, Subtraction
Add 6 and 4.
Switch the two digits of your answer.
Add 4 to the new number.
Secret Number:
5 5
Start with 3 less than 40.
Add 10.
Switch the two digits of your answer.
Secret Number:
7 4
46
Not Your Usual Workbook · Grade 1

Page 46

Use only the shapes shown in the box to make a drawing. Here are some ideas for your drawing: a house, a face, a pattern, a spaceship, a map.
QUICK DRAW
Skill: Drawing Shapes
Drawings will vary.
Not Your Usual Workbook · Grade 1
47

Page 47

Skill: Subtraction
For each puzzle, start at 20. Find a path that reaches 0 by subtracting each number you pass.
Math path
48
Not Your Usual Workbook · Grade 1

Page 48

Page 49

e(quation) sen+sation
Skills: Addition, Subtraction
Complete each number sentence. Fill in the missing numbers. Circle the correct math sign.
14 + − 5 = 19
22 + − 13 = 9
Not Your Usual Workbook · Grade 1
51

Page 51

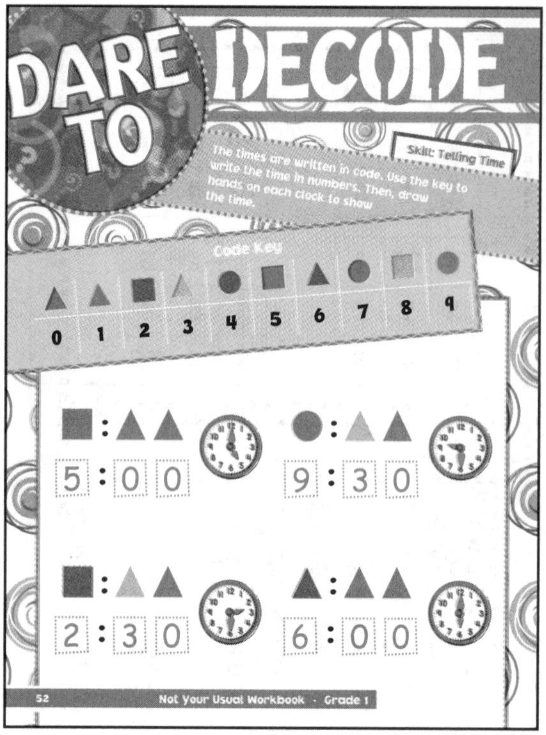
DARE TO DECODE

Skill: Telling Time

The times are written in code. Use the key to write the time in numbers. Then, draw hands on each clock to show the time.

Code Key

0 1 2 3 4 5 6 7 8 9

5:00 9:30

2:30 6:00

52 Not Your Usual Workbook · Grade 1

Page 52

MASTER SHAPE

Skill: Dividing Shapes

Cut out the red squares. Then, cut them into smaller pieces that match the blue shapes.

Not Your Usual Workbook · Grade 1 53

Page 53

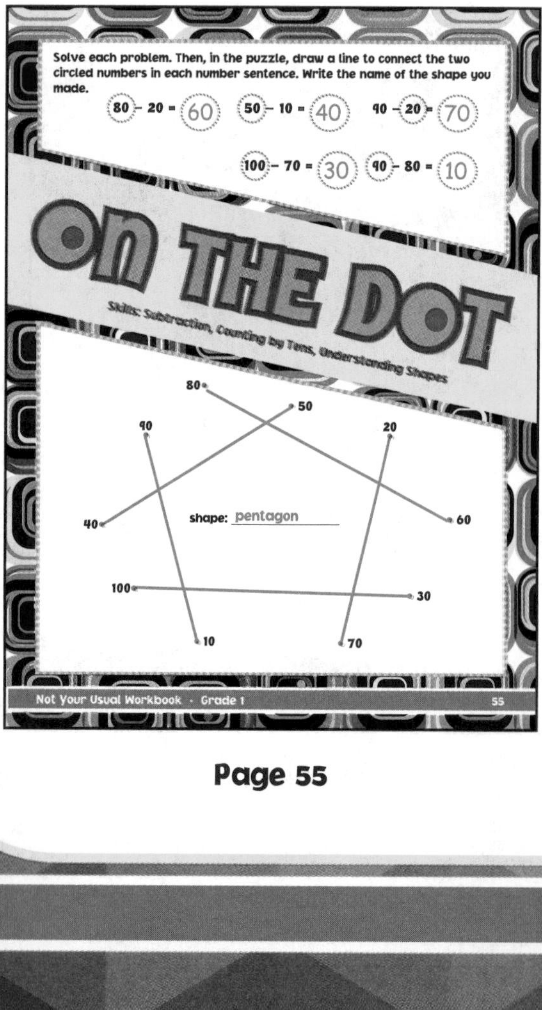
Solve each problem. Then, in the puzzle, draw a line to connect the two circled numbers in each number sentence. Write the name of the shape you made.

80 – 20 = 60 50 – 10 = 40 90 – 20 = 70

100 – 70 = 30 90 – 80 = 10

ON THE DOT

Skills: Subtraction, Counting by Tens, Understanding Shapes

Not Your Usual Workbook · Grade 1 55

Page 55

Skill: Addition

NUMBER CROSS

Across

77 + 7 = ____

27 + 8 = ____

65 + 6 = ____

89 + 6 = ____

91 + 9 = ____

Down

37 + 6 = ____

39 + 8 = ____

52 + 7 = ____

94 + 6 = ____

43 + 8 = ____

Solve the problems. Regroup tens as needed. Write the sums in the puzzle.

56 Not Your Usual Workbook · Grade 1

Page 56

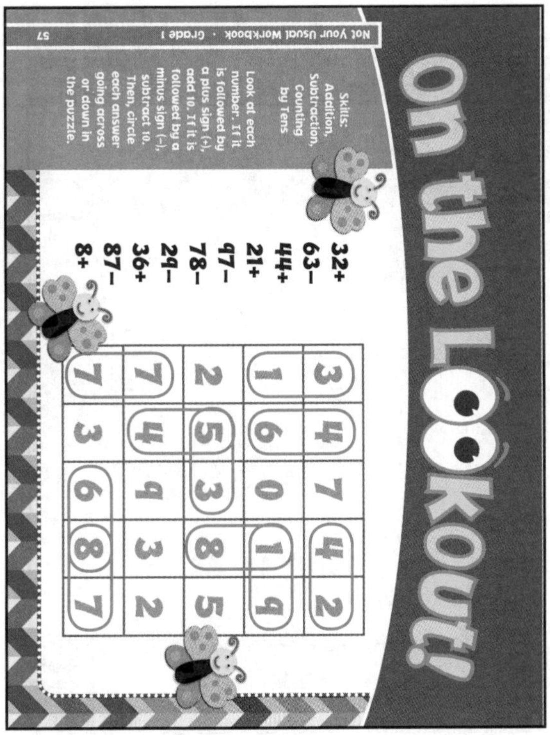

Page 57

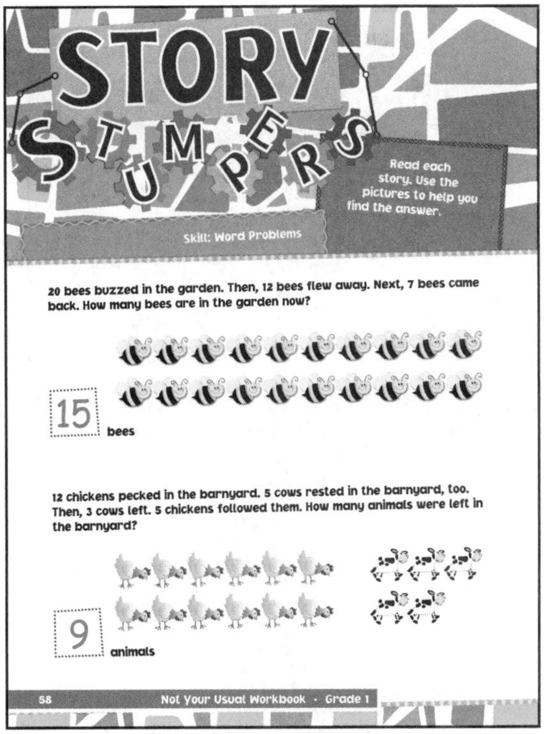

Page 58

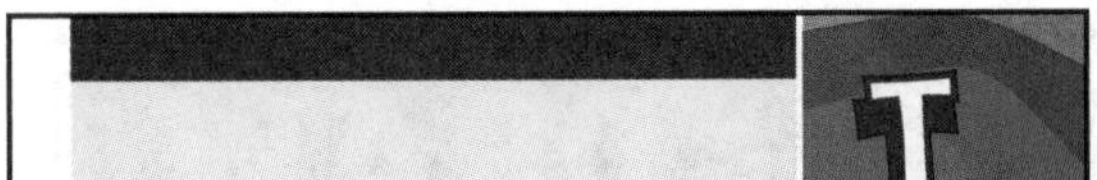

Page 59

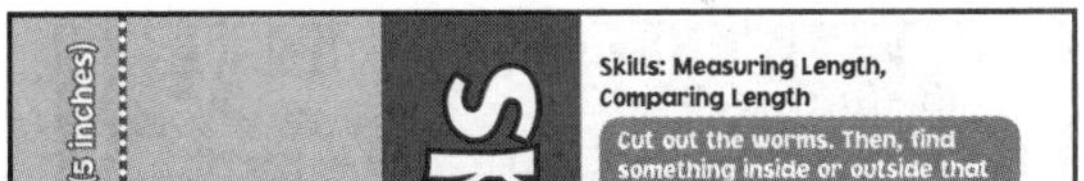

Page 61

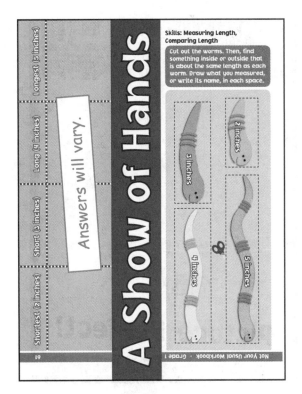

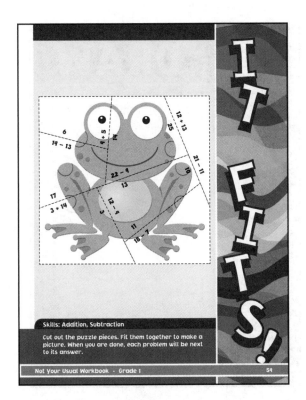

GUESS AGAIN

Use the clues to find each secret two-digit number.

It is more than 20.
It is less than 30.
Add its digits together, and you get 7.
Secret Number: 2 5
Tens Ones

It is less than 50.
It is more than 45.
Add its digits together, and you get 11.
Secret Number: 4 7
Tens Ones

Skills: Comparing Numbers, Addition, Place Value

It is less than 42.
It is more than 37.
Add its digits together, and you get 4.
Secret Number: 4 0
Tens Ones

It is more than 55.
It is less than 60.
Add its digits together, and you get 13.
Secret Number: 5 8
Tens Ones

Not Your Usual Workbook · Grade 1 63

Page 63

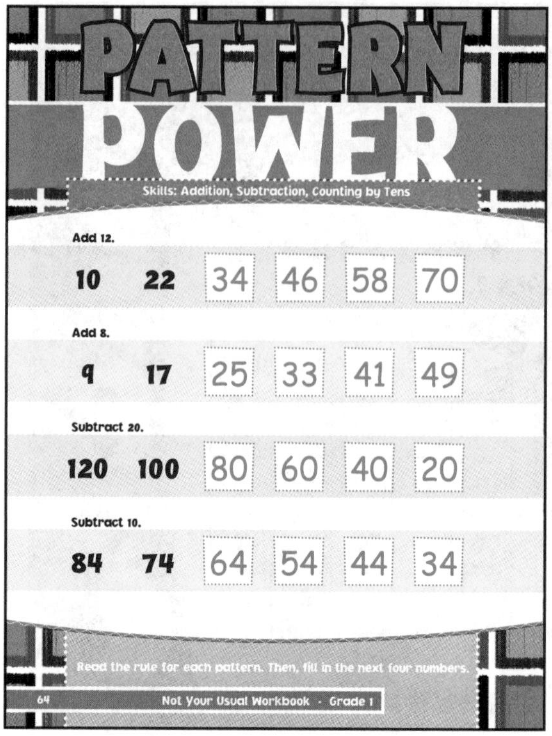
PATTERN POWER

Skills: Addition, Subtraction, Counting by Tens

Add 12.

10	22	34	46	58	70

Subtract 20.

120	100	80	60	40	20

Add 8.

9	17	25	33	41	49

Subtract 10.

84	74	64	54	44	34

Read the rule for each pattern. Then, fill in the next four numbers.

64 Not Your Usual Workbook · Grade 1

Page 64

Skill: Working with Data

Topp's Toy Store has a lot of bears! Count the bears of each color. Write the number at the bottom of the page after the equal sign. Then, circle the colored bear that has the largest group.

= 10 = 15 = 12

Picture Perfect!

Not Your Usual Workbook · Grade 1 65

Page 65

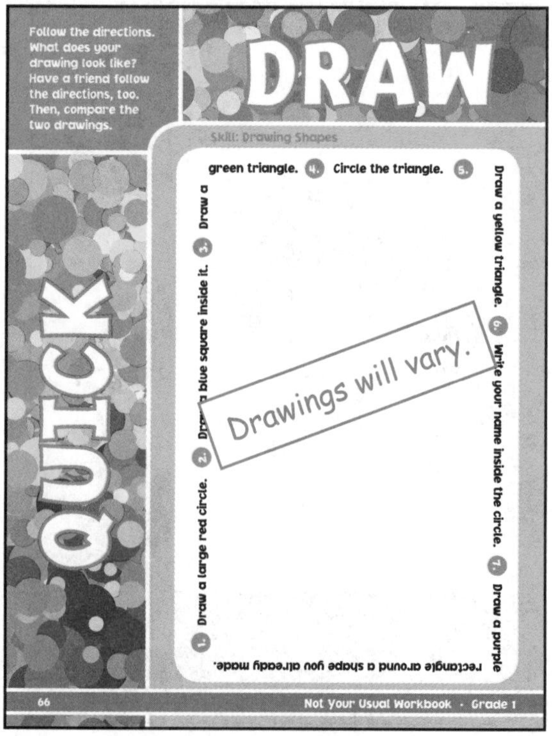
QUICK DRAW

Follow the directions. What does your drawing look like? Have a friend follow the directions, too. Then, compare the two drawings.

Skill: Drawing Shapes

1. Draw a large red circle. 2. Draw a blue square inside it. 3. Draw a green triangle. 4. Circle the triangle. 5. Draw a yellow triangle. 6. Write your name inside the circle. 7. Draw a purple rectangle around a shape you already made.

Drawings will vary.

66 Not Your Usual Workbook · Grade 1

Page 66

Page 67

Page 68

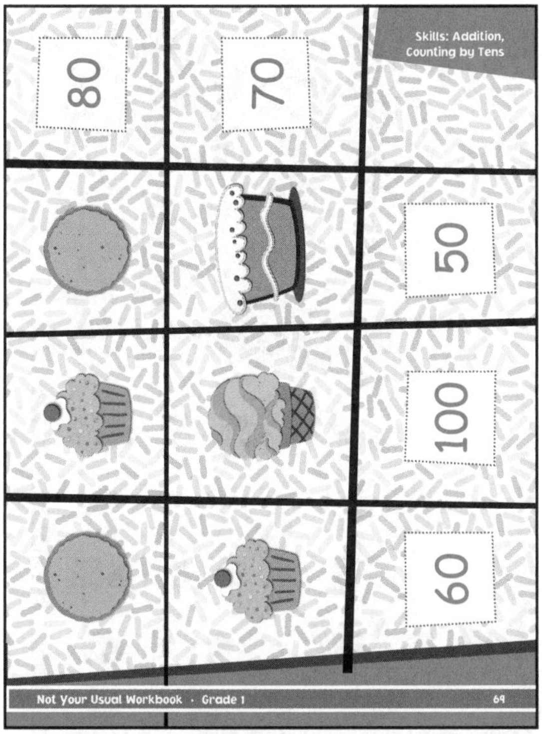

Page 69

e(quation) sen+sation
Skills: Counting by Tens, Place Value
Use the code to write each problem using numbers. Then, solve.
= 10
= 1
30 + 7 = 37
10 + 5 = 15
40 + 2 = 42
70 + 1 = 71
70
Not Your Usual Workbook · Grade 1

Page 70

PATTERN POWER
Skill: Telling Time
The times shown by the clocks in each row form a pattern. Draw hands on the last clock to complete the pattern.
Not Your Usual Workbook · Grade 1
71

Page 71

Page 72

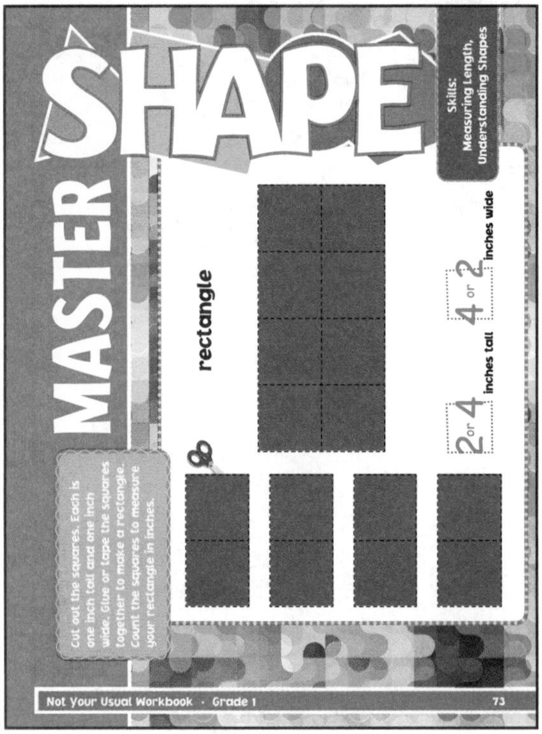

MASTER SHAPE
Skills: Measuring Length, Understanding Shapes
rectangle
4 or 2
inches wide
2 or 4
inches tall
Cut out the squares. Each is one inch tall and one inch wide. Glue or tape the squares together to make a rectangle. Count the squares to measure your rectangle in inches.
Not Your Usual Workbook · Grade 1
73

Page 73

Page 75

Skill: Subtraction
NUMBER CROSS
Across
Down
Think of a subtraction number sentence to describe each group of shapes. Write it in the puzzle. One is done for you.
22 − 15 = 7
18 − 4
12 − 3
24 − 15 = 9
19 − 6 = 13
15
20 − 9 = 11
3
76 Not Your Usual Workbook · Grade 1

Page 76

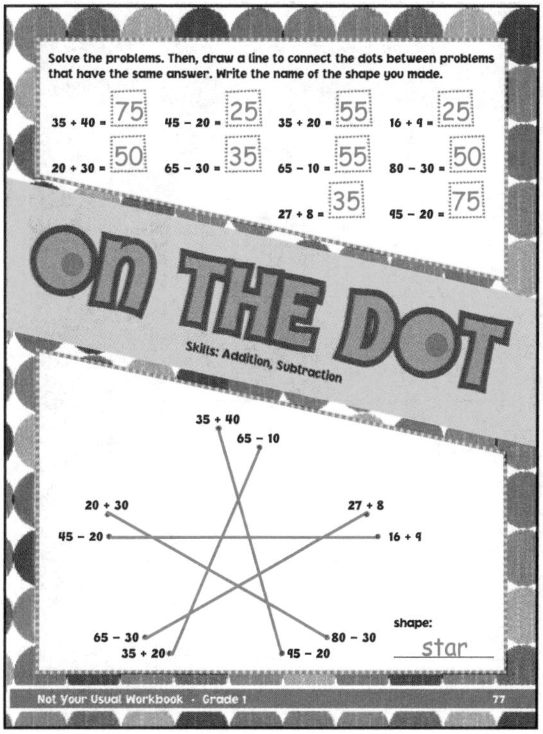

Solve the problems. Then, draw a line to connect the dots between problems that have the same answer. Write the name of the shape you made.
35 + 40 = 75
45 − 20 = 25
35 + 20 = 55
16 + 9 = 25
20 + 30 = 50
65 − 30 = 35
65 − 10 = 55
80 − 30 = 50
27 + 8 = 35
95 − 20 = 75
ON THE DOT
Skills: Addition, Subtraction
35 + 40
65 − 10
20 + 30
27 + 8
45 − 20
16 + 9
65 − 30
35 + 20
95 − 20
80 − 30
shape:
star
Not Your Usual Workbook · Grade 1 77

Page 77

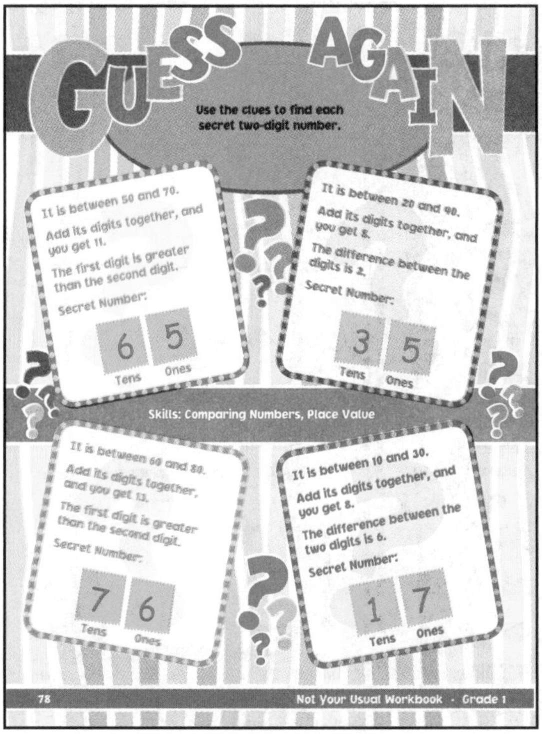

Page 78

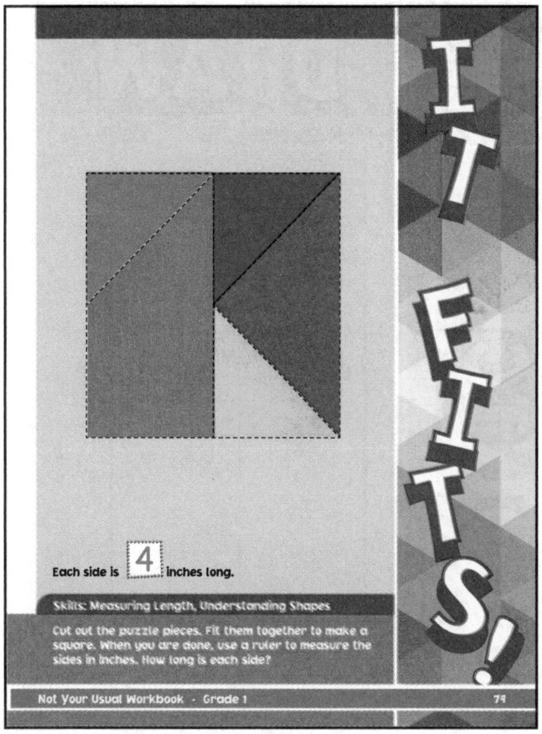

Page 79

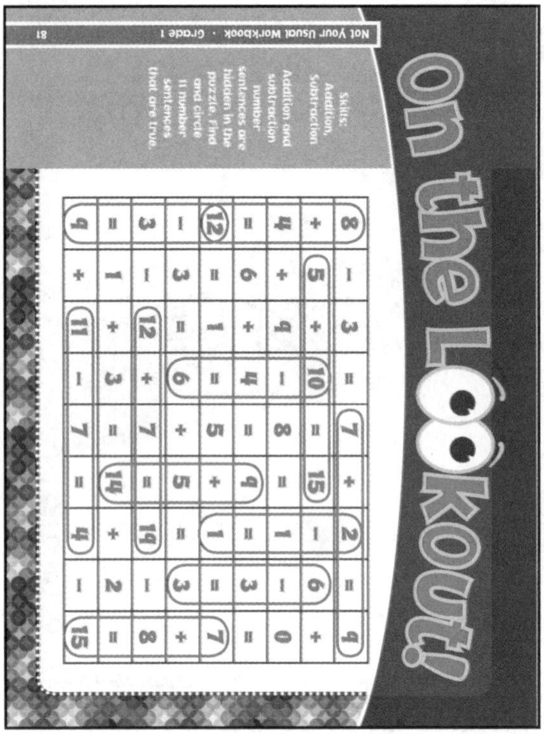

On the Lookout!
Skills: Addition, Subtraction
Addition and subtraction number sentences are hidden in the puzzle. Find and circle 11 number sentences that are true.
Not Your Usual Workbook · Grade 1
81

Page 81

Page 82

Page 83

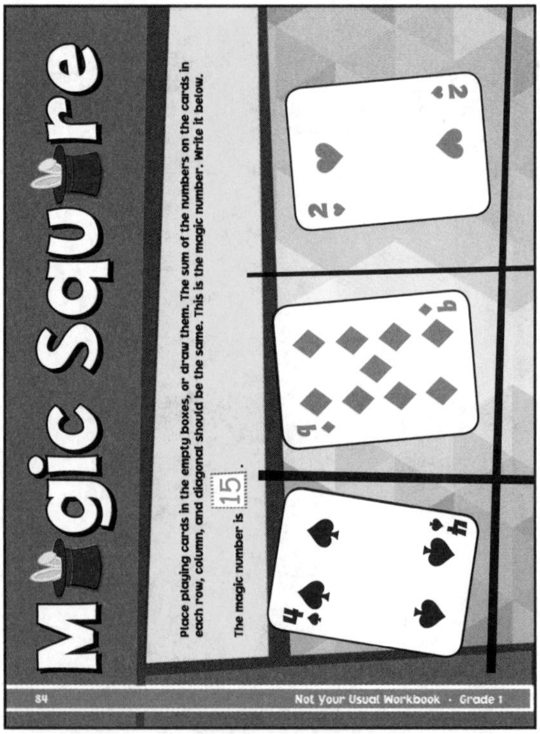

Page 84

Page 85

Page 86

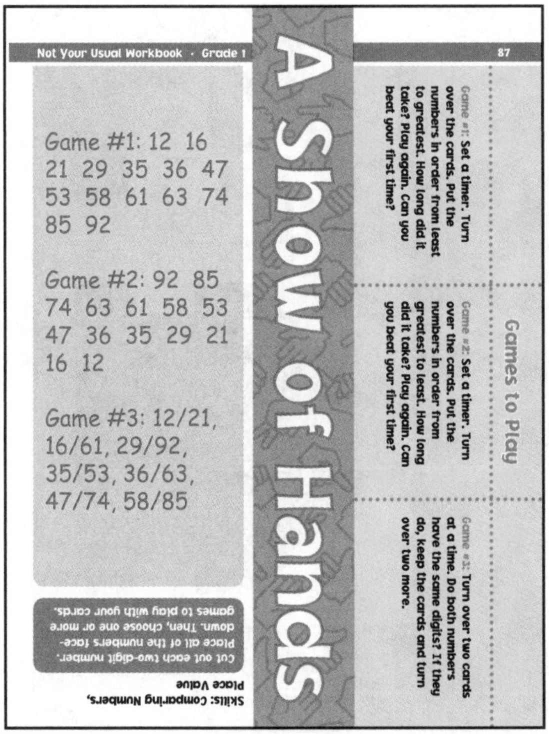

Page 87

PATTERN POWER
Skill: Addition
8 15 22 29 36 43
11 21 31 41 51 61
20 28 36 44 52 60
50 55 60 65 70 75
Find the pattern in each row. Write the missing numbers.
Not Your Usual Workbook · Grade 1
89

Page 89

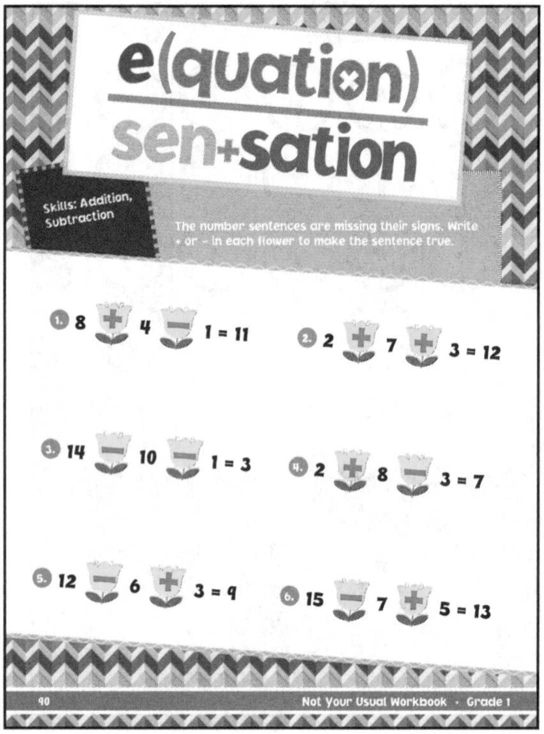

e(quation) sen+sation

Skills: Addition, Subtraction

The number sentences are missing their signs. Write + or − in each flower to make the sentence true.

1. 8 + 4 − 1 = 11
2. 2 + 7 + 3 = 12
3. 14 − 10 − 1 = 3
4. 2 + 8 − 3 = 7
5. 12 − 6 + 3 = 9
6. 15 − 7 + 5 = 13

90 Not Your Usual Workbook · Grade 1

Page 90

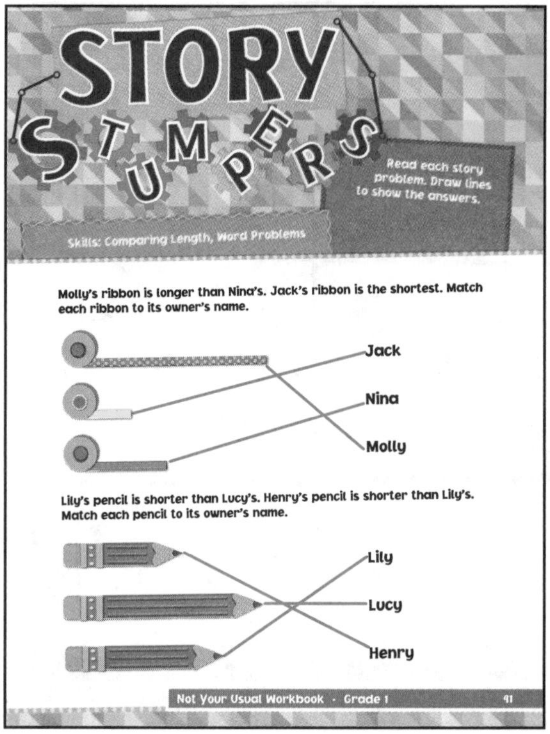

STORY STUMPERS

Read each story problem. Draw lines to show the answers.

Skills: Comparing Length, Word Problems

Molly's ribbon is longer than Nina's. Jack's ribbon is the shortest. Match each ribbon to its owner's name.

Jack
Nina
Molly

Lily's pencil is shorter than Lucy's. Henry's pencil is shorter than Lily's. Match each pencil to its owner's name.

Lily
Lucy
Henry

Not Your Usual Workbook · Grade 1 91

Page 91

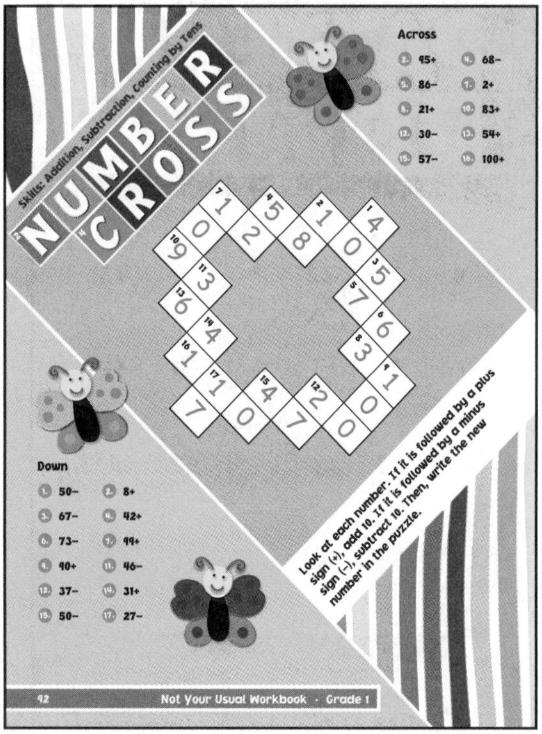

NUMBER CROSS

Skills: Addition, Subtraction, Counting by Tens

Across

1. 95+
4. 68−
5. 86−
7. 2+
8. 21+
10. 83+
12. 30−
13. 54+
15. 57−
16. 100+

Down

1. 50−
2. 8+
3. 67−
4. 42+
6. 73−
7. 99+
9. 90+
11. 46−
12. 37−
14. 31+
15. 50−
17. 27−

Look at each number. If it is followed by a plus sign (+), add 10. If it is followed by a minus sign (−), subtract 10. Then, write the new number in the puzzle.

92 Not Your Usual Workbook · Grade 1

Page 92

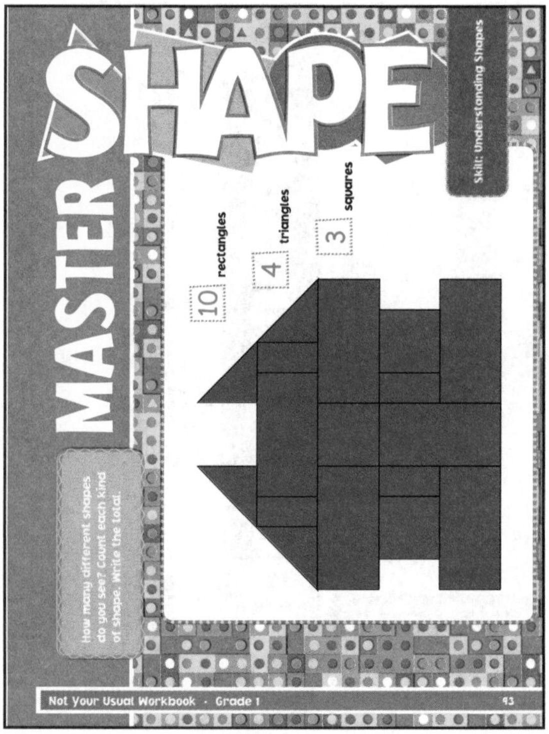

MASTER SHAPE

Skill: Understanding Shapes

How many different shapes do you see? Count each kind of shape. Write the total.

10 rectangles
4 triangles
3 squares

Not Your Usual Workbook · Grade 1 93

Page 93

Page 94

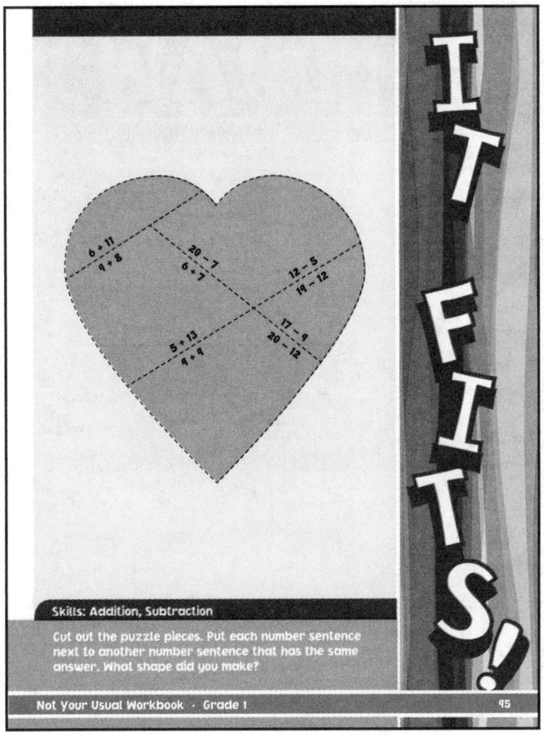

IT FITS!
Skills: Addition, Subtraction
Cut out the puzzle pieces. Put each number sentence next to another number sentence that has the same answer. What shape did you make?
Not Your Usual Workbook · Grade 1 95

Page 95

Page 97

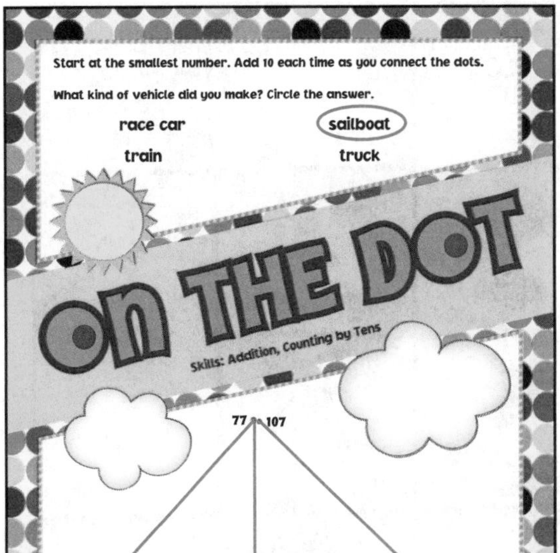

Page 98

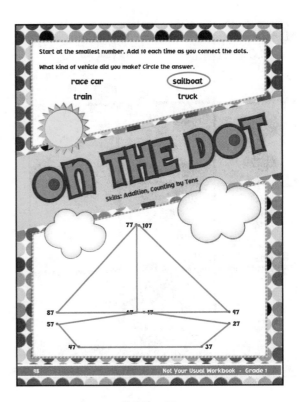

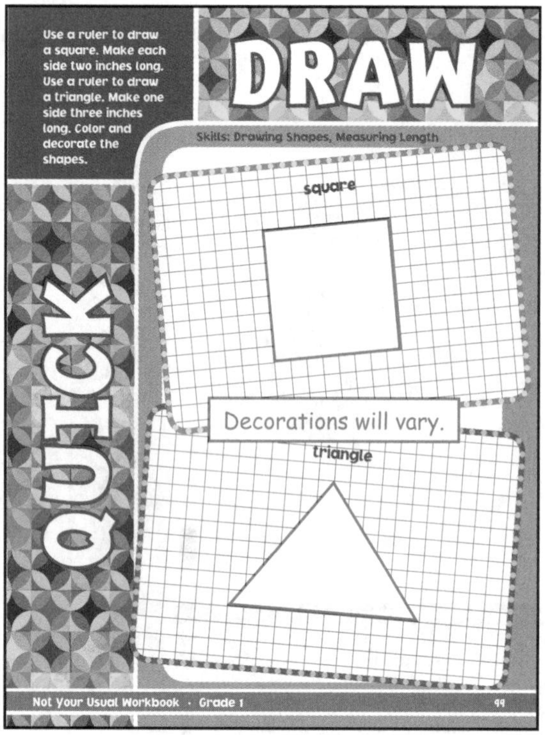

Page 99

Magic Square
Use the code to find the total in each square. Then, write the sum of the numbers in each row and column.
= 10
= 1
56
100
Not Your Usual Workbook · Grade 1

Page 100

Page 101

Page 102

A Show of Hands
Skill: Telling Time
Cut out each clock face. Glue or tape it onto the circle that shows the same time.
103
Not Your Usual Workbook · Grade 1

Page 103

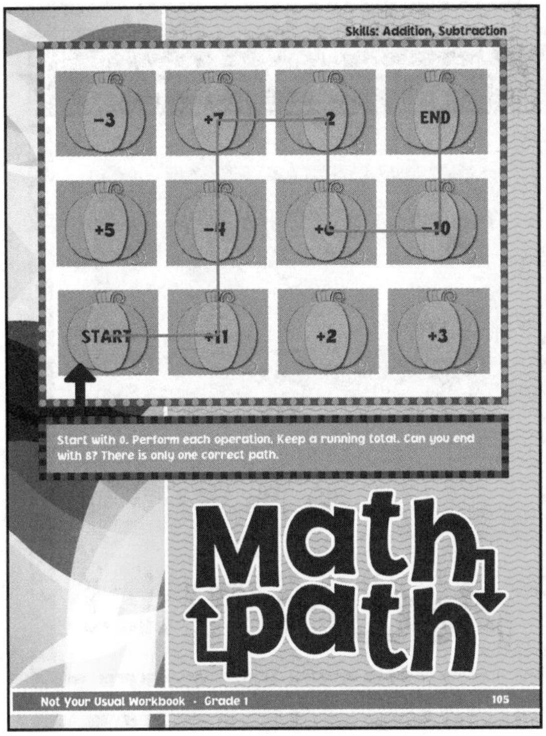

Page 105

Page 106

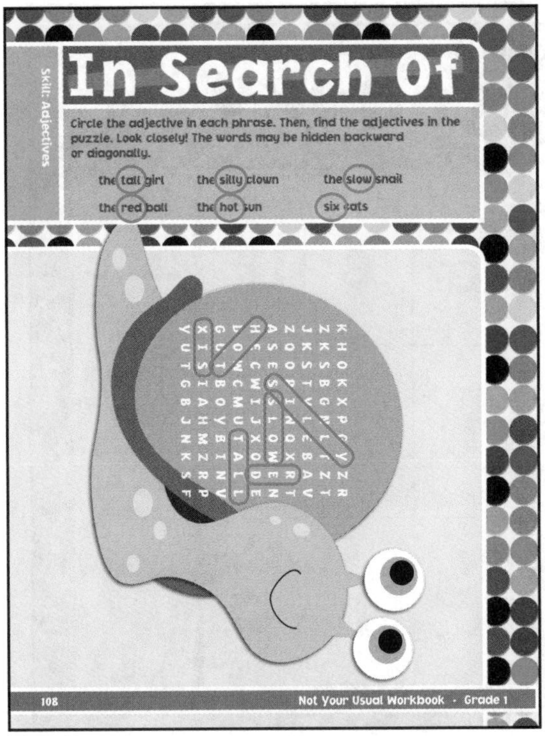

Page 108

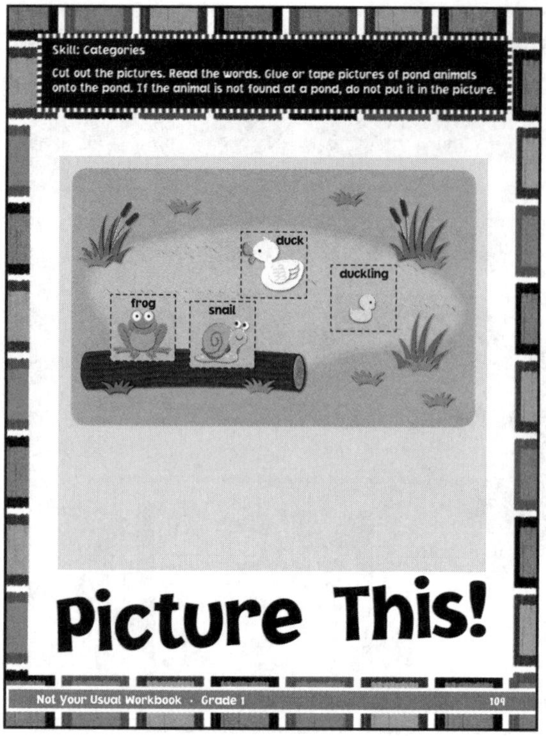

Page 109

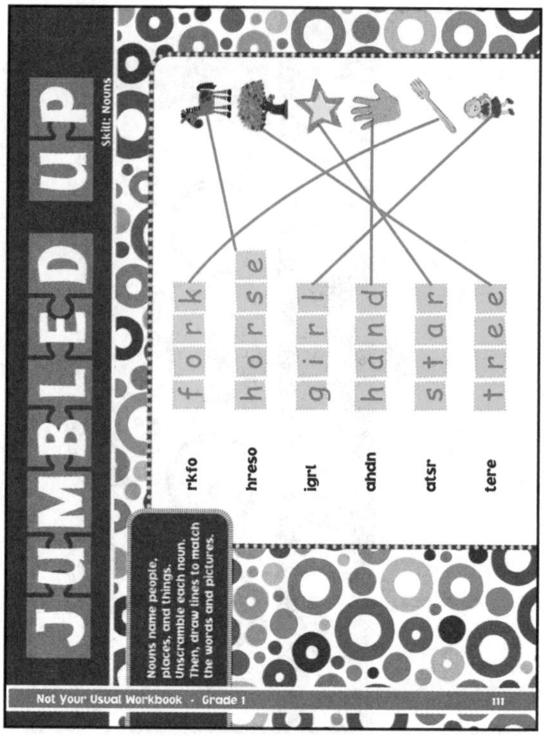

Page 111

Sudoku for You
Skills: Handwriting, Spelling
Write letters in the boxes so that each row and column has the letters to spell . Do not use any letter more than once in the same row or column.
a c t
t a c
c t a

Page 112

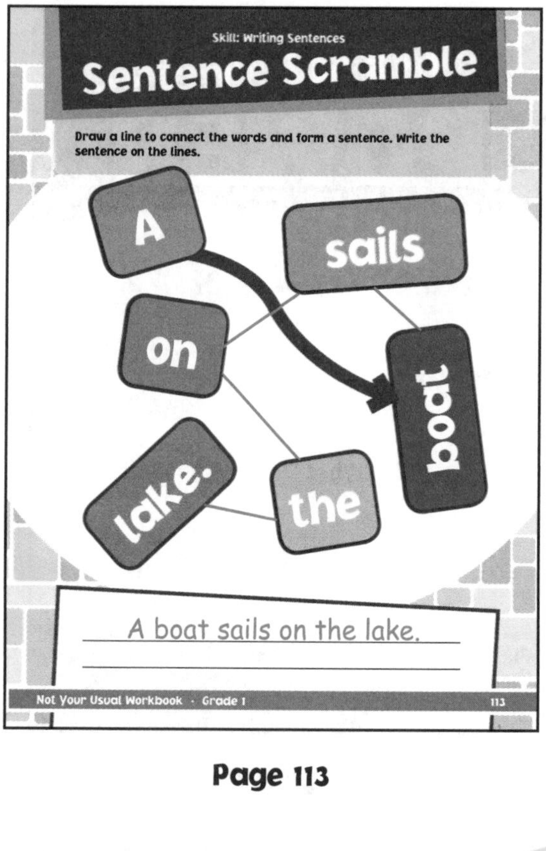

Page 113

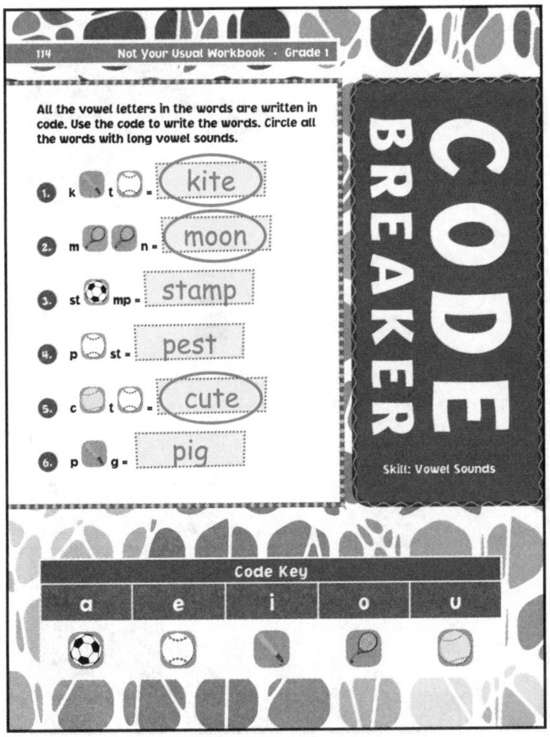
114 Not Your Usual Workbook · Grade 1

All the vowel letters in the words are written in code. Use the code to write the words. Circle all the words with long vowel sounds.

1. k _ t _ = kite
2. m _ _ n = moon
3. st _ mp = stamp
4. p _ st = pest
5. c _ t _ = cute
6. p _ g = pig

CODE BREAKER

Skill: Vowel Sounds

Code Key

a	e	i	o	u

Page 114

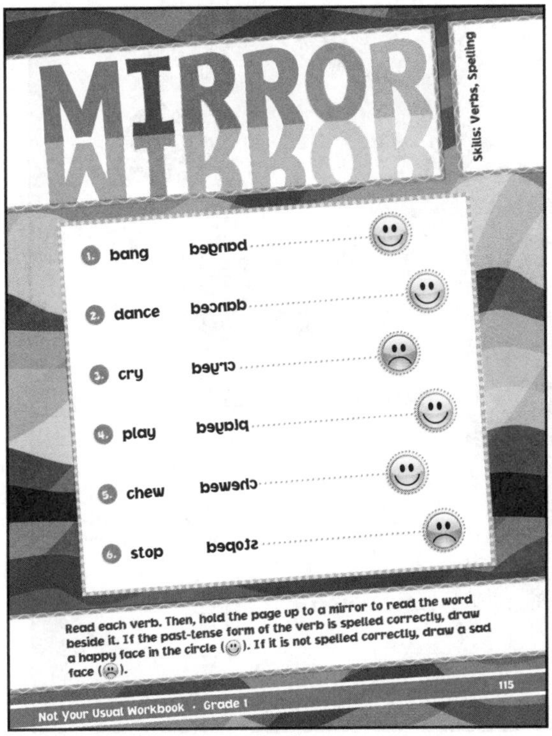
MIRROR

Skills: Verbs, Spelling

1. bang banged
2. dance danced
3. cry cryed
4. play played
5. chew chewed
6. stop stoped

Read each verb. Then, hold the page up to a mirror to read the word beside it. If the past-tense form of the verb is spelled correctly, draw a happy face in the circle (☺). If it is not spelled correctly, draw a sad face (☹).

115

Not Your Usual Workbook · Grade 1

Page 115

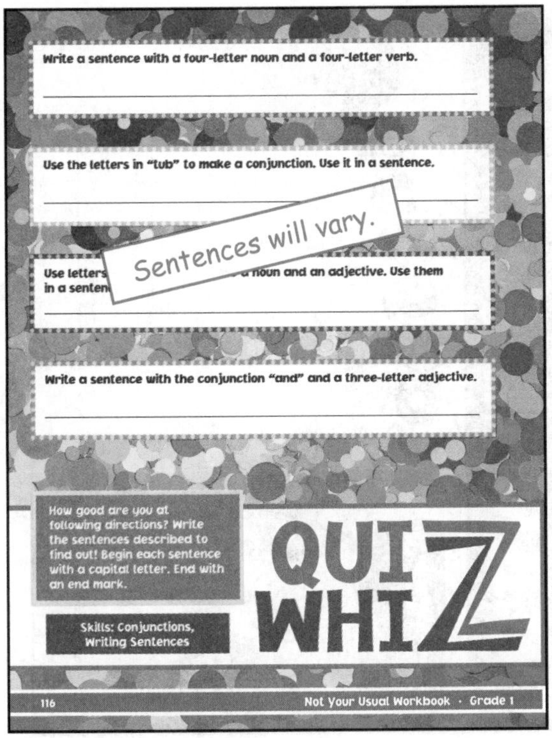
Write a sentence with a four-letter noun and a four-letter verb.

Use the letters in "tub" to make a conjunction. Use it in a sentence.

Use letters ... a noun and an adjective. Use them in a senten...

Sentences will vary.

Write a sentence with the conjunction "and" and a three-letter adjective.

How good are you at following directions? Write the sentences described to find out! Begin each sentence with a capital letter. End with an end mark.

Skills: Conjunctions, Writing Sentences

QUIZ WHIZ

116 Not Your Usual Workbook · Grade 1

Page 116

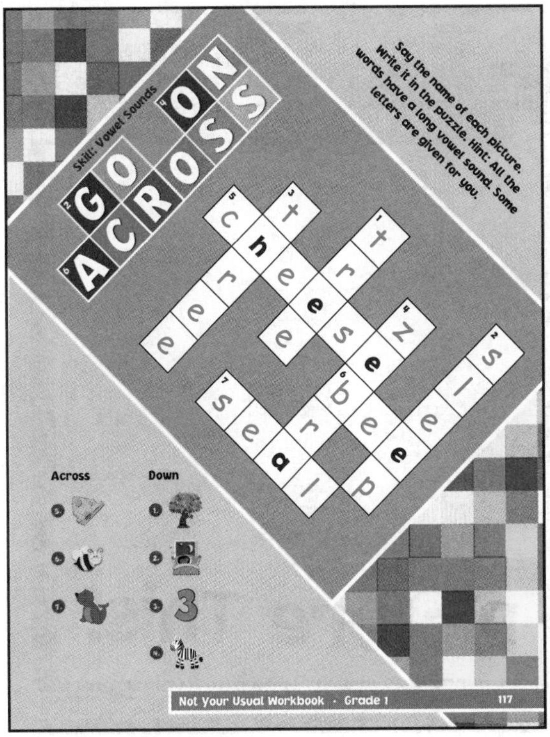
Say the name of each picture. Write it in the puzzle. Hint: All the words have a long vowel sound. Some letters are given for you.

Skill: Vowel Sounds

GO ACROSS

Across

Down

Not Your Usual Workbook · Grade 1 117

Page 117

Page 118

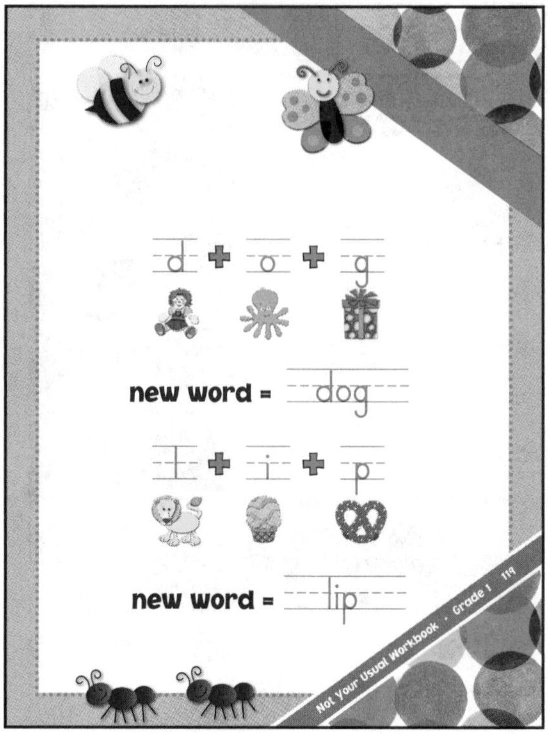

Page 119

Page 120

Page 121

RIDDLE ME
Use the clues to spell a word with a common prefix. On the line, write the base word.
Skills: Prefixes, Base Words
1 You never use the letter "q" without me. u
2 I am the first letter that makes a sound in "knife." n
3 I am the double letter in "hiss." s
4 I am the first letter of the alphabet. a
5 I am the first letter of the second month of the year. f
6 I am the silent letter in "wide." e
u n s a f e
Base Word:
safe
122
Not Your Usual Workbook · Grade 1

Page 122

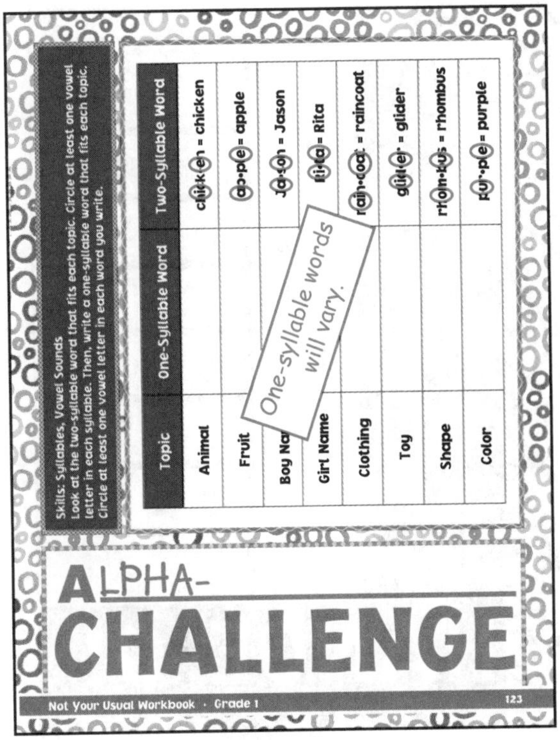

Page 123

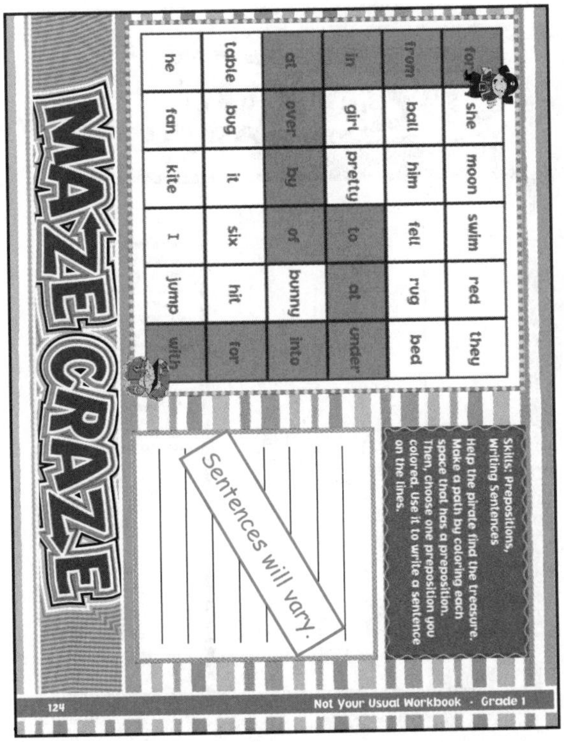

Page 124

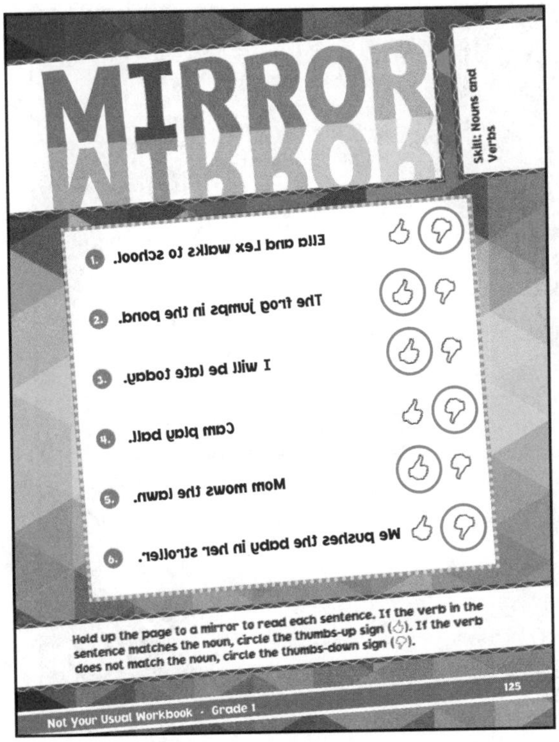

Page 125

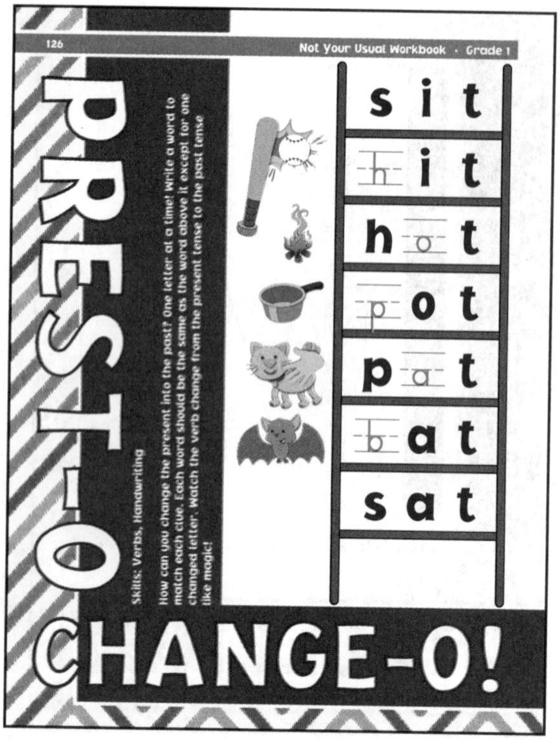
126 Not Your Usual Workbook · Grade 1

PREST-O CHANGE-O!

Skills: Verbs, Handwriting

How can you change the present into the past? One letter at a time! Write a word to match each clue. Each word should be the same as the word above it except for one changed letter. Watch the verb change from the present tense to the past tense like magic!

sit
hit
hot
pot
pat
bat
sat

Page 126

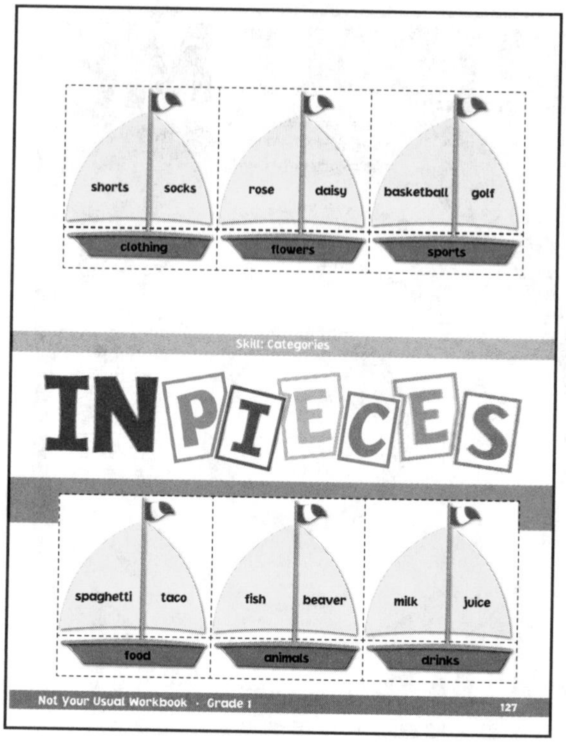
Skill: Categories

IN PIECES

shorts socks	rose daisy	basketball golf
clothing	flowers	sports
spaghetti taco	fish beaver	milk juice
food	animals	drinks

Not Your Usual Workbook · Grade 1 127

Page 127

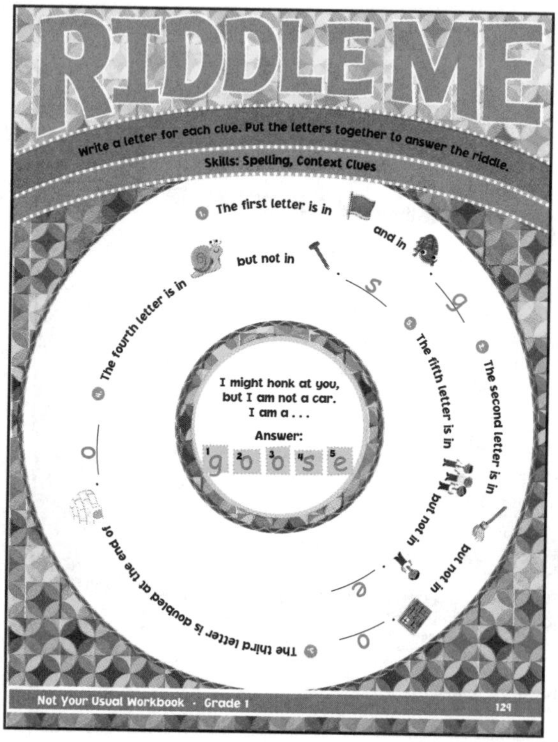
RIDDLE ME

Write a letter for each clue. Put the letters together to answer the riddle.

Skills: Spelling, Context Clues

1. The first letter is in (flag) and in (pig) but not in (snail). g
2. The second letter is in (boots) but not in (ax). o
3. The third letter is doubled at the end of (igloo). o
4. The fourth letter is in (snail) but not in (nail). s
5. The fifth letter is in (kites) but not in (kits). e

I might honk at you, but I am not a car. I am a . . .

Answer: g o o s e

Not Your Usual Workbook · Grade 1 129

Page 129

130 Not Your Usual Workbook · Grade 1

Sudoku for you

s	e	h
e	h	s
h	s	e

Skills: Pronouns, Handwriting

Write letters in the boxes so that each row and column has the letters to spell a pronoun that could take the place of "Hannah" in the sentence. Do not use any letter more than once in the same row or column.

Hannah kicked the soccer ball.

Page 130

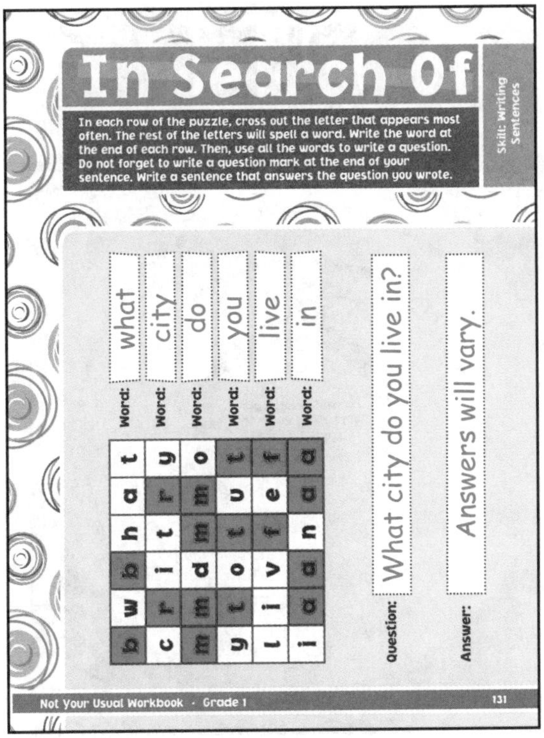

In Search Of

Skill: Writing Sentences

In each row of the puzzle, cross out the letter that appears most often. The rest of the letters will spell a word. Write the word at the end of each row. Then, use all the words to write a question. Do not forget to write a question mark at the end of your sentence. Write a sentence that answers the question you wrote.

b	w	b	h	a	t	Word: what
c	r	i	t	r	y	Word: city
m	m	d	m	m	o	Word: do
y	t	o	t	u	t	Word: you
l	i	v	f	e	f	Word: live
i	a	a	n	a	a	Word: in

Question: What city do you live in?

Answer: Answers will vary.

Not Your Usual Workbook · Grade 1 131

Page 131

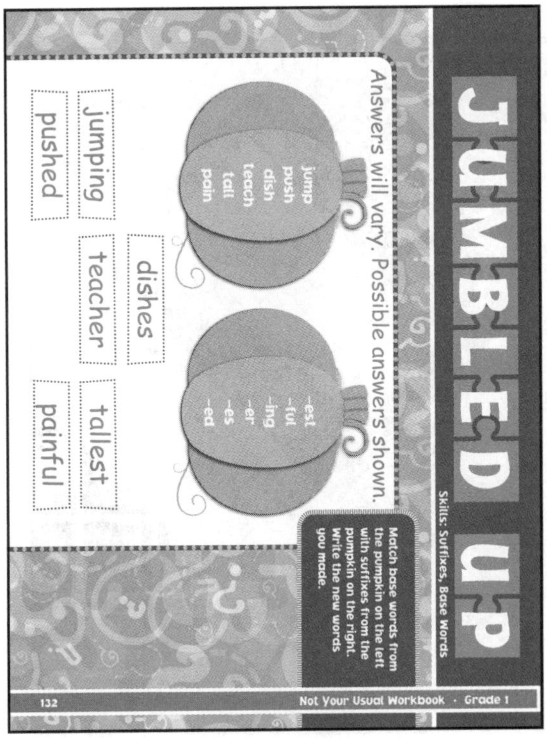

JUMBLED UP

Skills: Suffixes, Base Words

Match base words from the pumpkin on the left with suffixes from the pumpkin on the right. Write the new words you made.

Answers will vary. Possible answers shown.

jump
push
dish
teach
tall
pain

-est
-ful
-ing
-er
-es
-ed

dishes
jumping
teacher
tallest
pushed
painful

132 Not Your Usual Workbook · Grade 1

Page 132

Not Your Usual Workbook · Grade 1 133

CODE BREAKER

Skill: Using Capital Letters

Use the code to find the names of days and months. Begin each word with a capital letter.

May

Tuesday

November

Monday

June

Code Key

a b d e j m n o r s t u v y

Page 133

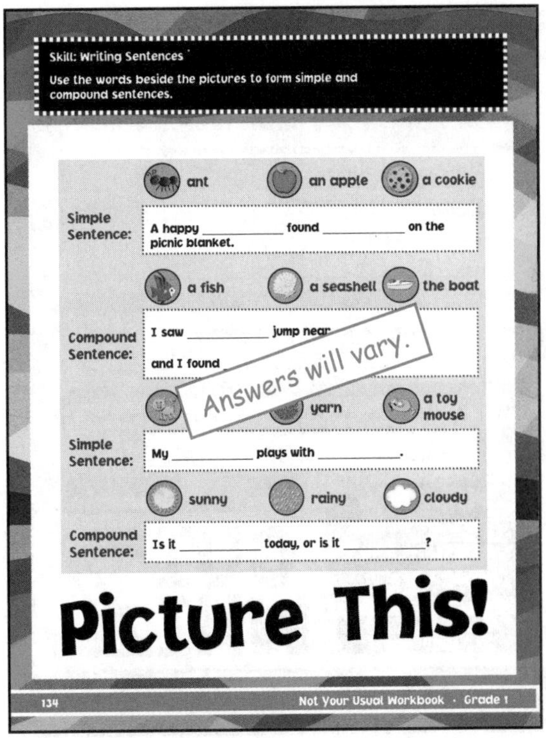

Skill: Writing Sentences

Use the words beside the pictures to form simple and compound sentences.

ant | an apple | a cookie

Simple Sentence: A happy ________ found ________ on the picnic blanket.

a fish | a seashell | the boat

Compound Sentence: I saw ________ jump near ________ and I found ________

Answers will vary.

yarn | a toy mouse

Simple Sentence: My ________ plays with ________.

sunny | rainy | cloudy

Compound Sentence: Is it ________ today, or is it ________?

Picture This!

134 Not Your Usual Workbook · Grade 1

Page 134

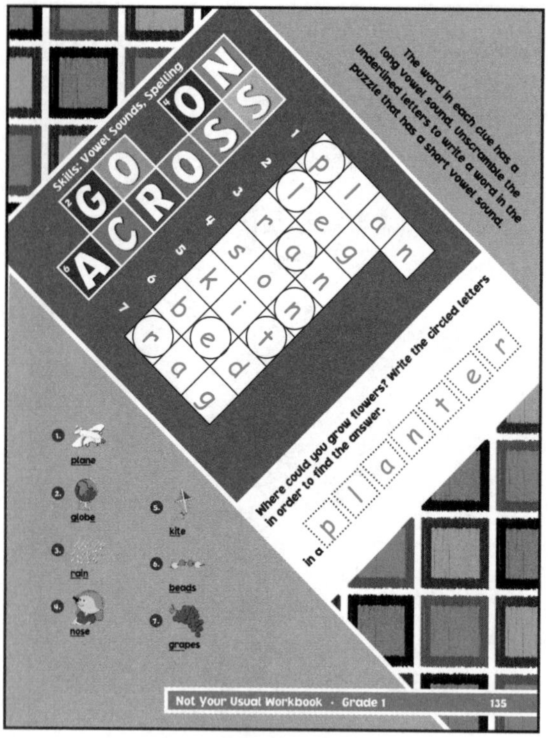

GO ACROSS

Skills: Vowel Sounds, Spelling

The word in each clue has a long vowel sound. Unscramble the underlined letters to write a word in the puzzle that has a short vowel sound.

1. plane
2. globe
3. rain
4. nose
5. kite
6. beads
7. grapes

1 plan
2 leg
3 ran
4 son
5 kit
6 bed
7 rag

Where could you grow flowers? Write the circled letters in order to find the answer.

In a p l a n t e r

Not Your Usual Workbook · Grade 1 135

Page 135

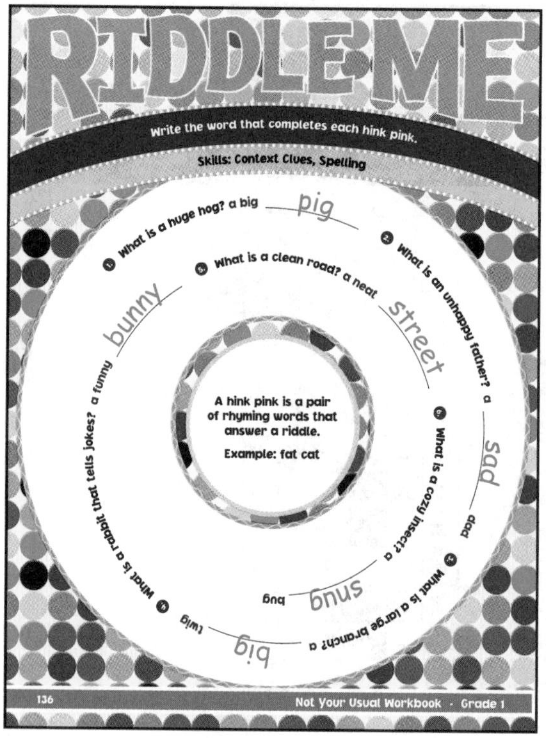

RIDDLE ME

Write the word that completes each hink pink.

Skills: Context Clues, Spelling

A hink pink is a pair of rhyming words that answer a riddle.

Example: fat cat

1. What is a huge hog? a big pig
2. What is an unhappy father? a sad dad
3. What is a large branch? a big twig
4. What is a rabbit that tells jokes? a funny bunny
5. What is a clean road? a neat street
6. What is a cozy insect? a snug bug

136 Not Your Usual Workbook · Grade 1

Page 136

Write a sentence using the word ending in silent e.

horse

Write a sentence using the word that ends with a vowel sound.

silly

Write a sentence using the word with a long a sound.

mail

Write a sentence using the word with a short i sound.

bring

Sentences will vary.

Read each direction. Write a sentence using a word from the box. Cross out each word as you use it. Write the two words that are left over: short tall

Word Box

short bring
mail tall
horse silly

QUIZ WHIZ

Skills: Writing Sentences, Vowel Sounds

Not Your Usual Workbook · Grade 1 137

Page 137

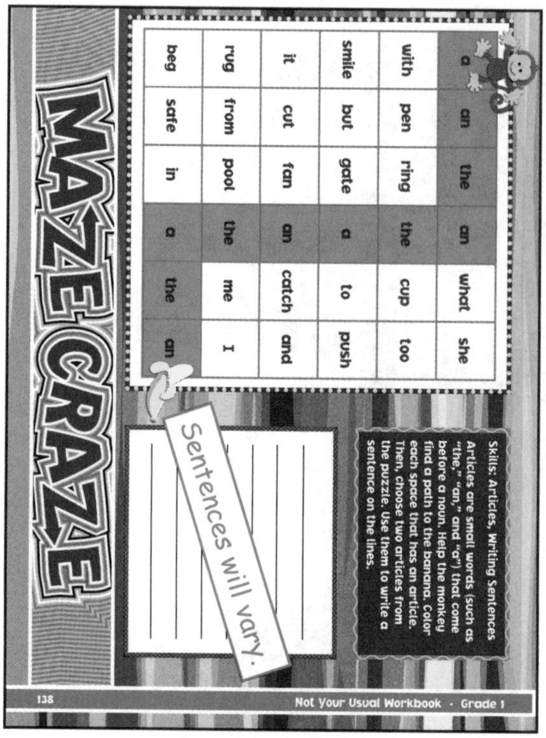

MAZE CRAZE

Skills: Articles, Writing Sentences

Articles are small words (such as "the," "an," and "a") that come before a noun. Help the monkey find a path to the banana. Color each space that has an article. Then, choose two articles from the puzzle. Use them to write a sentence on the lines.

a	an	the	an	what	she
with	pen	ring	the	cup	too
smile	but	gate	a	to	push
it	cut	fan	an	catch	and
rug	from	pool	the	me	I
beg	safe	in	a	the	an

Sentences will vary.

138 Not Your Usual Workbook · Grade 1

Page 138

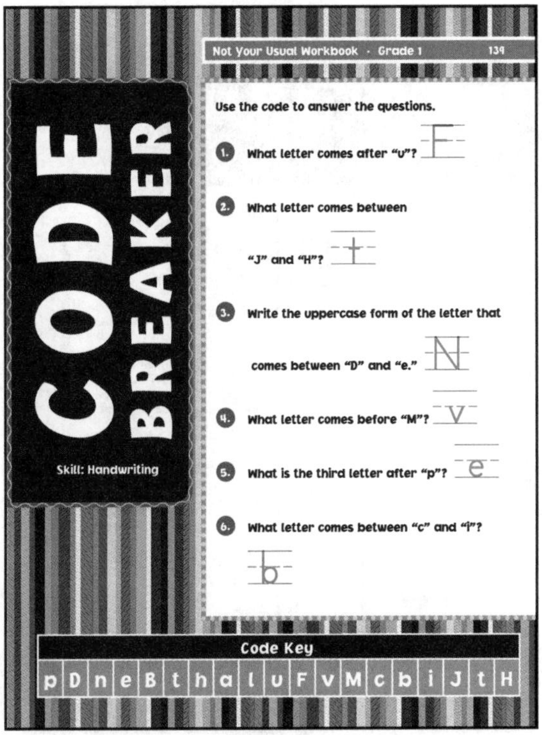
Not Your Usual Workbook · Grade 1 139

CODE BREAKER

Skill: Handwriting

Use the code to answer the questions.

1. What letter comes after "u"? F
2. What letter comes between "J" and "H"? t
3. Write the uppercase form of the letter that comes between "D" and "e." N
4. What letter comes before "M"? v
5. What is the third letter after "p"? e
6. What letter comes between "c" and "i"? b

Code Key

p D n e B t h a l u F v M c b i J t H

Page 139

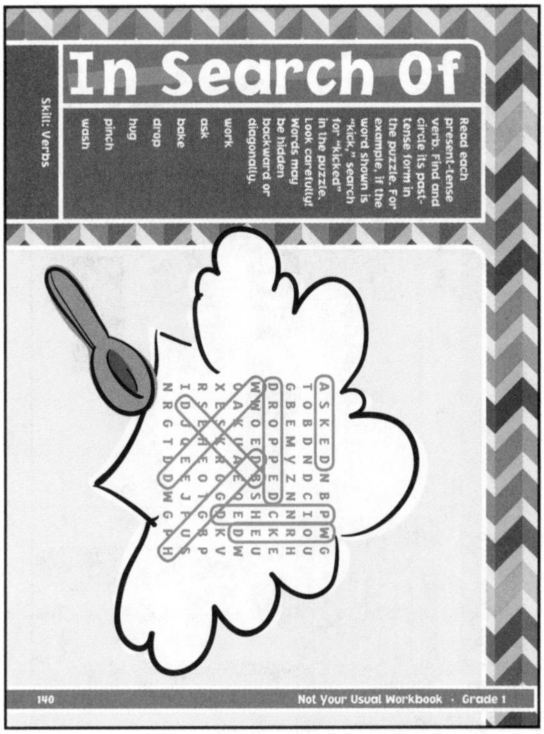
In Search Of

Skill: Verbs

Read each present-tense verb. Find and circle its past-tense form in the puzzle. For example, if the word shown is "kick," search for "kicked" in the puzzle. Look carefully! Words may be hidden backward or diagonally.

140 Not Your Usual Workbook · Grade 1

Page 140

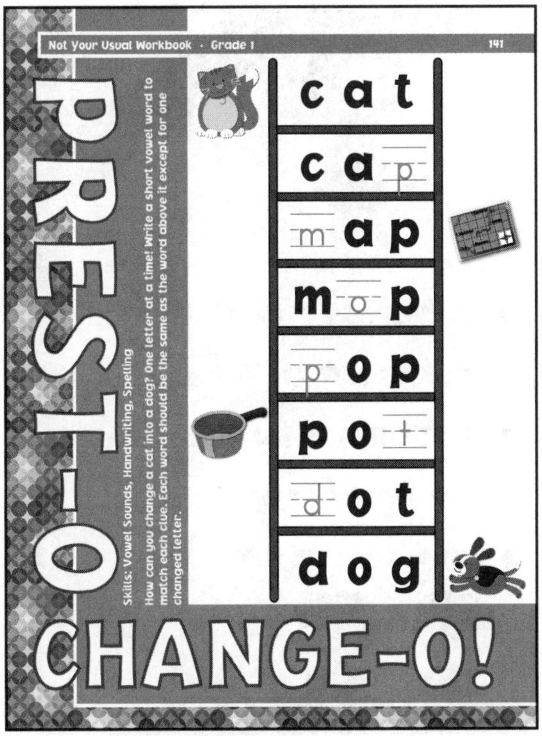
Not Your Usual Workbook · Grade 1 141

PRESTO-CHANGE-O!

Skills: Vowel Sounds, Handwriting, Spelling

How can you change a cat into a dog? One letter at a time! Write a short vowel word to match each clue. Each word should be the same as the word above it except for one changed letter.

cat
cap
map
mop
pop
pot
dot
dog

Page 141

Skill: Writing Sentences

Sentence Scramble

Draw a line to connect the orange words to make a question. Draw a line to connect the green words to make a command. Write the sentences on the lines. End the question with a question mark (?). End the command with an exclamation mark (!).

that for Have seen you Watch boots snake out my

Have you seen my boots?

Watch out for that snake!

142 Not Your Usual Workbook · Grade 1

Page 142

JUMBLED UP

Skill: Writing Sentences

A compound sentence tells two ideas. It contains a joining word such as "and" or "but." Cut out the tiles. Arrange them to make a compound sentence. Write the sentence on the lines.

Max's cat is all white, but my cat has stripes.

my ca | te, but | l whi | Max's c | t has st | at is al | ripes.

Not Your Usual Workbook · Grade 1 143

Page 143

Not Your Usual Workbook · Grade 1 145

Sudoku for you

p	l	y	a
y	a	l	p
l	p	a	y
a	y	p	l

Skills: Verbs, Handwriting

Write letters in the boxes so that each row and column has the letters to spell the verb that is missing from the second sentence. Do not use any letter more than once in the same row or column.

Yesterday, we played.

Today, we ______.

Page 145

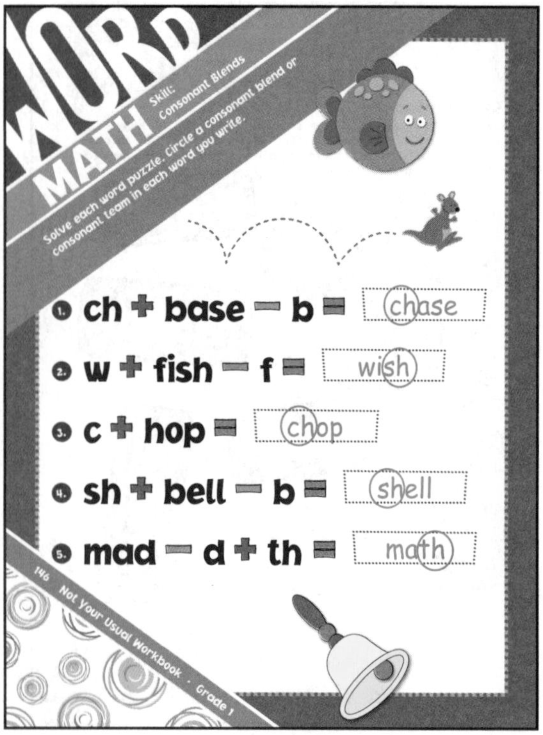
WORD MATH

Skill: Consonant Blends

Solve each word puzzle. Circle a consonant blend or consonant team in each word you write.

1. ch + base − b = chase
2. w + fish − f = wish
3. c + hop = chop
4. sh + bell − b = shell
5. mad − d + th = math

146 Not Your Usual Workbook · Grade 1

Page 146

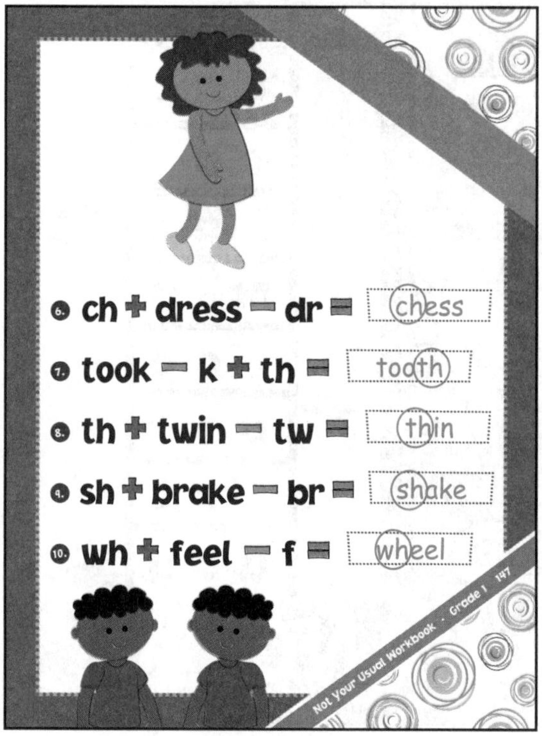
6. ch + dress − dr = chess
7. took − k + th = tooth
8. th + twin − tw = thin
9. sh + brake − br = shake
10. wh + feel − f = wheel

Not Your Usual Workbook · Grade 1 147

Page 147

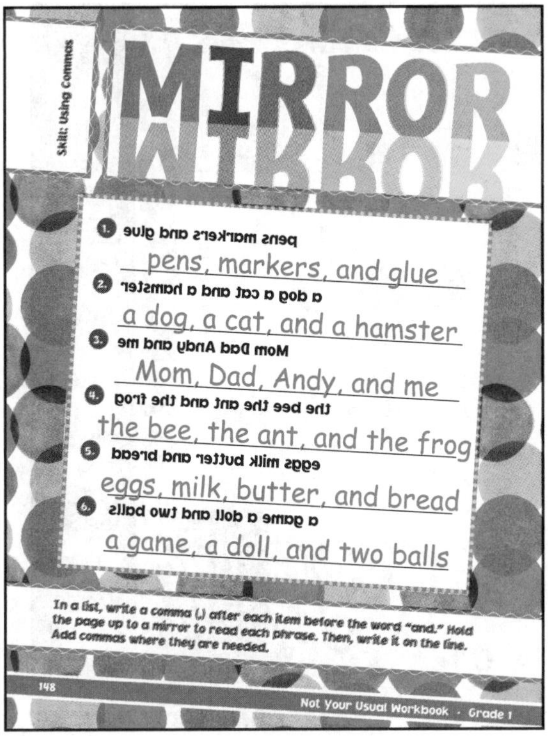
Skill: Using Commas

MIRROR

1. pens markers and glue
pens, markers, and glue
2. a dog a cat and a hamster
a dog, a cat, and a hamster
3. Mom Dad Andy and me
Mom, Dad, Andy, and me
4. the bee the ant and the frog
the bee, the ant, and the frog
5. eggs milk butter and bread
eggs, milk, butter, and bread
6. a game a doll and two balls
a game, a doll, and two balls

In a list, write a comma (,) after each item before the word "and." Hold the page up to a mirror to read each phrase. Then, write it on the line. Add commas where they are needed.

148 Not Your Usual Workbook · Grade 1

Page 148

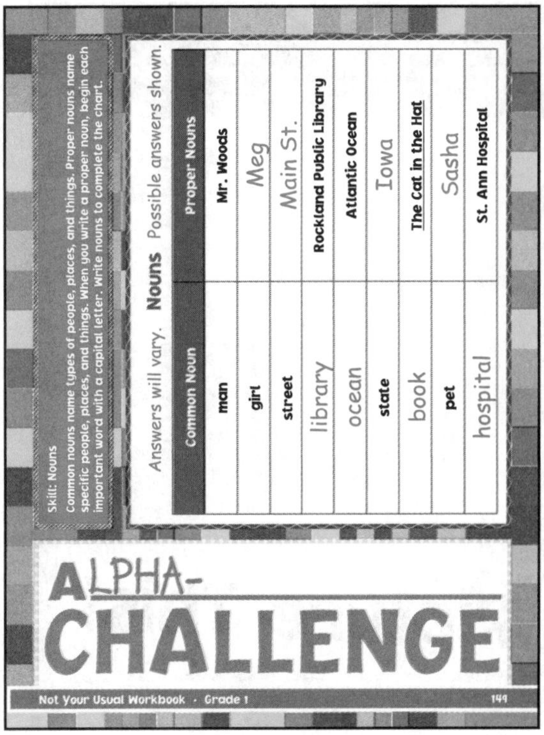
Skill: Nouns
Common nouns name types of people, places, and things. Proper nouns name specific people, places, and things. When you write a proper noun, begin each important word with a capital letter. Write nouns to complete the chart.

Answers will vary. **Nouns** Possible answers shown.

Common Noun	Proper Nouns
man	Mr. Woods
girl	Meg
street	Main St.
library	Rockland Public Library
ocean	Atlantic Ocean
state	Iowa
book	The Cat in the Hat
pet	Sasha
hospital	St. Ann Hospital

ALPHA-CHALLENGE

Not Your Usual Workbook · Grade 1 149

Page 149

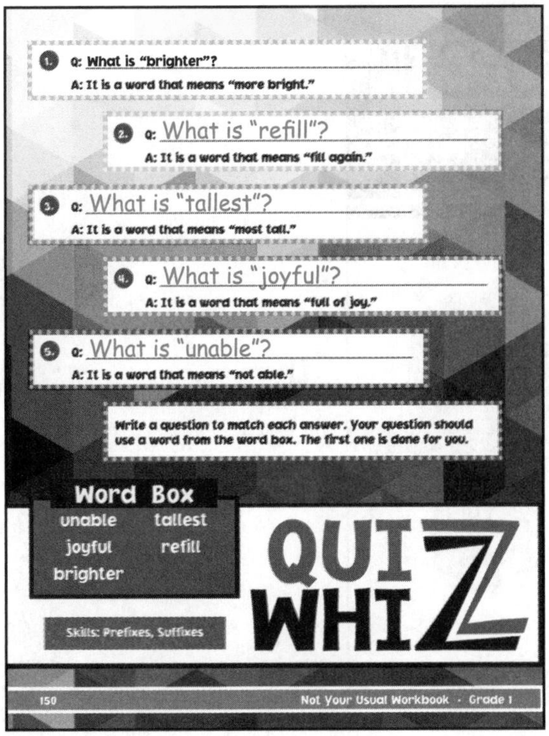
1. Q: What is "brighter"?
A: It is a word that means "more bright."
2. Q: What is "refill"?
A: It is a word that means "fill again."
3. Q: What is "tallest"?
A: It is a word that means "most tall."
4. Q: What is "joyful"?
A: It is a word that means "full of joy."
5. Q: What is "unable"?
A: It is a word that means "not able."

Write a question to match each answer. Your question should use a word from the word box. The first one is done for you.

Word Box
unable tallest
joyful refill
brighter

Skills: Prefixes, Suffixes

QUIZ WHIZ

150 Not Your Usual Workbook · Grade 1

Page 150

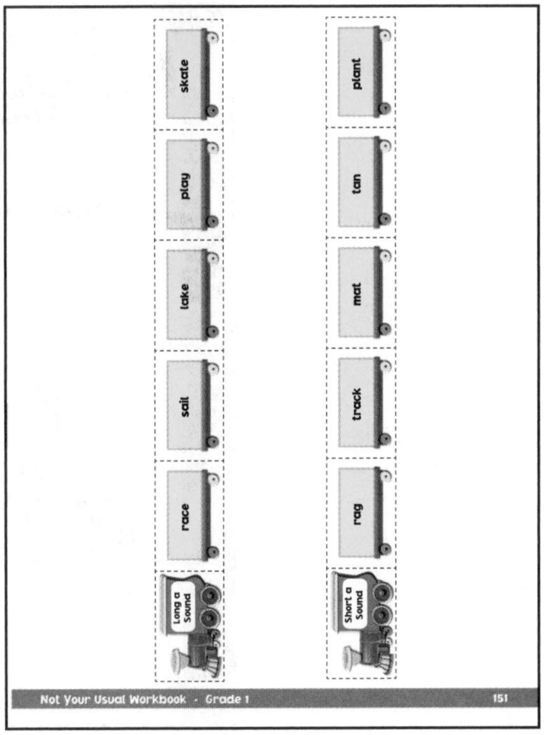

Not Your Usual Workbook · Grade 1 151

Page 151

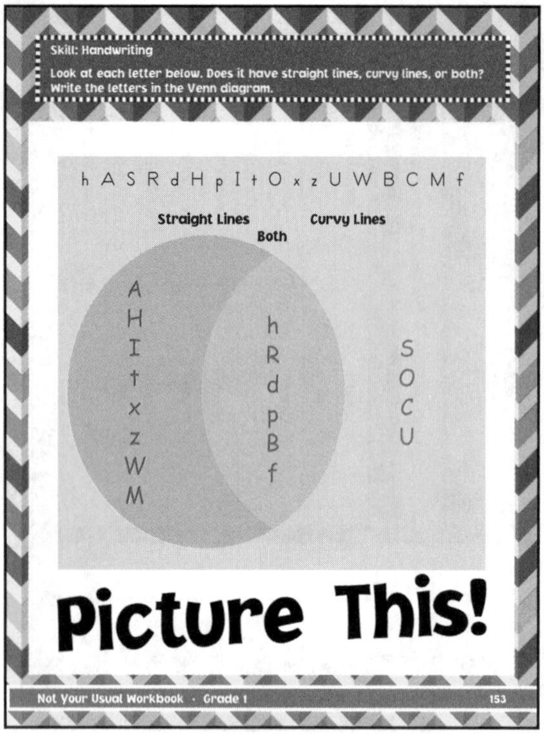

Page 153

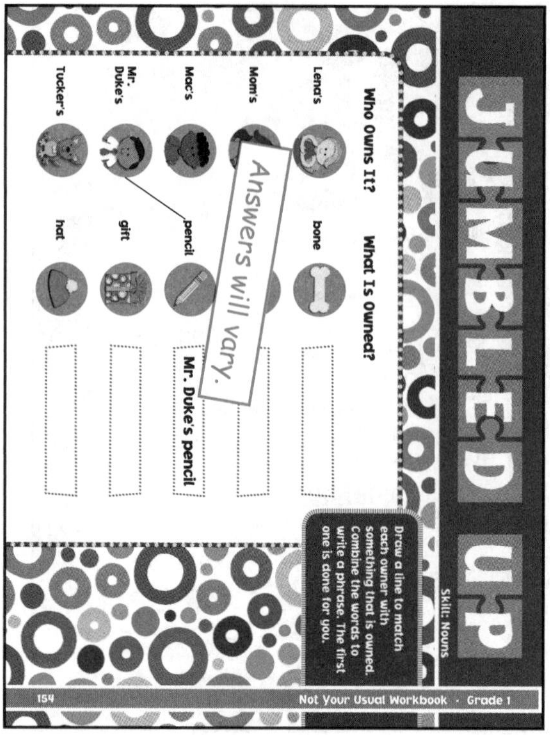

Page 154

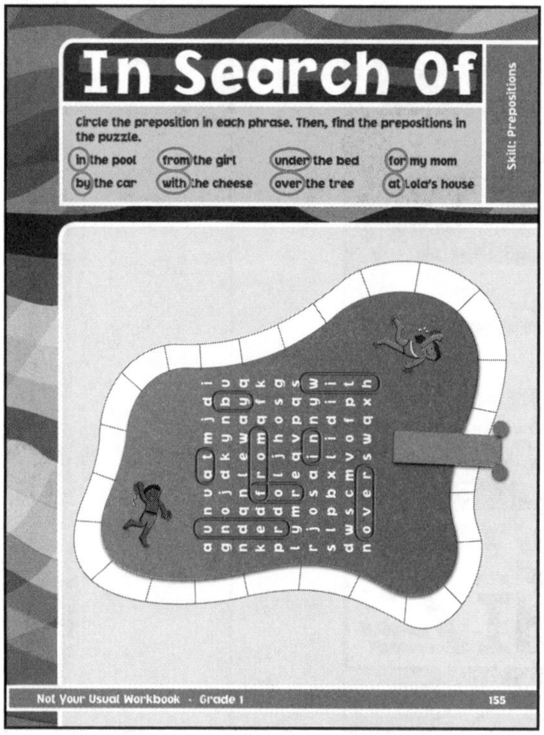

Page 155

Page 156

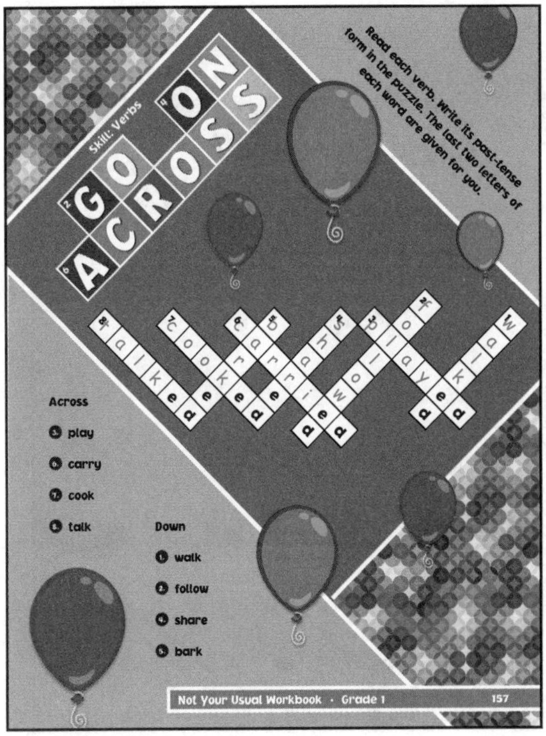

Page 157

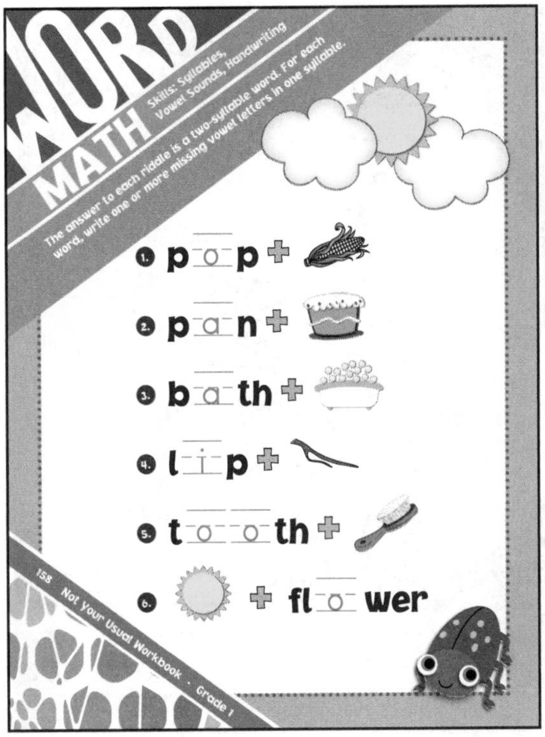

Page 158

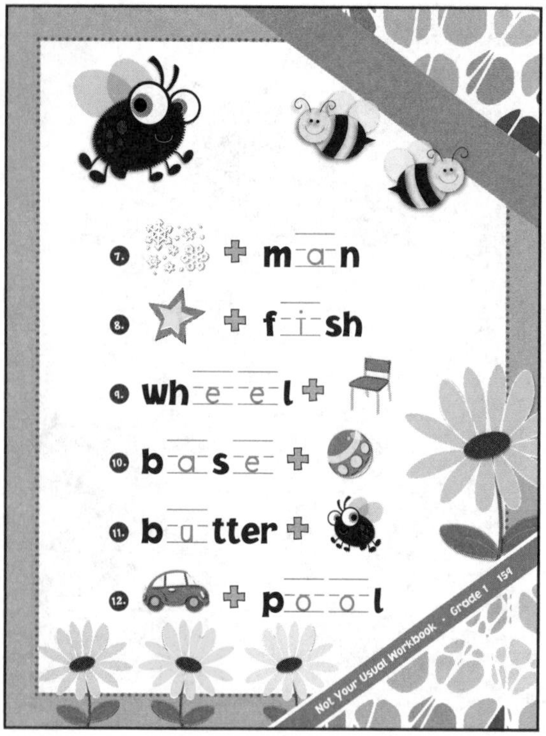

Page 159

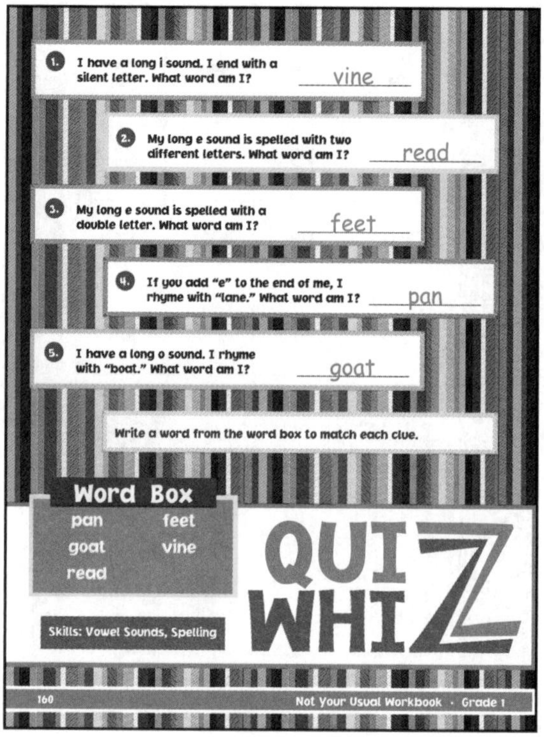

Page 160

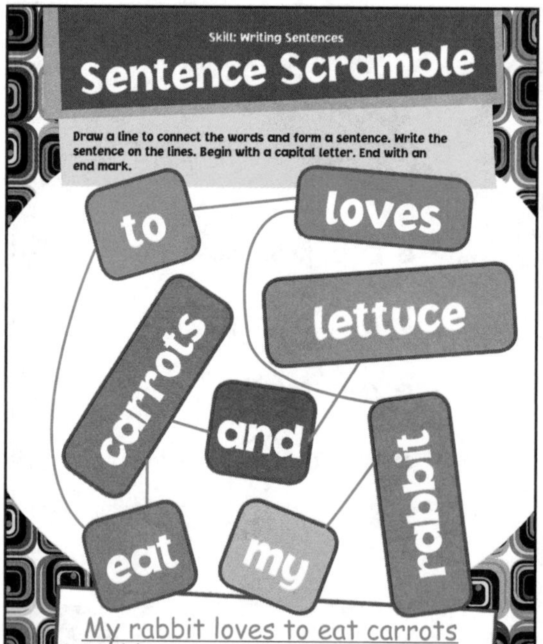

Page 161

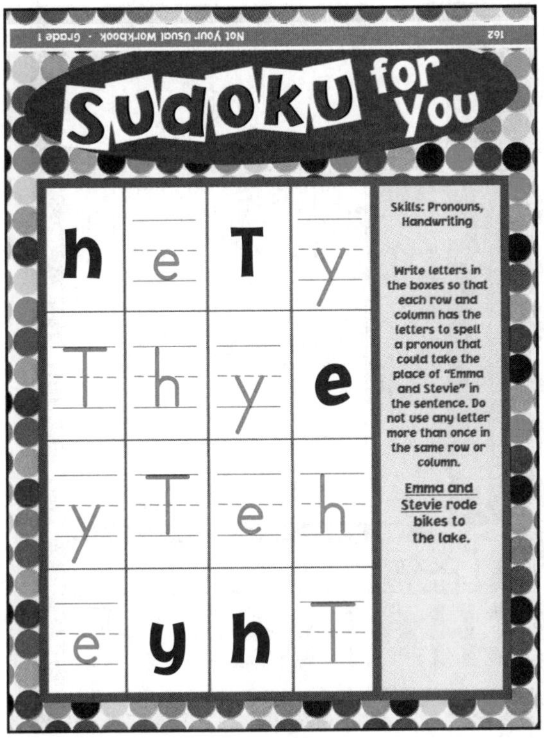

Page 162

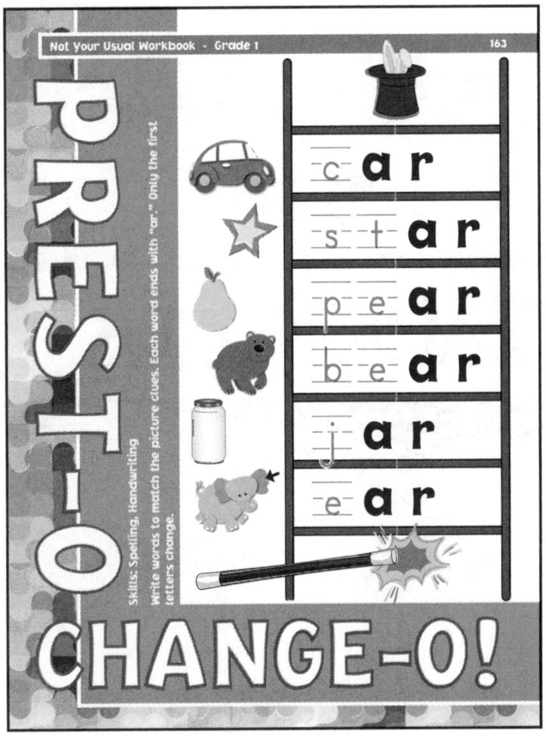

Page 163

Page 164

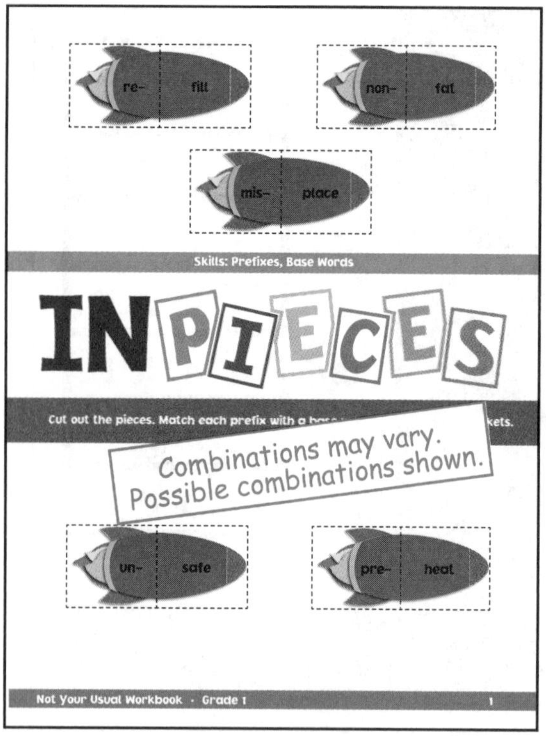
re- | fill
non- | fat
mis- | place
Skills: Prefixes, Base Words
IN PIECES
Cut out the pieces. Match each prefix with a bas… …kets.
Combinations may vary.
Possible combinations shown.
un- | safe
pre- | heat
Not Your Usual Workbook · Grade 1 1

Page 165

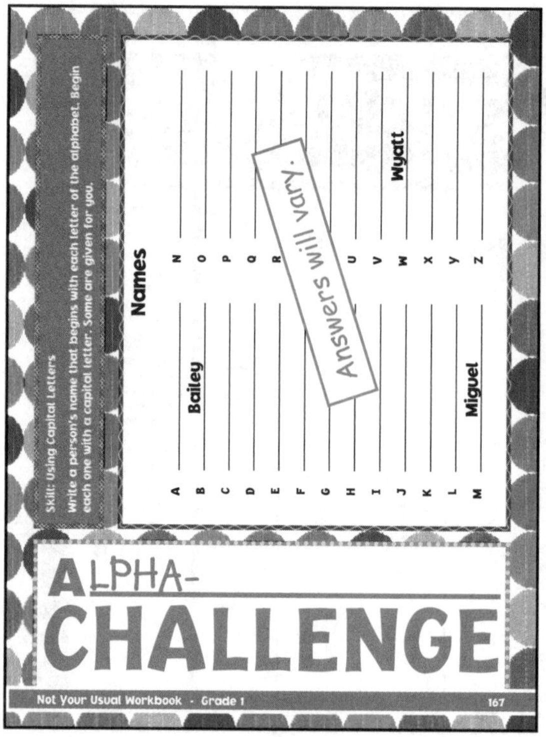
Skill: Using Capital Letters
Write a person's name that begins with each letter of the alphabet. Begin each one with a capital letter. Some are given for you.
Names
A
B Bailey
C
D
E
F
G
H
I
J
K
L
M Miguel
N
O
P
Q
R
S
T
U
V
W Wyatt
X
Y
Z
Answers will vary.
ALPHA-CHALLENGE
Not Your Usual Workbook · Grade 1 167

Page 167

168 Not Your Usual Workbook · Grade 1
CODE BREAKER
Skill: Nouns and Verbs
Use the code to write the verb in each sentence. If the noun and verb match, make a check mark (✔) at the end of the sentence. If they do not match, make an X.
1. Li kicks the ball. ✔
2. The cats pounce at the mouse. ✔
3. My bike have a flat tire. ✗
4. Will and Nico lives down the street. ✗
5. The chef makes soup for lunch. ✔

Code Key
pounce	lives	makes	kicks	have

Page 168

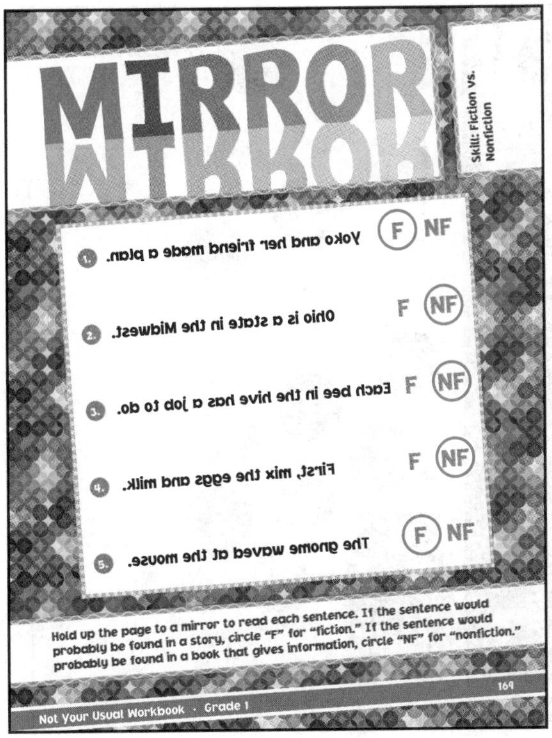
MIRROR MIRROR
Skill: Fiction vs. Nonfiction

1. Yoko and her friend made a plan. (F) NF
2. Ohio is a state in the Midwest. F (NF)
3. Each bee in the hive has a job to do. F (NF)
4. First, mix the eggs and milk. F (NF)
5. The gnome waved at the mouse. (F) NF

Hold up the page to a mirror to read each sentence. If the sentence would probably be found in a story, circle "F" for "fiction." If the sentence would probably be found in a book that gives information, circle "NF" for "nonfiction."

169
Not Your Usual Workbook · Grade 1

Page 169

Write an asking sentence that has two 3-letter words.

Write an exclamation that is five words lo...

Answers will vary.

Write a telling sentence that has a color word in it.

Write a sentence that is a command and has a number word in it.

How good are you at following directions? Write the sentences to find out!

Skill: Writing Sentences

QUIZ WHIZ

170
Not Your Usual Workbook · Grade 1

Page 170

GO ON ACROSS
Skills: Vocabulary, Spelling
Look at the picture clues. Write each animal's name in the puzzle.

Not Your Usual Workbook · Grade 1
171

Page 171

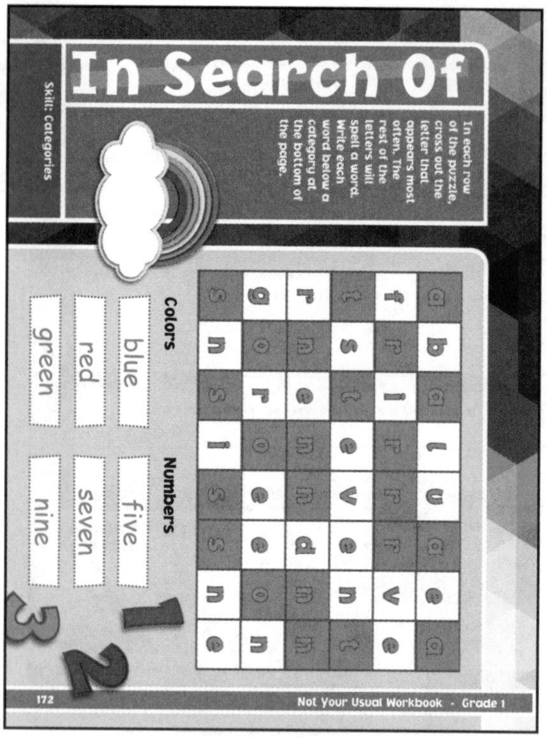

In Search Of
Skill: Categories
In each row of the puzzle, cross out the letter that appears most often. The rest of the letters will spell a word. Write each word below a category at the bottom of the page.
Colors
blue
red
green
Numbers
five
seven
nine
172
Not Your Usual Workbook · Grade 1

Page 172

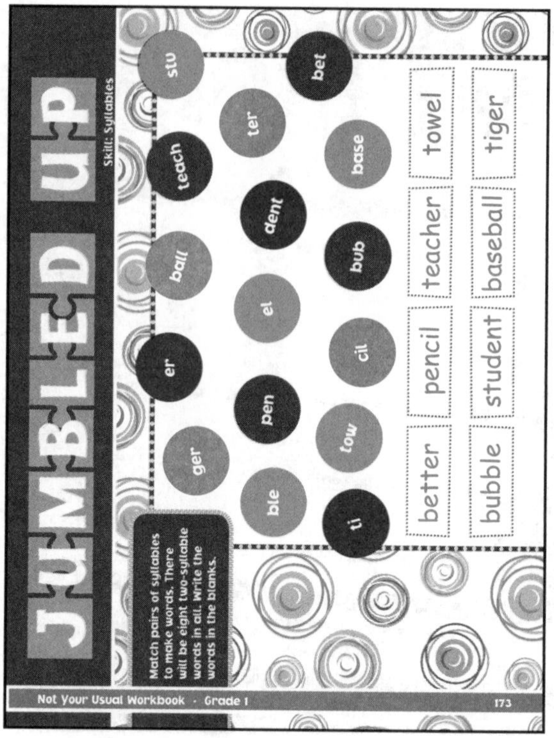

Page 173

RIDDLE ME
Use the clues to find the letters that spell a base word. Write the base word next to each prefix to complete the riddle. Then, guess the answer to the riddle!
Skills: Prefixes, Base Words, Spelling
The first letter of the base word makes the final sound in
The fourth letter of the base word is the only vowel letter in
The second letter of the base word is the only vowel letter in
The third letter of the base word is in but not in
You throw away my outside and eat my inside. Then, you eat my outside and throw away my inside.
What am I?
corn
174
Not Your Usual Workbook · Grade 1

Page 174

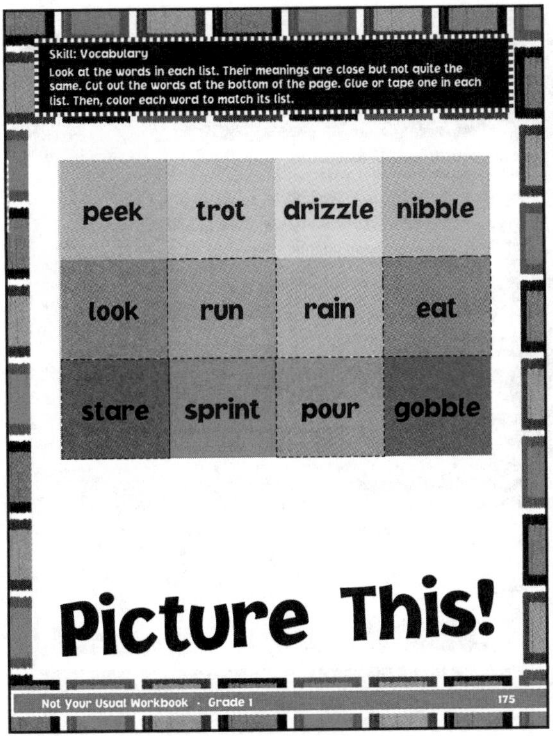
Skill: Vocabulary

Look at the words in each list. Their meanings are close but not quite the same. Cut out the words at the bottom of the page. Glue or tape one in each list. Then, color each word to match its list.

peek	trot	drizzle	nibble
look	run	rain	eat
stare	sprint	pour	gobble

Picture This!

Not Your Usual Workbook · Grade 1 175

Page 175

Not Your Usual Workbook · Grade 1 177

Sudoku for You

l	h	e	p
e	p	h	l
p	e	l	h
h	l	p	e

Skills: Verbs, Handwriting

Write letters in the boxes so that each row and column has the letters to spell a verb that completes the sentences. Do not use any letter more than once in the same row or column.

I ______ my family every day.

Yesterday, I ______ed sweep the floor.

Tomorrow I will ______ in the garden.

Page 177

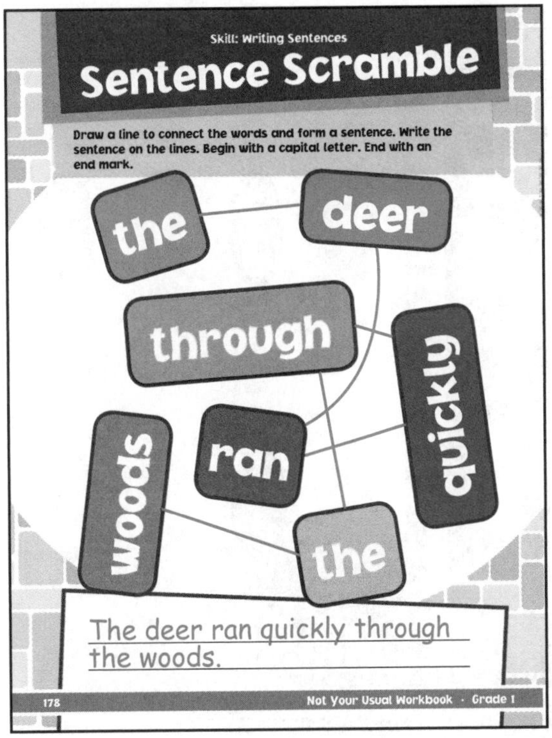
Skill: Writing Sentences

Sentence Scramble

Draw a line to connect the words and form a sentence. Write the sentence on the lines. Begin with a capital letter. End with an end mark.

The deer ran quickly through the woods.

178 Not Your Usual Workbook · Grade 1

Page 178

RIDDLE ME

Write the word that completes each hink pink.
Hint: Each word you write will include a consonant team.

Skills: Consonant Blends, Context Clues

1. What is a wiggly hen? a kickin' chicken
2. What is a bashful bug? a shy fly
3. Where do scary fish hang out? at a shark park
4. What do you call a fake horse? a phony pony
5. What do you call a red fruit with a beard? a hairy cherry
6. What do you call adding numbers in the tub? a math bath

A hink pink is a pair of rhyming words that answer a riddle.

Example: fat cat

Not Your Usual Workbook • Grade 1 179

Page 179

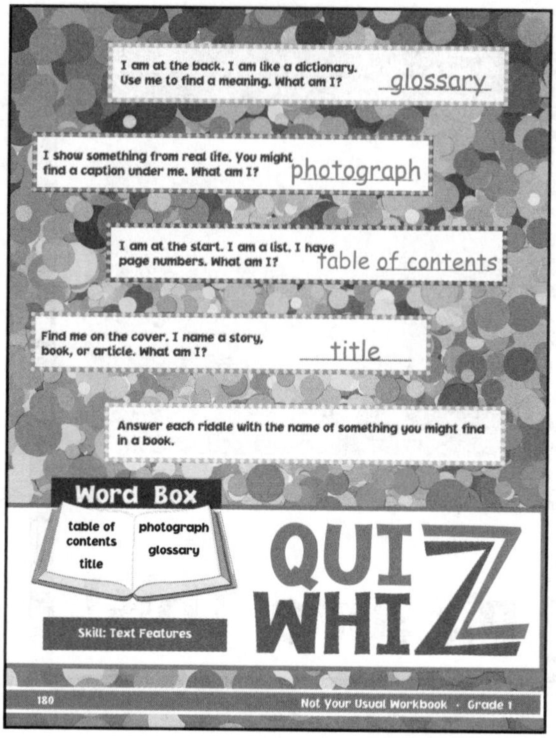

I am at the back. I am like a dictionary. Use me to find a meaning. What am I? glossary

I show something from real life. You might find a caption under me. What am I? photograph

I am at the start. I am a list. I have page numbers. What am I? table of contents

Find me on the cover. I name a story, book, or article. What am I? title

Answer each riddle with the name of something you might find in a book.

Word Box

table of contents, title, photograph, glossary

QUIZ WHIZ

Skill: Text Features

180 Not Your Usual Workbook • Grade 1

Page 180

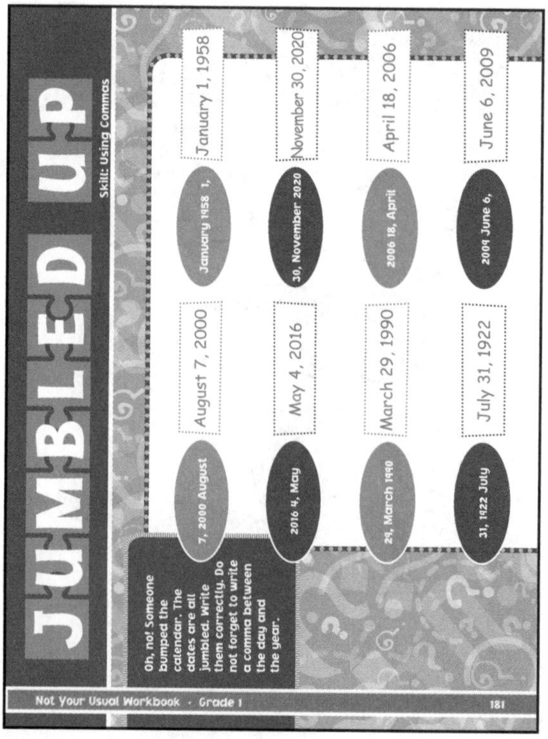

JUMBLED UP

Skill: Using Commas

Oh, no! Someone bumped the calendar. The dates are all jumbled. Write them correctly. Do not forget to write a comma between the day and the year.

Jumbled	Answer	Jumbled	Answer
7, 2000 August	August 7, 2000	January 1958 1,	January 1, 1958
2016 4, May	May 4, 2016	30, November 2020	November 30, 2020
29, March 1990	March 29, 1990	2006 18, April	April 18, 2006
31, 1922 July	July 31, 1922	2009 June 6,	June 6, 2009

Not Your Usual Workbook • Grade 1 181

Page 181

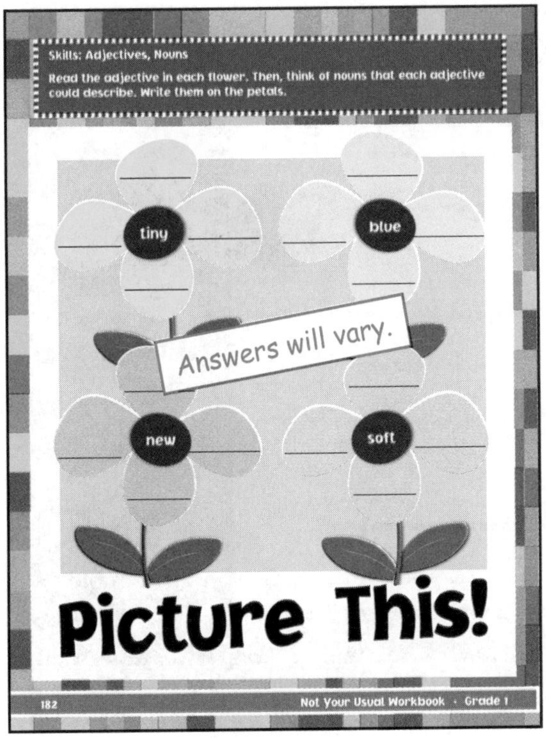
Skills: Adjectives, Nouns
Read the adjective in each flower. Then, think of nouns that each adjective could describe. Write them on the petals.
tiny
blue
new
soft
Answers will vary.
Picture This!
182
Not Your Usual Workbook · Grade 1

Page 182

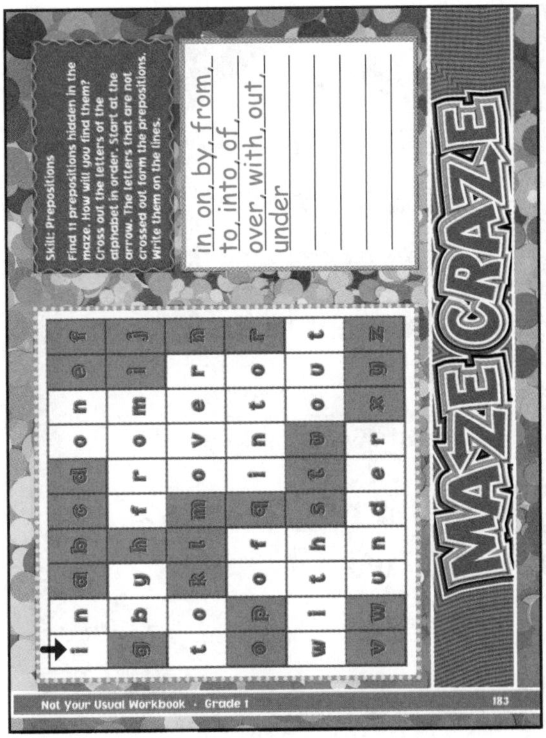
Skill: Prepositions
Find 11 prepositions hidden in the maze. How will you find them? Cross out the letters of the alphabet in order. Start at the arrow. The letters that are not crossed out form the prepositions. Write them on the lines.
in, on, by, from,
to, into, of,
over, with, out,
under
MAZE CRAZE
Not Your Usual Workbook · Grade 1
183

Page 183

WORD MATH
Skill: Writing Sentences
Decode each sentence. Write it in the blank. Add a period (.), question mark (?), or exclamation mark (!) at the end.
1.
I + − b
2 in the
I like to swim in the pool.
2. The s + − h on the
The cat sat on the table.
3. L + − h shout − sh 4 the
Look out for the snake!
184 Not Your Usual Workbook · Grade 1

Page 184

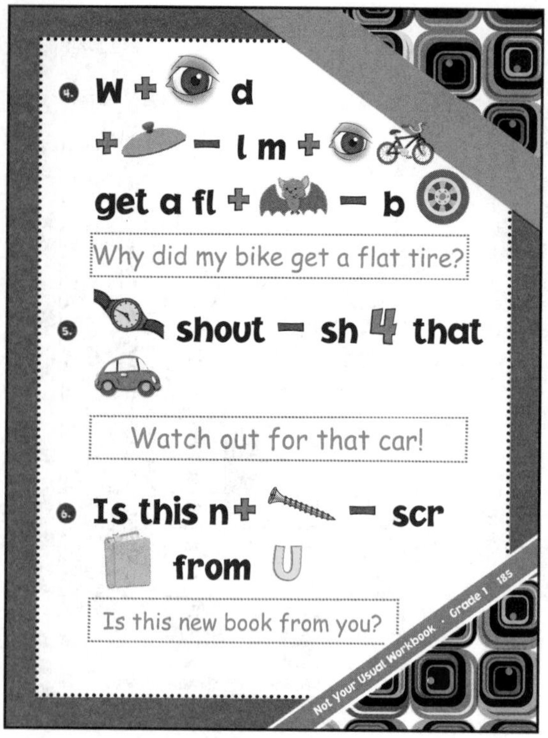

4. W + [eye] d
+ [lid] − l m + [eye] [bike]
get a fl + [bat] − b [tire]

Why did my bike get a flat tire?

5. [watch] shout − sh 4 that
[car]

Watch out for that car!

6. Is this n + [screw] − scr
[book] from U

Is this new book from you?

Not Your Usual Workbook · Grade 1 185

Page 185

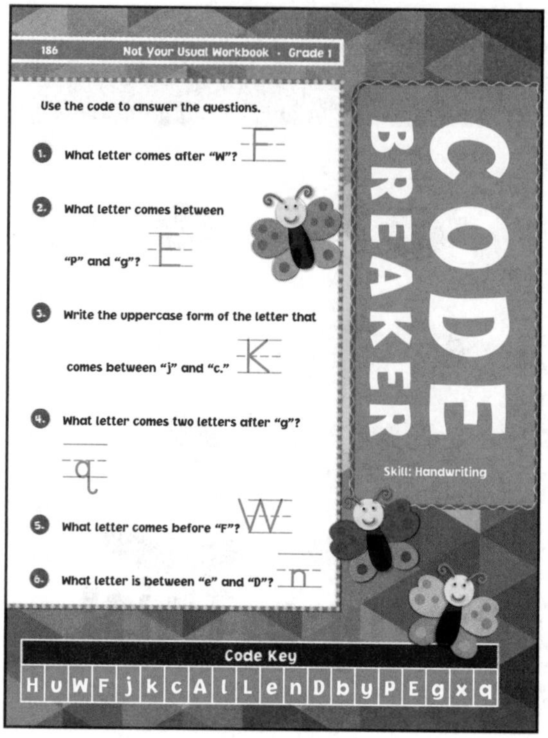

186 Not Your Usual Workbook · Grade 1

Use the code to answer the questions.

1. What letter comes after "W"? F
2. What letter comes between "P" and "g"? E
3. Write the uppercase form of the letter that comes between "j" and "c." K
4. What letter comes two letters after "g"? q
5. What letter comes before "F"? W
6. What letter is between "e" and "D"? n

CODE BREAKER

Skill: Handwriting

Code Key

H	u	W	F	j	k	c	A	l	L	e	n	D	b	y	P	E	g	x	q

Page 186

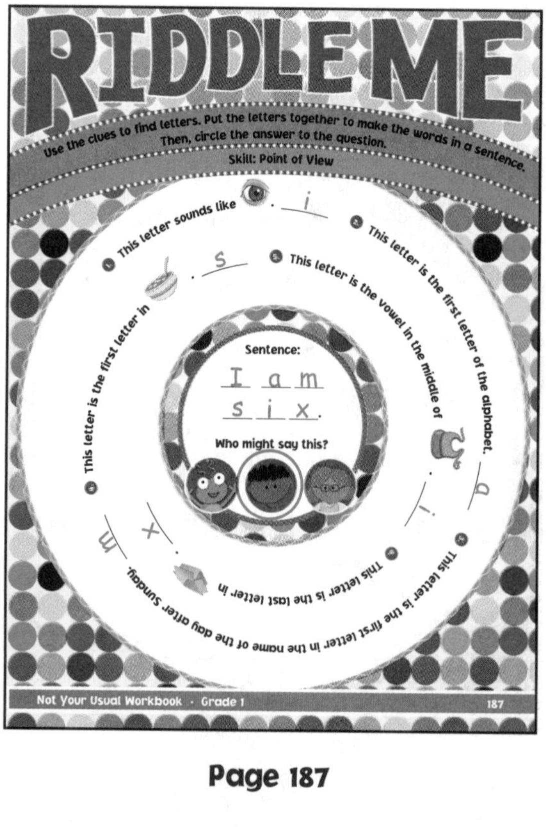

RIDDLE ME

Use the clues to find letters. Put the letters together to make the words in a sentence. Then, circle the answer to the question.

Skill: Point of View

1. This letter sounds like [eye]. i
2. This letter is the first letter of the alphabet. a
3. This letter is the vowel in the middle of [pot]. i
4. This letter is the first letter in the name of the day after Sunday. m
5. This letter is the last letter in [box]. x
6. This letter is the first letter in [soup]. s

Sentence:
I a m
s i x.

Who might say this?

Not Your Usual Workbook · Grade 1 187

Page 187

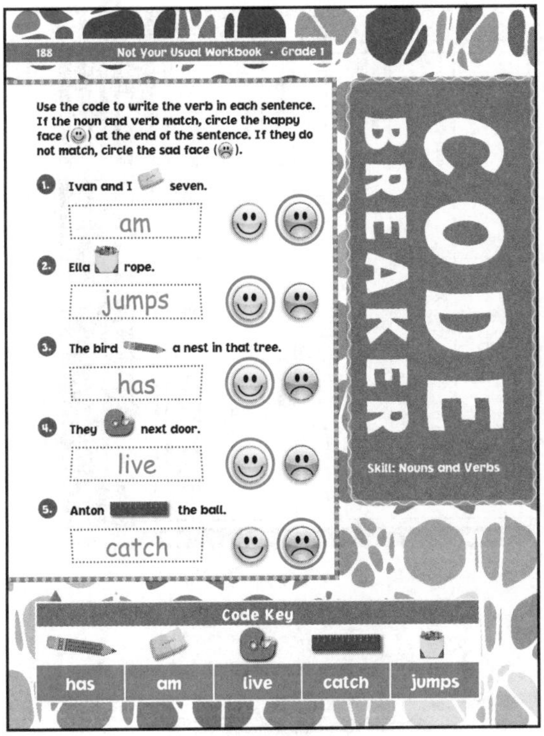
188 Not Your Usual Workbook · Grade 1

CODE BREAKER

Skill: Nouns and Verbs

Use the code to write the verb in each sentence. If the noun and verb match, circle the happy face (☺) at the end of the sentence. If they do not match, circle the sad face (☹).

1. Ivan and I ___ seven. am
2. Ella ___ rope. jumps
3. The bird ___ a nest in that tree. has
4. They ___ next door. live
5. Anton ___ the ball. catch

Code Key

has	am	live	catch	jumps

Page 188

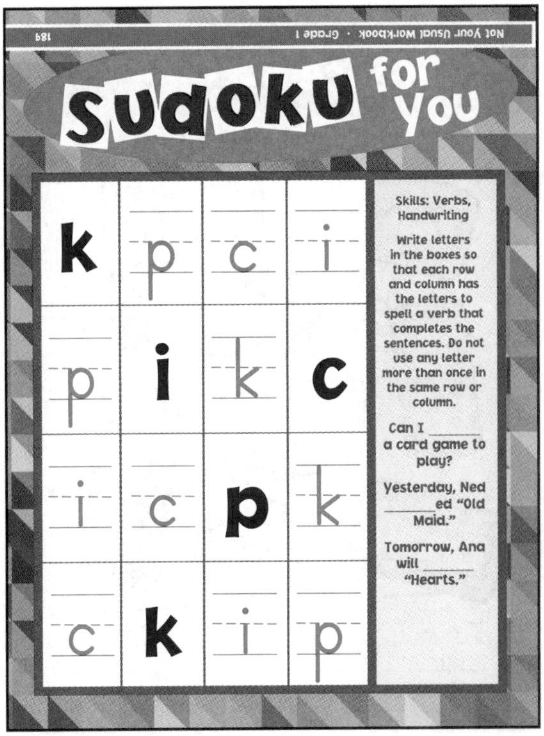
Not Your Usual Workbook · Grade 1 189

Sudoku for You

k	p	c	i
p	i	k	c
i	c	p	k
c	k	i	p

Skills: Verbs, Handwriting

Write letters in the boxes so that each row and column has the letters to spell a verb that completes the sentences. Do not use any letter more than once in the same row or column.

Can I ___ a card game to play?

Yesterday, Ned ___ed "Old Maid."

Tomorrow, Ana will ___ "Hearts."

Page 189

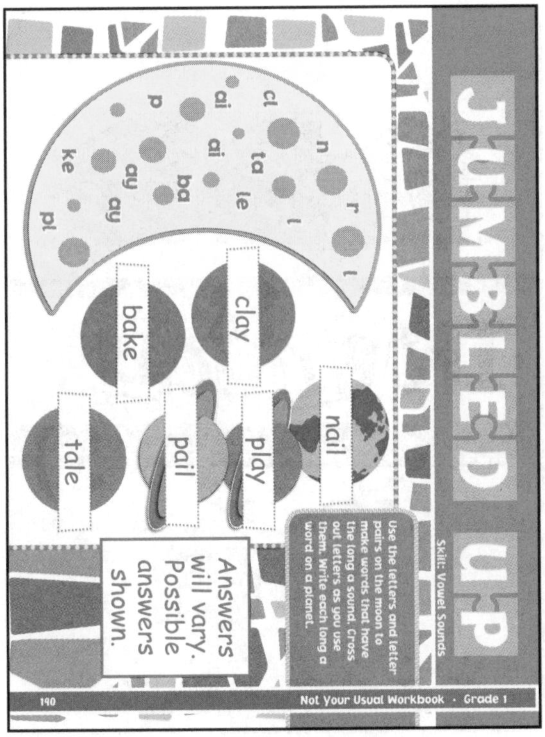

JUMBLED UP

Skill: Vowel Sounds

Use the letters and letter pairs on the moon to make words that have the long a sound. Cross out letters as you use them. Write each long a word on a planet.

Answers will vary. Possible answers shown.

190 Not Your Usual Workbook · Grade 1

Page 190

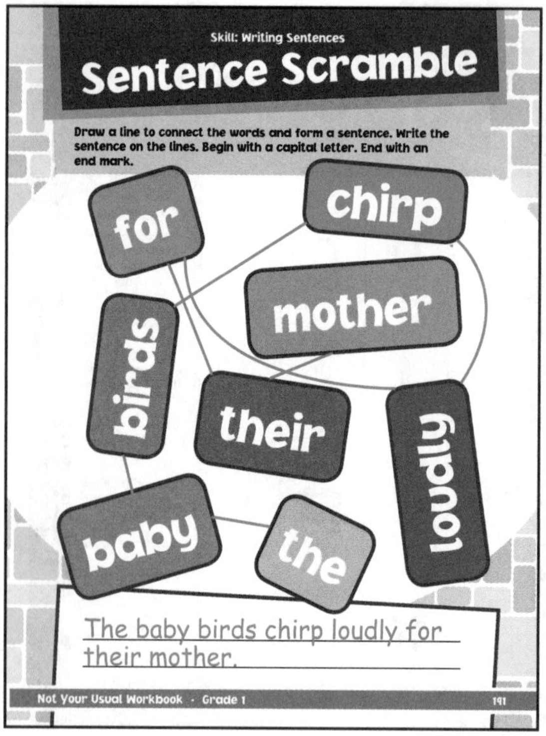

Skill: Writing Sentences

Sentence Scramble

Draw a line to connect the words and form a sentence. Write the sentence on the lines. Begin with a capital letter. End with an end mark.

The baby birds chirp loudly for their mother.

Not Your Usual Workbook · Grade 1 191

Page 191

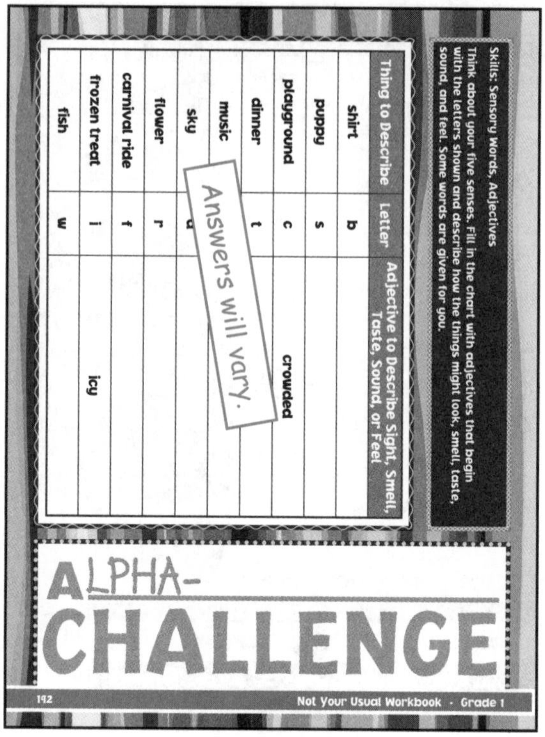

Skills: Sensory Words, Adjectives

Think about your five senses. Fill in the chart with adjectives that begin with the letters shown and describe how the things might look, smell, taste, sound, and feel. Some words are given for you.

Thing to Describe	Letter	Adjective to Describe Sight, Smell, Taste, Sound, or Feel
shirt	b	
puppy	s	
playground	c	crowded
dinner	t	
music	[illegible]	
sky	a	
flower	r	
carnival ride	f	
frozen treat	i	icy
fish	w	

Answers will vary.

ALPHA-CHALLENGE

192 Not Your Usual Workbook · Grade 1

Page 192

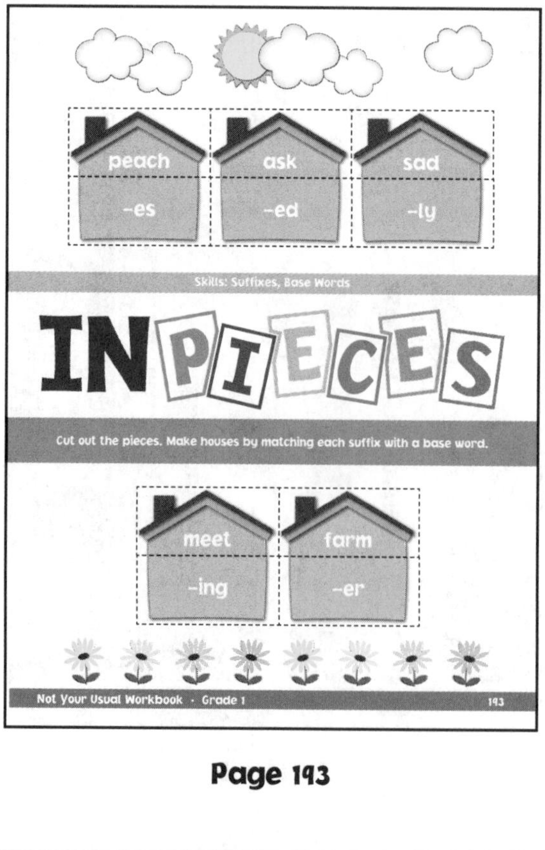

Skills: Suffixes, Base Words

IN PIECES

Cut out the pieces. Make houses by matching each suffix with a base word.

Not Your Usual Workbook · Grade 1 193

Page 193

MAZE CRAZE
sh l p f
r o d th
a ch w e
n c wh i
Skills: Consonant Blends, Spelling
Make as many words as you can with the letters in the box. You may use letters more than once. Each word should have a consonant team such as "sh," "ch," "wh," or "th." Write the words on the lines.
Answers will vary. Possible answers: whale, when, than, chin, chop, sheep, shop, fish, dash, inch, path, with
Not Your Usual Workbook · Grade 1 195

Page 195

Page 196

GO ON ACROSS
Skill: Vocabulary
What do you need to do each activity? Write the answers in the puzzle.
Across
cut paper?
eat soup?
check out a book at the library?
clean the floor?
Down
color a picture?
walk a dog?
rest your head?
get clean in the tub?
mail a letter?
Not Your Usual Workbook · Grade 1 197

Page 197

In Search Of

Skill: Spelling

Circle the correctly spelled word in each pair. Then, find it in the puzzle. Look carefully! The words may be hidden backward or diagonally.

mail, mayle
crait, crate
fliez, flies
hard, harde
opin, open
yellow, yelo
lewse, loose
rattle, rattul
stikur, sticker
mouse, mowse

198 Not Your Usual Workbook · Grade 1

Page 198

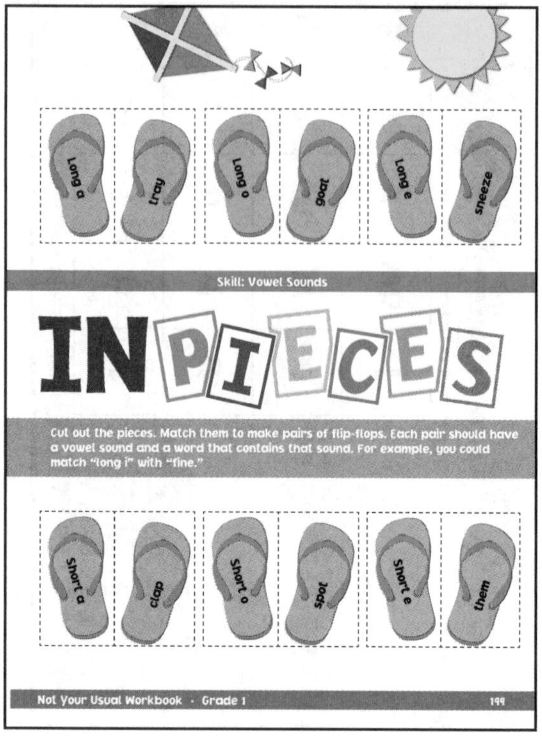

Skill: Vowel Sounds

IN PIECES

Cut out the pieces. Match them to make pairs of flip-flops. Each pair should have a vowel sound and a word that contains that sound. For example, you could match "long i" with "fine."

Not Your Usual Workbook · Grade 1 199

Page 199

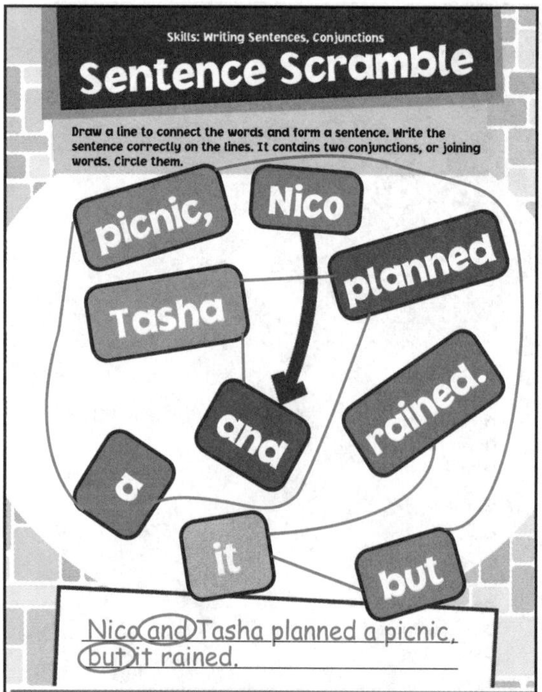
Skills: Writing Sentences, Conjunctions

Sentence Scramble

Draw a line to connect the words and form a sentence. Write the sentence correctly on the lines. It contains two conjunctions, or joining words. Circle them.

Nico and Tasha planned a picnic, but it rained.

Not Your Usual Workbook · Grade 1 201

Page 201

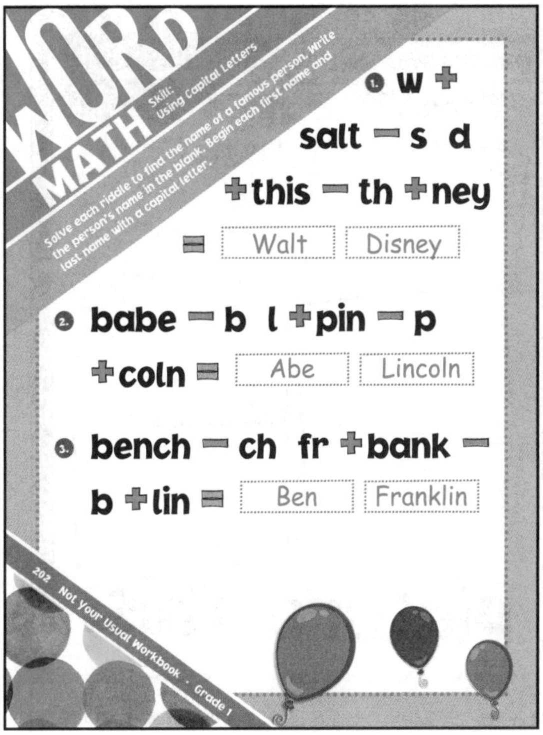

WORD MATH

Skill: Using Capital Letters

Solve each riddle to find the name of a famous person. Write the person's name in the blank. Begin each first name and last name with a capital letter.

1. w + salt − s d + this − th + ney = Walt Disney
2. babe − b l + pin − p + coln = Abe Lincoln
3. bench − ch fr + bank − b + lin = Ben Franklin

202 Not Your Usual Workbook · Grade 1

Page 202

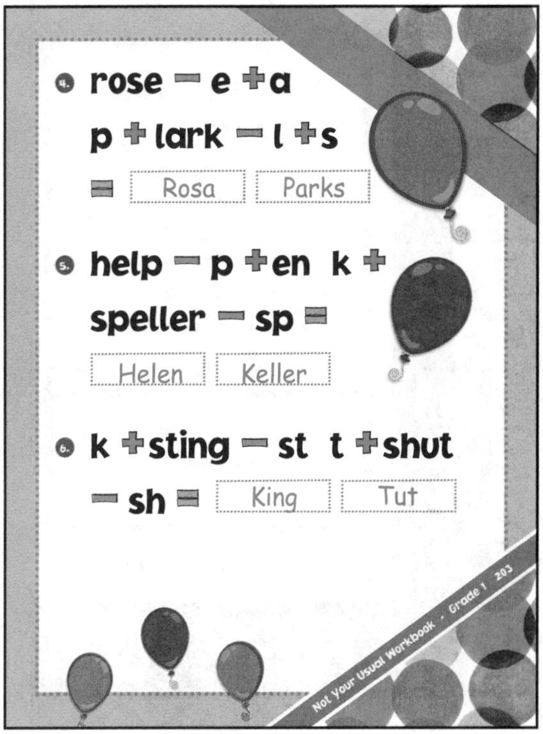

4. rose − e + a p + lark − l + s = Rosa Parks
5. help − p + en k + speller − sp = Helen Keller
6. k + sting − st t + shut − sh = King Tut

Not Your Usual Workbook · Grade 1 203

Page 203

RIDDLE ME

Use the clues to find letters that complete the name of a famous place. The word you write should begin with a capital letter.

Skills: Vowel Sounds, Using Capital Letters

1. This letter is in but not in . C
2. This letter spells the short vowel sound in . a
3. This letter spells the short vowel sound in . n
4. This letter spells the long e sound at the end of . y
5. This is the last letter in . o
6. This letter is in but not in . n

What famous American landmark is 277 miles long?

The Grand Canyon

204 Not Your Usual Workbook · Grade 1

Page 204

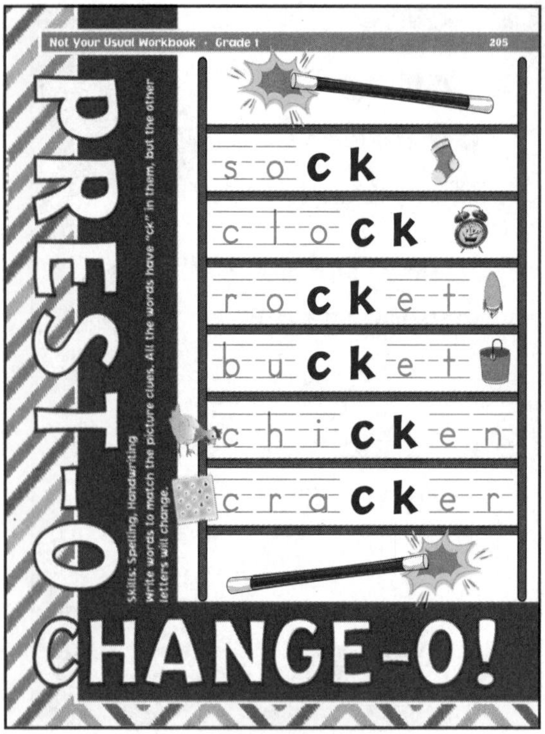
Not Your Usual Workbook · Grade 1 205

PREST-O CHANGE-O!

Skills: Spelling, Handwriting

Write words to match the picture clues. All the words have "ck" in them, but the other letters will change.

sock

clock

rocket

bucket

chicken

cracker

Page 205

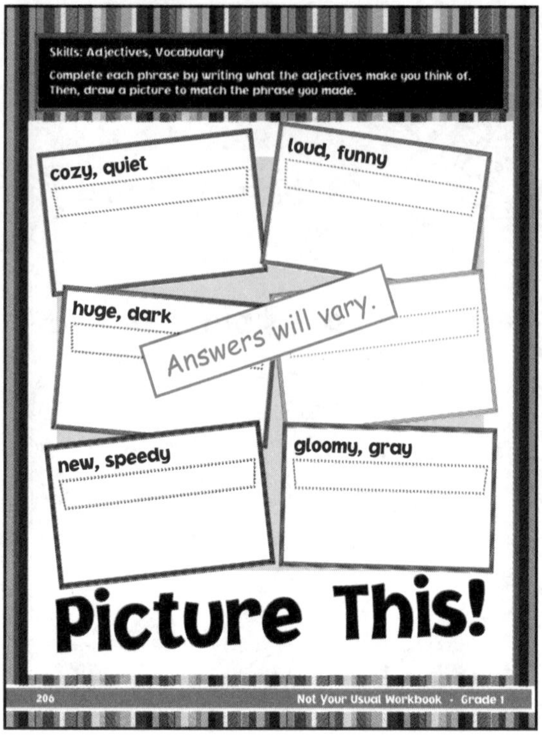
Skills: Adjectives, Vocabulary

Complete each phrase by writing what the adjectives make you think of. Then, draw a picture to match the phrase you made.

cozy, quiet

loud, funny

huge, dark

Answers will vary.

new, speedy

gloomy, gray

Picture This!

206 Not Your Usual Workbook · Grade 1

Page 206